MANAGING RISK
AND COMPLEXITY
THROUGH OPEN COMMUNICATION AND TEAMWORK

MANAGING RISK AND COMPLEXITY

THROUGH OPEN COMMUNICATION AND TEAMWORK

PHILLIP K. TOMPKINS

PURDUE UNIVERSITY PRESS, WEST LAFAYETTE, INDIANA

Cataloging-in-Publication data on file at the Library of Congress.

Paper ISBN: 978-1-55753-712-6
ePDF ISBN: 978-1-61249-383-1
ePUB ISBN: 978-1-61249-384-8

Contents

Introduction

When surgeries fail or airplanes crash, individual human error or technical failure is often assumed to be the cause. More often than not, coworkers fail to call out a warning at a critical moment. Or misguided managers ignore the report of an urgent problem because of the pressure to meet either a deadline or a budget. Organizational cultures often create in individual members a fear of reprisal should they send bad news up the hierarchy. Top managers frequently do not appreciate the degree of complexity and risk facing people at the bottom and hold to the sexist and paternalistic domination expressed in the old adage Father Knows Best. Few of us understand how many catastrophes and fatalities have resulted simply because the message was either sent too late, misunderstood, ignored, or not sent at all. Although organizations are both at risk and risky, the first concern in a capitalist economy is that of financial risk to the company. But organizations not only take chances that impact their financial status, they also risk the well-being of their workers, customers, and the world.

In the first chapter of this book I present a theory of organization—the theory of concertive control—which was originally inspired in part by my experience as a summer faculty consultant to NASA's Marshall Space Flight Center (MSFC) in 1967 and 1968. During those years I was able to observe and study some amazing, creative, and open communication practices that *worked*—one criterion being that the MSFC successfully developed the *Saturn V*, the rocket that landed astronauts on the Moon in 1969.

I was young but trained well enough to know that I was observing some amazing communication practices, exemplary ones I shall describe in chapter 2. I have written about those practices before, but they need restating here because I now understand them at a new and deeper level, allowing a new interpretation that helps introduce the theme of this book: managing complexity and risk through open communication and teamwork.

I have long been aware of the mathematical approach to risk analysis, an approach that helps a person or organization reduce or manage risks and uncertainties. I saw such approaches at work in NASA, of course, but with a new framework, I now better understand MSFC director Wernher von Braun's belief that verbal communication—that is, communication with words, oral and written—is an indispensable complement to the mathematical approach and should take place *prior* to that approach. The second stage of the *Saturn V* had the ultimate in complex requirements. In chapter 2 we shall see how that rocket stage succeeded against the odds by means of exemplary, aggressive forms of open communication that I now call collectively a "risk communication system."

My first attempt to theorize on those practices was done with the help of a colleague and former student, George Cheney. Together we developed the theory we called "concertive control" because it captured the essence of participatory, democratic decision making. I thought that if people were attracted to it, employed it, and verified it in empirical studies, it would become a grand theory of organization qua communication. Parts of concertive control theory had been tested in case studies conducted by me, graduate students, and colleagues before it was first published in a relatively complete form in 1985.[1] The coauthors were me, a professor of communication at Purdue University at that time, and George Cheney, then an assistant professor of communication at the University of Illinois, who had received his doctorate from Purdue University with me as his adviser.

The theory of concertive control was built on top of the tradition of organizational theory as we understood it, as well as some new trends—notably participation—in 1985. The year before, 1984, I had been invited to write a chapter about organizational communication for the *Handbook of Rhetorical and Communication Theory* edited by Carroll C. Arnold and John Waite Bowers. This would be the first time the subfield of organizational communication would have a place at the table along with traditional areas in the field of communication such as rhetorical theory and criticism, attitude change, and interpersonal, group, and mass communication. The editors assigned their functional theme to the title of my chapter as "The Functions of Human Communication in Organization."

The essay began by examining some major challenges to the dominant paradigm in the larger area of organizational studies, involving sociology, management, and public administration. The first challenge or critique was labeled the "action" critique of reification, the treatment of abstract concepts such as society or organization as concrete objects. Organizations were then treated as objective realities within which things happened. Textbooks, for example, talked about communication as being internal or external, as if the organization was a container. It was clear to me that the field of communication could handle this criticism easily, but the refutation was made more persuasive for me by the words of a Nobel Laureate in economics, Herbert Simon, who observed that anyone treating organizations as "something other than interacting individuals" was guilty of reification.[2] A communication scholar could not have said it better. My solution to the critique of organizational communication was this:

> Whether sociologists will resolve this issue is uncertain. In any case, organizational communication, by definition, should avoid the fallacy of reification by focusing on interacting individuals as the organization. Communication and organization should be conceived as synonyms: Communication *constitutes* organization rather than being something contained within the organization.[3]

I thought this was the first time, 1984, that the constitutive argument had been made, but Simon, of course, had beaten me to it without using the word *constitutive*. There may have been other writers who used the word itself before then, but with the constitutive conclusion in place, the essay quoted and summarized the communication contributions of organizational and management theorists such as Henri Fayol (who will play an important role in the Epilogue), Max Weber, the Human Relations Movement, Mary Parker Follett, Chester Barnard, and Herbert A. Simon. It also summarized the existing empirical research done in organizational communication as of that publication date made memorable by George Orwell: 1984.

These sources made up the vocabulary with which Cheney and I approached the development of the theory of what we called concertive control with the constitutive assumption. In addition, my 1984 "Functions" chapter had also noted a serious power critique of organizational studies. Little or no attention was paid to the phenomenon of power at that time, so we sought to correct that problem. But because power is an amorphous concept, we had to focus on control, the communicative manifestation of power and a commodity all organizations seek—whether we like it or not. The history of organizational control had been pursued by a temporal theory of it. Our theory of concertive control, with a new dimension or infusion dealing with risk, will be presented in a condensed form in chapter 1; it will also be illustrated and supported by case studies in later chapters. Organizational research in general clearly suffers from too many one-night stands—a single study of an organization with a fictional name that is never visited again. In this book, whenever possible, new data points will be entered on organizations studied in the past. Observations of organizations over time allow tentative generalizations about the life cycle of several organizations considered in this book.

As we follow the development of the concertive control theory, we shall see why I have chosen to change its name to open communication and teamwork theory. My ambitions for concertive control to become a grand theory were illusory, not pragmatic. In addition, by rethinking complexity and risk, I realized that a pragmatic theory would be more valuable and realistic than a grand theory. We live in what has been pronounced both the Age of Risk and the Age of Participation, and in this book the two streams achieve a confluence for the first time. Let's look now at the organization of the book, the brooks and streams.

Preview of Chapters

Chapter 1 summarizes theorizing about communication and control in organizations in the past. It describes why and how I became involved in a theory-and-research program called "concertive control." We consider the development of ideas in the earlier days of organizational communication such as control, decision making, and organizational identification. Because of the negative connotations and misunderstandings of the word *control*, I explain my decision to use the expression *open communication and teamwork* instead in this book. Ironically, the German sociologist Ulrich Beck declared that we have become a risk society in a book by the same name, *Risk Society: Towards a New Modernity*,[4] in which he would have the people regain *control* over big business and big science: "control, social," is an entry in the index to Beck's book.

In chapter 2 we encounter a first-hand account of my research at NASA's MSFC in 1967 and 1968, examining the extraordinary communication practices that made the Apollo Program such a success for all of humanity, and which inspired the original theory of concertive control, as well as the idea of promoting open communication and teamwork as a way to manage complexity and risk.

We see the professors at work, instead of watching others work, in chapter 3. We begin with a huge survey of perhaps the most highly complex intellectual work—academic research and publication—as well as several case studies that support the theory of participatory decision making in different kinds of organizations. Additional observations or data points—later visits—will be entered for three of the case studies.

A worldwide experimental study involving actual medical surgeries is found in chapter 4. This study was organized by Dr. Atul Gawande, a Harvard surgeon and medical professor. Gawande tested concertive control without calling it such, and this study provides invaluable evidence in support of the theory. Lists and checklists also enter the pragmatic theory I have chosen to call "open communication and teamwork." The Veterans Administration hospital makes a brief and scandalous appearance in this chapter.

Chapter 5 recreates the fire seminar I introduced and taught regularly at the University of Colorado and the subsequent research done by students studying firefighting teams, organizational identification, Fire Orders—lists of dos and don'ts—and of course risks. It also illustrates how discursive closure, so dreaded by the followers of critical theory, can stimulate discursive openness. The research on the U.S. Forest Service will give us an example of the dialectical organization, and how impossible rules were used by administrators to shift blame from themselves to the firefighters below them who were risking their lives. Drawing on Aristotle and the existential philosophy and theology of Paul Tillich, I offer a definition of "smart risk" in this chapter to provide a stance one can take instead of becoming paralyzed by concerns for safety in all dangerous situations.

Chapter 6 applies the theory of risk communication—or open communication and teamwork—in two case studies of the accidents involving the space shuttles *Challenger* and *Columbia*. In this chapter we learn from two more data points what communication practices that once worked became discontinued. We shall also consider the evidence supporting the idea that NASA may have developed a problem in common with the U.S. Forest Service, discussed in chapter 5.

Chapter 7 reports the effects my book *Apollo, Challenger, Columbia: The Decline of the Space Program* had on some managers in the aerospace industry and NASA itself. A top risk manager of an aerospace contractor read the book and invited me to translate open communication theory and practices into the terms of risk analysis, risk management, and risk communication theory—work that has not been published until now. The publication of that book also brought invitations from NASA to participate in two international conferences it sponsored in 2005 and 2006, in which I would be asked to explain why and how Apollo was such a phenomenal success. These presentations provided me once again with data points about organizational change in NASA that until now have not been expressed in print.

The reader is given a tour of a homeless shelter that practices open communication and teamwork in chapter 8. The chapter also explains how commissions and coalitions of diverse representatives adopted the Housing First reform in the cities of Denver, Phoenix, and Nashville, which actually *reduced* chronic homelessness during the Great Recession and in its aftermath. Additionally, this chapter discusses how discursive closure can at times be humane and pragmatically positive. Finally, it considers how the increasing inequality of income in this country can be related to the "privatization of risk" and homelessness.

The little-known Aviation Safety Reporting System is analyzed in chapter 9. It begins with my study of that open risk communication system created for an entire industry in order to reduce risk: ASRS. An update on this system will show that it has prevented so many accidents and saved so many lives that it has been accepted as a model in the United States and other countries; some of its principles have been adopted by individual industrial organizations, sectors of the economy, and most recently a group determined to protect schools from armed attack. The *principles* of ASRS derived from our study of it give us a model by which risky industries can *regulate themselves* with great success.

In chapter 10 we review the work of organizational consultants who announced in 1995, after looking at summaries of the academic research on participation, that the Age of Participation would soon begin. We then turn to the claims made by a practitioner of open communication, teamwork, and participation who introduced such practices in an international corporation headquartered in São Paulo, Brazil. Finally, we examine the claims of another practitioner and consultant who announced in 2014 that the Age of Participation had already arrived.

The Epilogue presents a new or at least different approach to communication theory of organizations: pragmatic-critical realism. We shall examine the relationship between the Age of Risk and the Age of Participation and how they might produce a reflexive *positive* modernization. The Epilogue also argues that the most ethical, practical, effective, and democratic approach to management is participation with open communication and teamwork, and it pulls together the conclusions necessary to fulfill the promise of the title of the book. Twelve conclusions are presented as lessons learned and emerging principles that can help us to manage complexity and risk more effectively today and in the future.

* * *

Although it may be an artless approach, I wish at this point to forecast my persuasive intentions in this book, my designs on the reader. As indicated earlier, the book argues that the most ethical, practical, effective, and democratic approach to management is participation with *open communication and teamwork*. My first hope is that managers will better manage risks in the future, and secondarily I hope that the academic field of organizational communication and other related areas of study will come to take risk seriously, to treat it as a *major factor* in both its descriptive and prescriptive theorizing.

Notes

1. Phillip K. Tompkins and George Cheney, "Communication and Unobtrusive Control in Contemporary Organizations," in *Organizational Communication: Traditional Themes and New Directions,* ed. Robert D. McPhee and Phillip K. Tompkins (Beverly Hills, CA: Sage, 1985), 179–210.

2. Herbert A. Simon, "On the Concept of Organizational Goal," *Administrative Science Quarterly* 9, no. 1 (1964): 1.

3. Phillip K. Tompkins, "The Functions of Human Communication in Organization," in *Handbook of Rhetorical and Communication Theory,* ed. Carroll C. Arnold and John Waite Bowers (Boston: Allyn and Bacon, 1984), 660. Emphasis in original.

4. Ulrich Beck, *Risk Society: Towards a New Modernity* (London: Sage, 1992).

1

Pragmatism and Critical Realism in Organizational Communication

*"In such [an ideal] society, communication would be domina-
tion-free, class and caste would be unknown, hierarchy would be
a matter of temporary pragmatic convenience, and power would
be entirely at the disposal of the free agreement of a literate and
well-educated electorate."*

—Richard Rorty, "Anticlericalism and Atheism"

R ichard Rorty, the author of the epigraph to this chapter, was well known as one of those most American of philosohers, a pragmatist. I chose this quotation because it strikes me as astonishing that an anticlerical atheist would have a vision of heaven—albeit on earth. But he did, and provided us with an ideal communication situation that deals with power, control, hierarchy, and open communication. This ideal communication situation can be used as an ideal type by which to evaluate current practices. It fits well with another philosophic approach we shall encounter: critical realism. They seemed to fit so well, these terms created a title for this chapter.

The Introduction promised that this chapter would review concepts developed in the early days of organizational communication such as power, control, decision making, identification, and others. A good place to begin is in a scholarly book by Richard Edwards, *Contested Terrain: The Transformation of the Workplace in the Twentieth Century*.[1] In it, Edwards shows that the history of organizations could be characterized as a struggle for control between the managers and the workers. Recent protests by fast-food workers and strikes by unions in the United States illustrate that the contest or struggle continues. Edwards identifies three strategies used by owners and management that developed over time as methods of controlling workers; here they are in his words:

> The first is what I call "simple control"; capitalists exercise power openly, arbitrarily, and personally (or through hired bosses who act in much the same way). Simple control formed the organizational basis of 19th century firms and continues today in small enterprises of the more competitive industries. The second is "technical control"; the control mechanism is embedded in the physical technology of the firm, designed into the very machines and other physical apparatus of the workplace. The third is "bureaucratic control"; control becomes embedded in the social organization of the enterprise, in the contrived social relations of production at the point of production.[2]

Simple control worked for owners until their organizations got too big for a single person to handle. They hired foremen to maintain simple control over the worker, but tyrannical supervisors could be obtrusive and unpleasant. This naturally caused labor and political unrest, something owners did not want. So they developed two different strategies for handling workers in different kinds of work. For manufacturing, the owners created technical control, the second of the three types. The apotheosis of this kind of control was put into action by Henry Ford at his Highland Park, Michigan, plant. The "endless conveyor" or assembly line used to make automobiles dictated the task and the speed of the work, not the foreman.

Supervisors were still needed to evaluate the work, but the span of control, or ratio of foremen to workers, in Ford's plant was 1 to 58, so large as to be in violation of all the existing "laws" and theories of organization and management of the day. Ford saved money in supervisors' salaries and gained something else as well. The change made control much less obtrusive than before. No one was hovering over workers all day long, threatening to fire them if they didn't meet personal expectations. The changes over time were described as moving from obtrusive control toward the unobtrusive. Technical control could, however, be set at such a high speed or rate that humans felt like cogs in a machine. Charlie Chaplin made a film in 1936, *Modern Times,* in which we watch him frantically tightening bolts while trying to keep up with the relentless assembly line. The United Auto Workers union was able to organize the workers on the assembly lines and engage in collective bargaining on their behalf, raising the owners' costs, and yet technical control continued. But how could one control the people in large corporations who do all the paperwork?

For the white collar workers, the owners and their managers developed the third strategy, bureaucratic control. It was the rule of trained and salaried experts, who enforced a set of rules codified and approved by management and handed down to the people in the various levels of the bureaucratic hierarchy. Supervisors now had little to do by way of ordering people about; even the evaluation of workers became a function of specified criteria well known to both parties. Productivity itself was measured by a person's compliance with the rules. Bureaucratic control became even less obtrusive than simple and technical control. But as every reader knows by experience, it is inevitable that situations arise in which the bureaucracy's goals and rules do not match. This is called "goal displacement"—that is, the rule displaces the goal and becomes a goal in itself—and is one reason the words *bureaucracy* and *bureaucrats* have such negative connotations. Another reason is that bureaucrats often feel caged or trapped by the rules they are forced to apply. In all of this, Edwards presents us with a dialectic or contest for control: owners and managers against the workers, and vice versa.

Edwards recognizes that bureaucratic control leads to boredom, frustration, and discontent for those under its rule. He states that it is still a contested terrain, with some intelligent bureaucrats wanting more control and flexibility in developing the rules and in making higher order decisions. Edwards argues that people are inevitably driven to want more participation, democracy, and individual satisfaction.

These facts, plus social and economic developments such as the civil rights and women's liberation movements, as well as my experience at NASA's MSFC, prompted Cheney and me to propose the fourth type of control: concertive control. Because both of those words—*concertive* and *control*—have created misunderstandings, in this book I often refer instead to *open communication* and *teamwork*, which are also descriptive of the control of decision making—that is, by the group or team. In some instances the neologism *concertive* is used because it provides denotative clarity and has the right connotation.

Cheney and I explain our attempt to account for the emergence of a new, post-bureaucratic and post-industrial system of control. Relying on the observations of other empiricists and theorists cited in the essay,[3] we carefully chose our words to capture the essence of concertive control: teamwork, coordination, flexibility, innovativeness, intensive face-to-face interactions, participatory decision making, "flat" hierarchies, and relative value consensus. Despite our use of these relatively liberating terms, we went out on a limb and hypothesized that organizations employing concertive control could, ironically, *increase* the total amount of control in the system because each individual and not just a supervisor would be exercising it; they would be controlling each other. Speaking for myself, I also believed that there would still be contested terrain between managers and workers that would tempt managers to create the mere *appearance* of participation, or a pseudo form of concertive control and cooptation.

The new term, *concertive,* was suggested by my wife, Elaine Tompkins, while Cheney and I were drafting the theory at the Tompkins dining room table; it was coined to communicate that people in such a system were *acting in concert.* Implicit in the theory was the notion that it was an adaptation to an increasing degree of complexity in which late 20th-century organizations had to function. Bureaucratic control's bundle of rules could not handle, could not anticipate, all of the new, dynamic, and perplexing problems presented by new technologies that could even take a man to the Moon and return him safely to Earth.

Decision Making and Decisional Premises

I had been using Herbert Simon's *Administrative Behavior* as a textbook in an undergraduate class when I got a call at home from a student in the class. "The author of our textbook has just won the Nobel Prize for Economics," the young man proudly reported. The Nobel committee released the statement that it could have used Simon's own theory of decision making to arrive at the decision to give him the award. Simon had theorized that choice or decision making in organizations was a process of drawing conclusions from premises, like the Aristotelian syllogism or enthymeme. Management has learned that if they control the premises their employees use in decision making they can control the conclusions. For example, the manager of a manufacturing company might try to inculcate in the mind of workers the premise of cutting costs—over the premises of ensuring quality or reliability—with the hope of influencing employees to use it in all of their decision making on the organization's premises (pun intended).

As mentioned earlier, unobtrusive control or communication such as the open and participatory kind relies on people having something close to value consensus on a major premise, even though some might have more specialized knowledge than others. In terms of decision making, this means they agree with each other about what value premises to use in making decisions—such as saving time. In chapter 3 we shall consider a case study in which engineers with high standards of reliability acted in concert and were successful in resisting a top management decision to decrease the quality or reliability of the company's products. How does an open, participatory organization achieve such value-premise consensus? Cheney and I added some items to Simon's list to explain how value consensus is achieved by a variety of methods: authority, education, recruitment, training, communication, and organizational identification all can be used to produce value consensus.

Organizational Identification

After my experience at NASA, I found myself increasingly intrigued by the concepts of hierarchy and identification. Using Kenneth Burke's notions of identification and mystery, I organized a study of the hierarchy of a university in the eastern United States and observed results similar to what one would predict from Burke's theory.[4] To paraphrase Burke, our "I" or personal identity is a unique set of "we's" that we carry around. The organizations with which we identify make up a part of each person's individual identity. Cheney and I combined Burke's rhetorical theory of identification with Herbert Simon's. We also refined Simon's operational definition of decision making and identification, and secured Simon's acceptance of this one: "A person identifies with a unit when, in making a decision, the person in one or more of his/her organizational roles perceives that unit's values or interests as relevant in evaluating the alternatives of choice."[5]

Why does organizational identification go with open organizational communication? Because an open organization is by definition freer of bureaucratic intrigue and deceit. The ability to question the conclusions of others, even those higher in the order, is more fulfilling, more natural in a democratic society. Participation approaches the neo-pragmatic ideal set forth in the epigraph at the beginning of this chapter written by Richard Rorty: "Communication would be domination-free . . . hierarchy would be a matter of temporary pragmatic convenience."[6] Yes, healthy human beings identify more with equality, democracy, and openness than with domination. Indeed, the process is one of identifying with someone or something and disidentifying with someone or something else, such as a domineering boss and dictatorial organization. As we shall see in chapter 9, there is also a quasi-religious or spiritual dimension suggested by participants themselves, Rorty's heavenly model of society, and Tillich's existential-participatory theology.

In chapter 3 we shall consider a study that found that workers in a system of concertive control identified more with the team than with the organization. This study seems to have created the misleading impression in many minds that concertive control theory applies only to small groups and teams and not to all levels of an organization. In addition, some scholars have found the very word *control* to have negative connotations. For these reasons I believe that even the term *concertive control* can be misleading. Therefore, as mentioned earlier, I tend to refer instead to *open communication* and *teamwork*. This is because organizations that practice concertive control are made up of teams that make significant decisions about their work. Teamwork and open communication add up to participation, and yet both still function as forms of control because power and control are inherent characteristics of organizations and exist at all levels within them. And as we shall see in chapter 5, open communication is the antidote to what has been called "discursive closure." There are contexts, nonetheless, when *concertive communication* is an appropriate descriptive term.

It should be clear that concertive control as a post-bureaucratic theory of open communication was meant to apply to an entire organization from the beginning because of its emphasis on flattening hierarchies and removing barriers to upward-directed communication. Using different terms—*open communication* and *teamwork*—to describe the theory will, however, lead to better understanding of the overall organizational context. The revised theory will also borrow a page from critical theory as it was introduced into organizational communication; that is, critical theory has been used in this field to criticize both theory and practice by means of an ideal type. Kuhn and Deetz, for example, wrote that their use of critical theory draws on "theorists following a Marxist tradition, such as Althusser, Marcuse, Horkheimer, Adorno, and Habermas."[7] They also use Habermas's ideal speech situation as the standard for criticizing corporate actions and theories of those actions. The ideal speech situation has been useful over the years, but I have chosen to include as the epigraph of chapter 1 the quotation from Richard Rorty. This quotation defines the ideal type for open communication and teamwork theory because it speaks not only to an ideal *speech* situation—"communication would be domination-free"—but also to the organizational aspects of "power," "hierarchy," and "free agreement" of the "electorate."

Critical theory has helped to enlighten organizational communication, but we must do more than sit back and criticize because many organizations as now constituted are a serious risk to society. Scholars and critics must promote, even fight for communication practices that reduce risk. Rorty's ideal type is backed up by his philosophic theory of neo-pragmatism and is well suited to serve as an evaluative standard for the theory and practice of organizations. It is also consistent with the views of the French philosopher Jacques Derrida, at least that part of his work which desires the *destabilization of hierarchies.* I urge the reader to return to the Rorty quotation while reading the present book about theory and practice. We shall also see how it is possible to take a step beyond critical theory or attempts at a grand theory by means of a combination of ideas drawn from Richard Rorty and Ulrich Beck that I call "pragmatic-critical realism."

Seventeen years after the theory of concertive control was written, Barker, Ashcraft, and I set out to write a paper that accommodated the opposition to the idea and materialization of control.[8] Before we were able to finish the paper, we did accomplish discussing the illusion of control and the hegemonic effect of identification, but we argued that what is ultimately important is the well-informed experience of members of organizations that are involved in open communication and control. Fulfillment could be one criterion, and another would be their record in regard to risk: risk to themselves, other workers, their organization, and the consumers of their goods and services as well as society as a whole. This leads us to a consideration of risk as it is conceived in this book, and how it functions in organizations.

Risk Communication

I now recognize that I had a long-unstated assumption that the practice of concertive control would help an organization better adapt to increasing complexity and risk. Complexity and risk were very much part of the excitement I experienced while working on the *Saturn V,* the Moon rocket vital to the Apollo Program. *Risk* and *complexity* are both words in the title of this book (and included in the Glossary of Acronyms and Technical Terms); the purpose of this section is to make them explicit so they can serve a structuring function for what is to follow. In 1986 the German sociologist Ulrich Beck published a book with this title, translated into English, *Risk Society: Towards a New Modernity.*[9] Those of us alive at that time lived in a risk society, which Beck defines as "a systematic way of dealing with hazards and insecurities induced and introduced by modernisation itself."[10] (I have inferred, therefore, that since his title describes movement toward modernity, it can be said we live in the *Age of Risk.*) If anything, this is more applicable today than when he made the claim 30 years ago because technologies have become more complex.

According to an important interpreter, Deborah Lupton, Beck had several approaches to interpreting the phenomena of the risk society. The one that best represents the view of this book is the "critical realist position,"[11] or critical realism—realism being highly similar to Rorty's pragmatism. I accept the traction of critical theory but also believe there are real-world organizations that need to be monitored, criticized, and changed to reduce the risks and hazards that most seriously threaten those of us with the least in our risk society. Hence, I embrace the critical realist approach because it allows us to accept some organizational practices as better than others for the people who are subjected to them. To sum up, my pragmatic-critical approach is supplied by the philosophy of pragmatism; the critical part is supplied largely by the ideal communication system described by Rorty;

my sense of realism is seen in my assumption that risks created by business and government organizations are out there, even when I can't see, smell, or taste them.

One other observation about this topic of risk: When first I studied organizational risk analysis I was dismayed to learn that threats and risks were often described in terms of economic harm to the owners of a company. I was again disappointed when I turned to my 1965 *Shorter Oxford English Dictionary*. The second definition of *risk* is "the chance or hazard of commercial loss." I turned to my 1973 *Webster's New Collegiate Dictionary*, its second definition begins, "In insurance, hazard of loss. . . ." Capitalism has influenced our language in financial shapes and forms I had not completely appreciated. But these definitions remind us that risk management by both mathematics and words can be beneficial to organizations for financial reasons as well as being the right thing to do for people and their society.

In their book, *Managing the Unexpected: Assuring High Performance in an Age of Complexity*, Karl Weick and Kathleen Sutlcliffe discuss risk and organizations and refer to the work of Aaron Wildavsky[12] before taking their own considered position that not all risks can be anticipated and that resilience is also therefore needed. They also quote the position of James Reason[13] on risk: "Achieving safety from risk is elusive because it is a nonevent." But they go on to list the factors that presage some findings that will appear in this book:

> Mutual adjustments like this preserve reliability and are accomplished only through a combination of respectful interaction, communication, trust, firsthand knowledge of the technology, attentiveness, familiarity with another's roles, and experience. This combination of capabilities enables people to deal with dynamic nonevents, and to keep the unexpected as a nonevent.[14]

In a footnote to that paragraph, Weick and Sutcliffe refer to the cluster of attitudes and activities by a tantalizing phrase: "team mind."

Paul's Law

I stored my notes about Paul's law in a file folder housed with many other file folders containing interview notes from my days as a researcher at NASA, when my interviewees' work was high in both risk and complexity. The interviewee was Hans Paul, a division chief in the Propulsion and Vehicular Engineering Laboratory of the MSFC when I interviewed him in the summer of 1968. As I sat down for our interview, he showed me a diagram that I copied into my notes. He called it simply "Paul's law." Today I can find no evidence that he ever published the diagram and theory either before or since then, but members of the engineering culture of that time communicated important ideas with each other by means of informal state-of-the-art papers containing ideas that would be passed around the labs rather than taking the time to have them published as scientific papers in journals.

Figure 1 shows the diagram he drew with the terms he used. He believed that the law applied to all problem-solving situations humans confront.

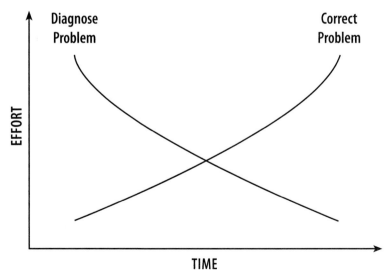

Figure 1 Paul's law

The vertical plane represents the amount of effort required to solve a problem. The horizontal plane represents the passage of time. The arc beginning at the top left of the graph and curving down toward the right symbolizes the effort required to diagnose a problem: to diagnose a problem in the early stages of a project requires much more effort than is required later on because over time the problem becomes increasingly obvious and therefore is easier to diagnose. The arc starting at the bottom left and moving upward to the right symbolizes the amount of effort required to correct a problem: to correct a problem in the early stages of a project requires much less effort than is required later on.

To use an example from medicine, diagnosing cancer in its earliest stages requires great effort; as time passes it becomes easier to recognize it. Eliminating cancer, however, requires less effort in its early stages than in its later stages. Diagnosing cancer requires less effort over time, but greater effort over time is required to cure or eliminate it.

Some students and others I have shown this to over the years have hypothesized that the point at which the two curves intersect must be the *optimal point* for diagnosing and solving problems. I believe that life may be more complicated than that, but I would like to hear from readers of this book before making a final decision. Some conditions do, however, demand expending extra effort at an early diagnosis because of the seriousness of the consequences.

Paul-Tompkins Law of Risk Communication

Let me first introduce some definitions, not from risk communication, but from a paper by Dr. Stein Cass, an expert on the mathematical approach to risk. Before doing so I must add that to me, risk is more than threats to an organizational objective as defined by Cass: it includes injury or death to an employee, consumer, or anyone else. The dozens of people killed over the past few years by faulty ignition systems in cars made by General Motors ought to be alive today, particularly because we know that employees recognized the problem, its riskiness, and expressed that in e-mail correspondence.

Here now are the Cass definitions:

Risk is defined as the "likelihood and impact of potential problems or undesirable events which might occur and prevent meeting an objective."

Risk analysis is defined as "attempts to define what could go wrong and what to do about it."

Risk management is defined as the "program framework for risk analysis and uses the results to make decisions and take action. Risk management is an *iterative* process which starts at program inception and ends with program close-out."[15]

In Figure 2, the vertical plane is the energy required to diagnose a risk, both its likelihood and impact to the organization and its goals; the horizontal plane again represents the passage of time. The arc beginning at the top left of the graph curving down toward the right indicates that it takes less and less energy to diagnose a risk over time. The arc starting at the bottom left and moving upward to the right suggests that to reduce risk, an organization, like an individual, ought to invest energy at the beginning

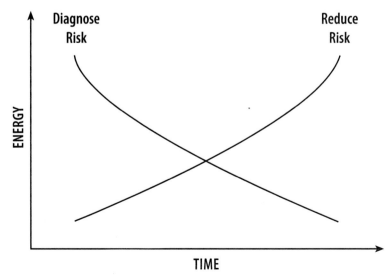

Figure 2 Paul-Tompkins law of risk communication

of new projects in order to discover risks early on and fix them so as to (1) avoid the higher costs of energy over time or (2) face the possibility over time that the risk cannot be fixed because sufficient energy is not available within the organization.

Now look at Figure 3 with the same eye used to view Figure 2—that is, to see it in terms of organizational risk communication. The vertical plane still visually suggests energy expended in communicating, diagnosing, and fixing a risk. It also represents the hierarchy of the organization, the chain of command from bottom to top. In this case each level of supervision is a marker for the semantic-information distance between two levels of the hierarchy. The horizontal plane would be the temporal economy of deadlines in an organization. Looking at the diagram this way, we can see at a glance that the speed of the upward-directed communication of risk (as represented by the diagonal arrow) is related to organizational success or failure because the sooner a risk is recognized at the bottom of an organization and sent up the line, and resources such as a task force or working group are appointed if necessary to fix it, the better it is for the organization. If it needs to go all the way

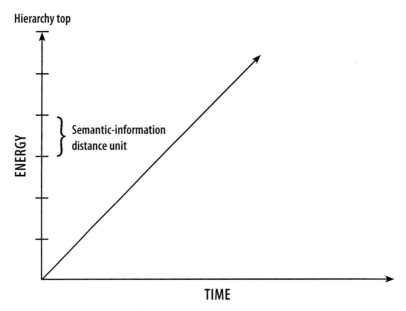

Figure 3 Semantic-information distance

to the top of a multilayered hierarchy, the cost is much more energy and time.

Imagine the message going from the worker on an assembly line reporting a problem to a first-level supervisor. That is one semantic-information distance unit. The supervisor must now take the potential risk to the next higher supervisory level. At each level the explanations must traverse the semantic-information distance between the two levels. Hence, one must take into account the vertical distance and the amount of time messages about risks require in the process of being moved and translated to a higher level of abstraction by people at the bottom to those at the top of the hierarchy. What if the organization allowed the worker to take the potential risk *all the way to the top* with her or his first message? Or fix it and then report it up the line?

After composing the paragraphs above, I happened to turn to Cynthia Stohl's book *Organizational Communication: Connectedness in Action.* I was astonished to read in it a quotation from my own PhD dissertation, a study of an international labor union in which I reported that rank and file members had completely different meanings for and attitudes about certain crucial words and phrases than did the union headquarters staff. Stohl wrote: "Tompkins (1962) termed this disparity of interpretation *semantic-information distance.*"[16] Hierarchy, or the vertical plane of communication and its distance, has been both mysterious and fascinating for me from the very beginning of my formal studies of organizations. Perhaps that is why I watch *Downton Abbey* religiously. The program's worldwide popularity proves that many others experience the same fascination. (For readers not familiar with *Downton:* There is the hierarchy upstairs, with Lord Grantham at the top, and the hierarchy downstairs, headed by Carson, the butler. Semantic-information distance exists *within* the hierarchy of each floor—kitchen maids know much less than other servants—and *between* the upper and lower levels of the Abbey. Ironically, the upper-class folks reveal things to and in front of servants they don't say to each other! It is as if servants are assumed not to understand the English language. Carson flouts his authority over valets and footmen more than does Lord Grantham. The maids and cooking staff are also locked in, as are the Lord's relatives upstairs. It makes for a humorously sad way of living: bowing and barking.) Getting back to the quotation in Stohl, I am reminded to stress the semantic-information distance that exists in the readers' own various hierarchies and alert them to the chance that it might be shortened to reduce risk.

In a partition titled "The Compression of Time and Space" in her essay "Globalization Theory," Stohl observes that the speed of new communication technologies that has hastened globalization, this "time-space compression involves the shortening of time and a shrinking of space."[17] This idea fits here for two reasons: the first to help us recall and keep in mind the effects of globalization on risks and risk management; the second is to remind us that the vertical distance on the risk diagram can be shortened by the use of new electronic communication technologies as well as other shortcuts.

Looking Ahead

The fuller meaning of the revised theory of open communication will become clearer as we analyze case studies and examples throughout the rest of the book. In chapter 2, for example, we shall see why hierarchies that "flatten" or shorten themselves have an advantage over those that don't. The analysis of theory and practice will interact to produce additions and refinements that will be gathered in the final chapter of this book.

In the past, organizational and management theories and practices were expected to demonstrate benefits to the organizations adopting them. Rorty's ideal type for open communication encourages us to ask what effect their practice has on the members of these organizations as well as on our society, its citizens, and all others in this world.

Notes

1. Richard Edwards, *Contested Terrain: The Transformation of the Workplace in the Twentieth Century* (New York: Basic Books, 1979).

2. Ibid.,161.

3. Phillip K. Tompkins and George Cheney, "Communication and Unobtru-

sive Control in Contemporary Organizations," in *Organizational Communication: Traditional Themes and New Directions,* ed. Robert D. McPhee and Phillip K. Tompkins (Beverly Hills, CA: Sage, 1985), 179–210.

4. Phillip K. Tompkins, Jeanne Y. Fisher, Dominic A. Infante, and Elaine L. Tompkins, "Kenneth Burke and the Inherent Characteristics of Formal Organizations: A Field Study," *Speech Monographs* 42 (1975): 135–42. doi: 10.1080/03637757509375887.

5. Tompkins and Cheney, "Communication and Unobtrusive Control," 183.

6. Richard Rorty, "Anticlericalism and Atheism," in *The Future of Religion,* ed. Santiago Zabala (New York: Columbia University Press, 2005), 40.

7. Timothy Kuhn and Stanley Deetz, "Critical Theory and Corporate Social Responsibility: Can/Should We Get Beyond Cynical Reasoning?" in *The Oxford Handbook of Corporate Social Responsibility,* ed. Andrew Crane, Abigail McWilliams, Dirk Matten, and Donald S. Siegel (Oxford: Oxford University Press, 2008), 177.

8. Phillip K. Tompkins, James Barker, and Karen Lee Ashcraft, "Communication, Unobtrusive and Concertive Control in Contemporary Organizations: A Theoretical and Empirical Update" (unpublished paper, 2002).

9. Ulrich Beck, *Risk Society: Towards a New Modernity* (London: Sage, 1992).

10. Ibid., 21.

11. Deborah Lupton, *Risk,* 2nd ed. (London: Routlege, 2013), 42.

12. Aaron Wildavsky, *Searching for Safety* (New Brunswick, NJ: Transaction, 1991).

13. James Reason, *Managing the Risks of Organizational Accidents* (Brookfield, VT: Ashgate, 1997).

14. Karl E. Weick and Kathleen M. Sutcliffe, *Managing the Unexpected: Assuring High Performance in an Age of Complexity* (San Francisco: Jossey-Bass, 2001).

15. Stein Cass, "Risk Management in the Aerospace Industry: Past and Present" (paper presented at the quarterly meeting of the Colorado Chapter of the International Council of Systems Engineering, December 2, 2004).

16. Cynthia Stohl, *Organizational Communication: Connectedness in Action* (Thousand Oaks, CA: Sage, 1995), 56. Emphasis in original.

17. Cynthia Stohl, "Globalization Theory," in *Engaging Organizational Communication: Theory and Research,* ed. Steve May and Dennis K. Mumby (Thousand Oaks: Sage, 2005), 251.

2

A Call from the Moon: Exemplary Communication Practices at NASA's Marshall Space Flight Center

"Its hazards are hostile to us all. Its conquest deserves the best of all mankind, and its opportunity for peaceful cooperation may never come again. But why, some say, the moon?

"Why choose this as our goal? And they may well ask why climb the highest mountain? Why, 35 years ago, fly the Atlantic? Why does Rice play Texas? We choose to go to the moon in this decade and do the other things, not because they are easy, but because they are hard, because that goal will serve to organize and measure the best of our energies and skills, because that challenge is one that we are willing to accept, one we are unwilling to postpone, and one which we intend to win, and the others, too."

—President John F. Kennedy, Speech at Rice University, September 12, 1962

The phone call came in January 1967 from a total stranger with a slight German accent who said he was calling from NASA's Marshall Space Flight Center (MSFC) in Huntsville, Alabama. He said his name was Walter Wiesman, coordinator of internal communication at MSFC, and then he invited me to serve as a summer faculty consultant in organizational communication. MSFC was the NASA field center developing the *Saturn V,* the rocket intended to take us to the Moon, and the director there was the legendary rocket scientist and all-around genius, Dr. Wernher von Braun. I jumped at the opportunity. I was 33 years old, an associate professor at Wayne State University in Detroit, and as excited as anyone about the audacity of President Kennedy's challenge: the peaceful exploration of space. But pragmatically, the young associate professor thought he might also learn a thing or two from those exotic space scientists while teaching them some basic communication theory and research findings.

Wiesman helped me get through the exhaustive security check conducted by the FBI and arranged for me to move into a furnished apartment in Huntsville. I showed up, got my security badge, and went through a thorough orientation program that included watching a mighty F-1 engine test that produced the loudest sound I have ever heard and a blast that bent trees to the ground over hundreds of yards. I toured all of the laboratories in Research and Development (R&D), studying the complex organization chart in my free moments. I even read some of Dr. von Braun's earlier correspondence as translated into English.

Many readers might wonder how a German rocket scientist happened to be developing the rocket that would take the United States of America to the Moon. The United States was drawn into World War II in 1941 when Japan attacked our military forces at Pearl Harbor. Japan was in an alliance with Italy and Germany, collectively known as the Axis or Fascist Powers, and so the United States joined its Allies, Great Britain, France, and other smaller countries attacked by Germany. Germany was under the control of Adolf Hitler and his Nazi political organization.

The Germans, led by the Nazis, developed amazing new weapons to subdue all of Europe. Their jet planes, the first, were important tools of conquest, capable of much faster speeds than propeller-driven aircraft. So was the V-2 rocket, capable of raining bombs on the lowlands of Europe and even Great Britain.

One of my mentors was horrified when I told him I was going to work for Dr. Wernher von Braun. "Why?" I asked.

"Because he tried to kill me," explained Professor Bruce Kendall. He had served in Great Britain during the war as an intelligence officer for the U.S. Army, and some of von Braun's V-2 bombs had landed near where he was working in London.

While readying myself for my new assignment, I learned that von Braun was working for us. Knowing about him and his work during WWII, the United States assigned an Army colonel, Ludi Toftoy, to head up part of what was known as Operation Paperclip. Its job was to find von Braun and his top scientists and engineers and bring them to the United States from Nazi Germany after we won the war. Toftoy's mission was a great success.

During my orientation period and before I met him, I could sense the charismatic presence of von Braun among the 120 Germans who came with him as well as the Americans, who accounted for the rest of the payroll of about 7,200 people, most of whom were engineers and scientists. I had even seen Hollywood's film biography of him. Born in Wirsitz, Germany, in 1912, by the age of 22 von Braun had earned two engineering degrees and a PhD in physics. He had a pilot's license, and in addition to his native German he spoke English and perfect French. He played the cello and piano and had composed music for those instruments. In addition, he was the genius among rocket scientists and had thought his way into a sophisticated view of the theory and practice of organizational communication, which I had studied while earning my doctorate at Purdue University. His reputation was more than a bit intimidating, but Wiesman told me not to worry about working with him.

Wiesman and I quickly became close friends, and he fascinated me with stories about the days making the V-2 rocket in Nazi Germany. Heinrich Himmler, head of the notorious SS, had ordered von Braun to join the SS but later had von Braun committed to prison for talking about exploring outer space after the war. Himmler labeled that kind of talk "defeatism." When von Braun was released from prison by Hitler, he went back to Peenemünde, the German Army base on the Baltic Sea. As the Soviet forces neared Peenemünde, Himmler gave orders for the V-2 forces, scientists, and engineers to defend their base to the last man. The Soviets, however, were looking to take von Braun and his top people back to the USSR (Union of Soviet Socialist Republics) to boost their program. Von Braun held a meeting with his top people and opened up a round of participatory decision making. They came to the conclusion that that they had endured enough of totalitarianism and elected to disobey Himmler's orders and make their escape to Bavaria, where they would surrender to the advancing U.S. Army. It was Wiesman's job to commandeer a train and load it with rocket designs, other important documents, and rocket scientists headed to Bavaria. *To be thrown in prison by Heinrich Himmler, head of the SS,* I thought, *is not a bad character reference.*

After interrogation by Toftoy's team—to filter out the Nazi true believers—the Germans were brought by the U.S. Army to Fort Bliss, Texas, for five years, their period of "wandering in the desert" as von Braun later wrote, while they tested and uprated the V-2 and learned to speak Southern American English with a German accent. (Wiesman later taught me to say "Wie gehts, y'all" when greeting people at MSFC in Alabama.) When the Cold War heated up, they were transferred to the Army's Redstone Arsenal in Alabama, where they developed the Redstone missile and the rest of our Cold War arsenal of intercontinental ballistic missiles. Von Braun and the rest of the Germans, 120 in all, fit right in with the Army's arsenal concept. The Army, unlike the Navy and Air Force, believed in having an arsenal with in-depth technical knowledge, enough to do the R&D for a weapon and *only then* farming out the manufacturing to an independent defense contractor.

When President Eisenhower created NASA, the "German team," as the group was called, quickly moved over to the brand new MSFC in Huntsville, not far from the Redstone Arsenal. Now they could pursue von Braun's lifelong dream of exploring the heavens as well as actualizing President Kennedy's goal of landing a man on the Moon and bringing him back safely within the decade. When I joined them in 1967 we had just a couple of years left in which to meet that deadline. The Soviets had beaten us into space with Sputnik, giving us deep national self-doubts, but now there was a heated space race to reach the Moon first, before the other superpower did.

Walt Wiesman explained to me that von Braun, as the manager of the V-2 Rocket Program, the U.S. Army missile development program, and now the leader of NASA's largest field center, had come to the conclusion that *the best way to understand and manage complex organizations was as a communication system.* Walt added that while searching for a faculty consultant in communication, he had gotten my name from W. Charles Redding, one of the founders of the field of organizational communication and a professor at Purdue University. Walt's information about approaching Redding to find a faculty consultant validated my opinion of von Braun's genius in organizational communication as well as rocket science because his people were ahead of the academics. It was said that I was the first faculty consultant to MSFC from the "soft" sciences; the others were all from engineering and the hard sciences.

The time came for me to have my first appointment with the boss, a large, athletic, handsome, and charming man. Walt walked me over to introduce me to von Braun, who then sat me down and explained his system of communication. (Readers can find a fuller description of von Braun's system of communication in my previously published articles and books listed in the Bibliography. I shall take a close look at some of the communication practices he created later in this chapter.) Two quotations from that meeting will suffice here. The first is this: "Communication up must be free, not tied to channels, if management is to be kept informed. However, there must be a clear action and command channel." Thus, my expression *open communication* derives in part from observing the success of *upward-directed communication that is "free, not tied to channels."* I cannot stress how important this was to the personnel at NASA-MSFC, and to my thinking about open communication and the management of risk. The second is a brilliant analogy: "This is like being in the earthquake prediction business," he said in a slight German accent as I furiously took notes. "You put out your sensors. You want them to be sensitive enough, but you don't want to be drowned in noise. We have enough sensors, even in industry."

Later in the meeting, von Braun gave me an assignment: to interview 55 top and middle managers in depth to discover which communication practices worked and which ones didn't. While typing up my notes from the meeting, I realized that von Braun had a profound understanding of *constitutive* communication. He had let me know that he understood the crucial importance of open loops of upward-directed communication in an organization facing tremendous complexities. He also understood the importance of *risk communication*—communicating about risks, and the earlier the better—as the earthquake prediction analogy demonstrated. Researchers in risk communication tend to concentrate on the negative connotations of the word *risk,* forgetting at times the thrills and excitement people get out of mountain climbing or making and riding a rocket to the Moon—risks people believe are worth taking. I was already caught up in the excitement and noticed I had begun using the "we" of organizational identification, as in *we* are going to the Moon!

Von Braun's analogy of being in the earthquake prediction business and having sensors within the space center and even in industry let me know his job was to predict and avoid risk by means of upward-directed communication from the sensors: his own NASA associates and the employees of private contractors. This essentially created or constituted a new *interorganizational communication system.* I took my job as a consultant to the head of a system of sensors seriously as I began interviewing in depth some of the world's top rocket scientists. Von Braun had written a letter to each one of my interviewees, providing my credentials, advising them that they would have anonymity, and instructing them to tell me the truth. They were ready for me, and some of the interviews lasted several hours and sometimes involved more than one long appointment.

The Mushroom Problem

I showed up for one of my interviews with a lab director early one summer morning and was shown into his office.

"Ah, Dr. Tompkins," he said in a German accent. "I understand you are here to see me about the mushroom problem."

"There must be some misunderstanding," I replied. "I don't know any-thing about a mushroom problem."

"Aren't you interested in organizational communication?"

"Yes."

"Do you know how to grow mushrooms?"

"No," I said, wondering what was happening to my interview.

"The way mushrooms are grown illustrates a common problem of orga-nizational communication. You put them down in the basement and keep them completely in the dark. Every once in a while you open the door and throw some horseshit on them."

We both laughed heartily and then had a productive interview, talking about other problems and how to solve them. It was obvious to both of us that von Braun was not trying to grow a crop of mushrooms.

I discovered 11 problems (including growing mushrooms) and came up with recommendations, which I reported back to von Braun. Characteristic of his communication style, he invited me back in October to address an audience of his top 55 administrator-engineers so I could tell them about their problems, make recommendations for improvement, and then take their questions, a process that lasted over two hours. (Later I was told that a top German rocket brain had commented, "He knows us better than ve do.") After the problems and recommendations discussion, I provided the audience with their answers to the most fascinating question I had asked them in the interviews: "What works?" The rocket scientists I interviewed were almost as excited as I while they described the powerful communica-tion practices we shall now examine.

What Works?

The Monday Notes

The first answer to the question "What works?" was invariably "the Monday Notes." The origin of the notes began when Dr. Kurt Debus, one of the 120 members of the German team, moved from Huntsville to Cape Canaveral to oversee the construction of launch facilities for the *Saturn V*. Von Braun missed interacting with him so he asked Debus to send him a weekly one-page note from the Cape in which he was to describe the week's progress and problems. Finding that he looked forward to reading the weekly note, von Braun decided to ask two dozen middle managers, lab directors, and project managers in this matrix organization to send him a weekly note summarizing the week's progress and problems, *skipping a layer of management*. As to format, simplicity was the key. The single page was headed by the contributor's name and the date, no NASA Form Number or other heading. The note was to reach von Braun's office each Monday morning. The layer of managers skipped could read them but could not edit them nor make any changes.

As von Braun read each note, he initialed it with a "B" and wrote the date in the upper right-hand corner. (The first time I saw a set of Monday Notes, the teacher in me automatically flipped through the pages looking for an "A" paper.) He put a check mark at the end of each paragraph, as if to let the reader know he had read every word. He also printed in a clear hand some marginalia from time to time—asking questions, making suggestions, and occasionally dishing out praise. The notes of July 10, 1967, included a question directed to a manager about some vehicle cost figures he had included in his note: "Have we passed this on to Mueller [a NASA Headquarters official]? B." To a lab director whose earlier recommendations about the superiority of one kind of weld over another had been rejected, and who then conducted additional tests which supported his original position, von Braun wrote, "Looks like you won after all! Congrats. B."

The next step was highly important. The collected and annotated notes, arranged alphabetically by author's surname, were reproduced and returned as a package to *all* 24 of the contributors. What was the effect of these notes? I put that question to each of the contributors. The answers came back as almost totally unqualified praise. "Best thing we do here," and other such compliments. The reasons given are worth considering.

First, the director was kept informed of progress and problems that needed his attention. This was, of course, in addition to the briefings, appointments, telephone calls, lab visits, and memoranda that took up much of his day.

Second, as the managers emphasized to me, the notes provided a crucial horizontal or lateral communication function in this matrix organization. Each lab director learned what all the other directors and project managers had been up to in the preceding week. The notes stimulated additional interaction among them. A lab director I was interviewing said the recently returned Monday Notes contained a comment from von Braun suggesting that he, the interviewee, needed to telephone a project director in the other part of the matrix about a mutual problem. By chance, my next interview happened to be with that very project manager. Without prompting from me, he volunteered that he discovered a suggestion in the notes that he needed to telephone the lab director. I emphasize this because the most serious communication problem I found in my study was competitiveness and a lack of lateral openness among the labs and project offices. The notes helped to overcome this.

Third, the marginalia supplied by this brilliant, charismatic leader made the notes "the most diligently read document" at the MSFC, as one interviewee put it. This crucial feedback function was mentioned by nearly everyone. They saw the feedback others got as well as their own. And any praise was treasured.

Fourth, von Braun had in the past visited the labs, listened to researchers give reports about their projects, and demonstrated the incredible depth of his knowledge and understanding. As he spent more and more time in Washington, DC, and other locations, the notes kept the channels of communication open during periods of decreased face-to-face interaction.

Fifth, the notes also served as an antidote to the sterile, formalized, bureaucratic procedures that NASA Headquarters produced. No code-numbered NASA-MSFC format was dictated: just the person's name, date, information about problems and progress, and then the boss's hand-printed feedback. Terms they used to describe the notes included *informality, quickness,* and *frankness.*

Sixth, curious about how a writer could summarize in one page a week's worth of such complex work, I asked each of them how they did it. This allowed me to discover something that von Braun did not know but was absolutely delighted to learn. The lab directors said they asked their division chiefs for a Friday Note. Division chiefs told me they asked branch chiefs for a Thursday Note. Von Braun's simple request for a one-page Monday Note caused most of the personnel at this space center to pause at least once a week and ask what the boss, and colleagues, most needed to know about progress and problems. This provided a rigorous and regularly recurring discipline of communication within this organization.

George Cheney, Lars Thoger Christensen, Theodore E. Zorn Jr., and Shiv Ganesh discussed the Monday Notes in their book, *Organizational Communication in an Age of Globalization: Issues, Reflections, Practices*. They began by noting that I had referred to the "process through which stories change as they are communicated to different levels in the organization as *uncertainty absorption*." Then, as if prescribing an antidote for the disease, they described the Monday Notes as a "regular feedback mechanism," and as being one of the most "useful channels of communication" in NASA during the Apollo Period.[1] Uncertainty was reduced by the process.

Frederic Jablin and Linda Putnam invited Karl Weick and Susan J. Ashford to contribute a chapter on learning in organizations for a voluminous handbook of organizational communication they edited. The two authors, Weick and Ashford, gave a theoretical treatment of the subject and then used my description of the Monday Notes as a model of organizational learning. They thought the flow of the notes fostered "faster learning" than did more routine practices. They found them more "conversational" because of the regularity and feedback. Because each lab producing a note spoke a different technical jargon, the participants became aware of different ways of expressing problems and solutions. With Stohl's reminder in chapter 1 about the problems introduced by vertical semantic-information distance, we can see that there was also a *horizontal* semantic-information distance that was reduced by this practice, which also promoted organizational learning, important in managing risk. The frequency would, as Weick and Ashford wrote, also reduce hindsight bias as well as "masking," and learning is facilitated where "conflicting forces are tolerated." In an astute, memorable statement, they wrote this about the Monday Notes: "Since drafting the notes is done in part by people who are actually doing the work . . . , the drafting is *constitutive* as well as representative. People do things they can talk about."[2] The Monday Notes thus facilitated learning by constitutive and open communication and a source of motivation.

Automatic Responsibility

I had not heard of the concept of automatic responsibility, which had long been part of von Braun's communication toolbox, until my interviewees told me about it. It had started with lab directors and then moved deeper into the organization, right down to the floor of the labs where engineers got their hands dirty with the components of the Moon rocket. It meant this: if anyone in the organization discovered a problem—let's call it a risk to the rocket and program—he was expected *automatically* to participate in all projects that involved his discipline and to carry his own work through to its conclusion. That meant that if an engineer in Lab A found a risk in a project in his area of competence, even if assigned to Lab B, he had to drop what he was doing and accept responsibility for finding a solution to the risk if possible. There was also a communicative principle in automatic responsibility. The person who discovered the problem was automatically responsible for communicating the problem up the line, whether he could fix it or not. That is what von Braun meant when he told me in our first interview that "communication up must be free, not tied to channels." Automatic responsibility included free and open upward communication.

If the person reported a problem or risk he could not fix, von Braun would study it and create a working group made up of people representing all of the relevant disciplines and specialized knowledge that could be applied to the problem. Working groups would do exactly as the name implies: work together to find a solution acceptable to the entire group. These were among the most complex problems tackled, and solving them required knowledge from all the different relevant disciplines. At times there were compromises, which were inevitable, but as von Braun put it to me, what we had to avoid was a "*foul* compromise," a phrase I have tried to use in my own decisions ever since. The recommendations of these working groups could rarely, if ever, be overturned. No single individual had all of the knowledge from all the different disciplines involved to make the decision with any confidence. Group members were open and assertive, but they also listened to each other and made "tradeoffs." (This was the first time I had heard that word used for compromise.) These working groups were models of intelligent, informed, effective participatory teamwork.

Penetration

Organizational penetration is the process in which a member of one organization enters the communication system of another, say a supplier, for the purpose of learning whether the second organization's work meets the criteria of risk, cost, and quality of the penetrating organization. Shortly after learning about this practice from the managers I was interviewing, I found documentation for it in a book by H. L. Nieburg published just a year before I went to work at MSFC—a hard-hitting volume entitled *In the Name of Science*. This book provides a catalogue of atrocities committed by what the author calls the "contract state." The book reviews systematic waste, profiteering, technical failures, cost overruns, and plain ineptitude on the part of corporate contractors, mainly in the defense industry and the government agencies that were supposed to monitor them. Nieburg describes a congressional subcommittee inquiry into how a specific contractor, General Dynamics Astronautics, could have made some fundamental mistakes in its development of the Centaur rocket for the U.S. Air Force. The project was later referred to NASA, the mistakes were fixed, and von Braun was called to the subcommittee to testify. According to Nieburg, von Braun's testimony "euphemized the situation, yet succeeded in conveying a sharp indictment of the Air Force management."[3] Von Braun's testimony was this: "I think what we felt was a lack of depth of *penetration* of the program on the part of the government personnel, in very general terms. We believed that this staff of eight people . . . [was] just an inadequate coverage on the part of the government, no matter whether it is NASA or the Air Force."[4] When NASA assumed the management of the project, von Braun assigned 140 technical personnel to supervise the contractor—in contrast to the Air Force's 8.

An even more dramatic illustration of the practice of penetration emerged during one of my interviews in 1967. This top ranking manager at the MSFC explained to me that a contractor's first experience with the Marshall Center was usually "traumatic" because the MSFC managers and engineers were so aggressive in making sure they were going to get exactly what they had ordered. One such contractor delivered its first attempt to fabricate the complex second stage for the *Saturn V* to the MSFC in Huntsville. This stage had rigorous heat leak specifications that virtually required a vacuum seal; the requirements were so exacting that an ice cube placed inside it at a temperature of 70 degrees Fahrenheit would take eight and a half years to melt and another four years for the water temperature of the resulting puddle to rise to 70 degrees. The Marshall personnel quizzed the contractor's representatives in a conference room at the MSFC, asking them about the possibility of cracks in the stage.

After many denials, the contractor's people finally admitted there might be some cracks in the stage they had delivered.

"How many cracks?

"Twenty-one," was the answer.

"No, there are 26 cracks," asserted the MSFC engineer.

"No, no, no," the contractor averred with sincerity.

The rocket stage was then X-rayed and found to have 26 cracks—along with a few workers' tools and lunch boxes and other debris that should not have been there. The contractor was nonplussed. Its representatives had begun by, well, hedging at least, but then admitted some mistakes, only to learn that the customer knew more about their own merchandise at the moment of delivery than they, the manufacturer, did. The MSFC had penetrated the contractor's organization, observed the production process, and developed rapport with the contractor's personnel, who knew not to send bad news up the line of their own organization, but were willing to open up to the MSFC personnel.

Organizational penetration is a very important practice. How important? I introduce here the most persuasive evidence of the damage of a failure to execute organizational penetration by U.S. government agencies.

On Sunday, February 16, 2014, the television program *60 Minutes* reported that the F-35 fighter jet was $160 billion over budget, seven years behind schedule, and will cost taxpayers $400 billion—twice as much as it did to put a man on the Moon. The Pentagon's weapons buyer stated that this was a case of "acquisition malpractice" and that the Pentagon should have followed the "fly before you buy" adage.

It also should have practiced von Braun's cost- and risk-cutting practice of penetration.

My interviewees told me they had learned on the job at MSFC to practice an internal, or vertical, variation of penetration. As a lab director put it, it was helpful to penetrate two layers up, to the office of the boss's boss, and two layers down, through the division chief to the branch chief. I found this useful in my own career as professor, department chair, and associate dean—penetrating *at least* two levels up and two down.

Manned Flight Awareness Program

There were other effective risk communication practices by NASA during the Apollo Program. For example, the Manned Flight Awareness program was developed because, counting both the government personnel and the many more contractor employees, more than 200,000 people were working on some aspect of the Apollo Program. Many had no idea what they were making or that it might be part of a Moon rocket. So, NASA sent astronauts out to the private contractor plants to give a pep talk to the workers. The astronauts used to joke about the risks they faced by asking their audience how they would feel about going up in spacecraft built by the lowest bidder. The workers were said to be delighted to learn about the importance of what they had previously considered to be meaningless work.

I must also mention organizational identification because of its importance to the theory of open communication. I saw it in the MSFC employees, both those I got to know well and those I didn't. They worked long hours without overtime pay. They sought responsibility. Their salaries were at times half those of comparable contractor technical personnel. Today all this would be considered a dysfunction of identification by some writers of the critical school. It did not occur to me or to them that their working conditions were at all unfair. I felt it myself—the emotional, quasi-religious feeling—while slipping into the "we" of identification. The organization became a part of me as I was a part of it. We all knew we had *voice*, knew that we would be heard whenever we had an important message to express. That knowingness increases the degree of oneness with the organization and with all involved.

It is important to note that I observed Simon's model of decision making (identifying and listing alternatives, determining the consequences that could result from each alternative, and applying the criteria of efficiency, time, and cost to each set of consequences) at work at the MSFC. It was obvious if one knew to look for it. The main premises (and criteria) for decisions and the arguments in the working groups trying to reach a compromise were cost, reliability, and time. The schedule was important, dictated by President Kennedy's goal to get to the Moon within the decade, and so was the budget. But as highly qualified engineers who identified with the product, their highest value consensus was reliability. Tradeoffs they had to make at times, but they were instructed to avoid the "foul" compromise. By agreeing that reliability was more important than the other two premises, they had the value consensus defined in chapter 1.

Implications for Risk Communication

The presentation of theory in chapter 1 allows us to use it as a structuring mechanism to better understand the case studies presented in this book. In this case, as I assume my readers know, we did go to the Moon and return the astronauts safely to the Earth. The communication practices described in this chapter helped NASA to overcome the extreme complexity and risky nature of the enterprise. The first observation is that it was open communication at both the organizational and team levels that worked. The working groups showed the intense teamwork at the group level that was vitally important. In addition, the exemplary communication practices constituted openness. Recall that one of the aspects of the original theory was "flattening" or minimizing the hierarchy. The Monday Notes did this by skipping a level of management, reducing both vertical and horizontal semantic-information distance. Automatic responsibility was a liberating concept allowing a person to bypass any intervening steps of the hierarchy when he or she perceived a risk to the technology, skipping all layers between the reporter and top management.

Consider also how penetration flattened the hierarchy. MSFC personnel penetrated the contractors' organizations, talking to the people on the lab floor and listening to their problems—problems they were fearful of communicating up the hierarchy of their own company. Instead of relying on later reports of risks to go all the way up the bureaucratic levels of the contractor and then be communicated to the MSFC, the Marshall Center representatives were there at the labs where some of the action was taking place. In addition, penetrating two levels up and two down within the MSFC also had a flattening effect. All of these hierarchy-flattening practices enabled messages about risks to move much faster and sooner than would have been possible had the protocol of bureaucratic control been observed. The risk communication diagram (Figure 2) presented in chapter 1 reminds us of the advantage to the organization in recognizing a risk at the earliest possible moment so that working groups or teams can be created to solve it if beyond the competence of the individual who discovered it. At the MSFC, penetration, hierarchy flattening, and open communication allowed the risks to be discovered early and fixed in time. Recall also that Weick and Ashford said that the Monday Notes facilitated faster organizational learning, thus saving time in recognizing and managing risks.[5] An additional perspective and appreciation is gained by the remark made to me by an engineer at the time: "All of this in an organization governed by civil service regulations!"

Figure 2 in chapter 1 also gives structure to this case study by making us notice the redundancy built into the system. Redundancy can be defined from a communication perspective as more information than is ideally necessary. Repetition and restatement of a message are simple examples that aid communication until the receiver reaches an advanced state of boredom, but we can also talk about the redundancy of communication channels. Redundancy is important to engineers in designing and building risky technology, as is illustrated when backup components are built into the design in case the original part fails.

Dr. Atul Gawande, whose work is important to chapter 4 about the medical establishment, complexity, and risk, discusses the importance of redundancy to human health in his most recent book, *Being Mortal: Medicine and What Matters in the End.* In it he writes about how engineers build backup systems to backup systems and points out that we have two kidneys, two lungs, two breasts, two gonads, and extra teeth. Our most complex machines, then, imitate the human body to a limited degree. Gawande mentions that "Leonid Gavrilov, a researcher at the University of Chicago, argues that human beings fail the way all complex systems fail: randomly and gradually."[6] But the redundancy does give those complex organizations some extra years of life and reliability.

The same principle was at work with von Braun's redundant channels of communication. For example, the Monday Notes not only flattened the hierarchy, but they also provided an *additional* channel in addition to the normal upward-directed reports, appointments, briefings, telephone calls, and other methods. Within the Monday Notes for one week, one might read several reports of the same successful or failed test of a weld of two exotic metals. Automatic responsibility also provided redundancy for messages that would go up the line through the routine channel. Penetration allowed MSFC management to receive reports from Marshall Center personnel who had direct contact with the contractors, as well as to quickly hear about what personnel who penetrated within the MSFC had learned. Having redundant channels of communication, by analogy to technology, could again save time if one channel failed and the backup worked.

Finally, let me add another dimension that is not purely communicative in nature but fits the risk communication scheme we have employed. The MSFC had the reputation among high tech organizations as being by far the most frequent tester of all. They tested the mighty F-1 engines early and often, one of which I observed and *heard.* They even had a giant "shake table" that would literally shake the rocket vigorously, emulating the vibration of the controlled explosion of a lift-off. The personnel at all levels told me that they learned more from the failed tests than from the ones that passed. They also tested much earlier than other organizations, as if following the lesson of the intersecting curves on our risk communication model (Figure 2): the earlier the better. Again, the system worked.

What about the effects on society? I need not dwell on the lift, the increase in pride, the sense of unity the people of the United States of America and beyond experienced when astronaut Neil Armstrong told Houston the *Eagle* had landed. We won the space race in a peaceful competition that also gave warning about our technical competence to attack an enemy. People around the world went to the Moon with us.

What about the individuals involved? There can be no question that the astronauts benefited from the MSFC's risk communication practices. What about rocket scientists and engineers? One could make a case that by encouraging a sense of identification with the organization, astronauts, and the common good, the open communication was beneficial to the individual. Why otherwise would the MSFC engineers work closely with, and accept much less pay than, their counterparts in contractor organizations? They identified with and were responsible for and proud of their collective achievements.

Before moving on, I must acknowledge and repeat that I would not have become a summer faculty consultant to von Braun if Professor W. Charles Redding had not been sought out by Walter Wiesman, internal communication coordinator at NASA's MSFC. Redding had been my dissertation adviser at Purdue University. He was also the author of the theoretical concept "ideal managerial climate"[7] or IMC, which has five components. My professorial calling now compels me to assign grades to the MSFC on all five of those criteria.

Supportiveness: A-
Participative decision making: A+
Trust, confidence, and credibility: A+
Openness and candor: A+
Emphasis on high performance goals: A+

All five criteria add up to what this book advocates: *reducing risks to organizations, employees, customers, and the public.* I give the MSFC an A- on Supportiveness because of the competition among labs and project offices that caused them to be at times somewhat opaque with each other instead of completely transparent.

I was invited back to the MSFC in 1968 and I accepted. This time von Braun wanted me to help him anticipate the future, project to the post-Apollo period, and come up with an organizational chart for the future and ways of strengthening the Marshall Center's approach to systems engineering. (The MSFC had a tendency to over-engineer components, making later integration of those components more difficult.) I was invited again in 1969 but had to say no because I had received a wonderful grant from my new employer, Kent State University, to travel to the National Museum and Library in Dublin, Ireland, to continue my research into the work of the Irish novelist James Joyce, a piece of the other side of my scholarly life.

Kent State University: "Four Dead in Ohio"

I was invited back to the MSFC in 1970 to help again with organizational problems created by NASA Headquarters' desire to strengthen systems engineering. Again I had to say no because the president of Kent State University had appointed me to a task force on communication and the general commission to study the events of May 4, 1970. At that time it was riskier to be on a university campus than in a space center with all those controlled explosions known as rocket engine tests.

"Four dead in Ohio," sang Crosby, Stills, Nash, and Young on "Ohio," recorded and released just weeks after the shootings. They might have added some words along this line: "And nine wounded in Ohio." I still feel a sense of outrage about the killings, fired up again yesterday—in 2014—when a friend sent me an e-mail message that a well-known clothing store was offering bloodstained Kent State University sweatshirts. I said no to NASA in order to find out why it all happened on May 4, 1970. The president of KSU, Robert I. White, not only appointed me to two groups doing research and making recommendations, he also gave me a grant to finance a study in which we would interview 225 students, 120 faculty members, administrators, and himself. Helping me with the project was a young instructor in communication, Elaine V. Anderson, who became my coauthor when it was obvious that a book should be written about the case.

But I must describe the reason such a communication study was needed. Colleges and universities in the United States in 1970 were different than they are today. Communication was different. There were no cell phones or social media, of course. And the students looked different. Their dress and appearance were intended to communicate, to be a counterstatement of opposition to the "establishment," consisting of President Nixon, Congress, the Defense Department, other people in power, and their war in Vietnam. Long hair, beards, headbands, tie-dyed tee shirts, and unkempt clothing pinned with slogan-bearing buttons came to every class meeting: all of this was a "we-ness" in opposition to the war, and the norms and mores of those who supported it. Kent State University was no noisy Berkeley; it had been relatively quiet in comparison with other campuses. There had been, however, an incident in 1969, a case in which the administration suspended members of the SDS, Students for a Democratic Society, and revoked their organization's charter without hearings. But we had gotten past that and the administrators had a feeling of relief and confidence in the spring of 1970.

But in April of that year we learned that the United States had expanded the war against Communist North Vietnam by an incursion into Cambodia. President Nixon addressed the American public via television on April 30, 1970, in an attempt to quiet protestors and justify the apparent reversal of his policy to bring the war to an end. Students and others rallied on the KSU campus the next day and promised some "street action" in the downtown section of the city of Kent. As prophesied, store windows were smashed, a bonfire was set, and police cars were pelted. The mayor of Kent declared a state of emergency and closed all the bars, turning a lot of Friday night partiers into an angry and growing mob.

The mayor called the governor to get him to send the Ohio National Guard to protect the city and the campus with the hope of reducing the risk to all of us there; the Guard arrived to find damage done to the city and a wooden ROTC building blazing on campus. The many KSU students who spent Friday and Saturday elsewhere, out of town, returned to campus on Sunday, May 3, to find it encircled by uniformed and armed guardsmen and their military vehicles. A crowd of people gathered that night and were told that the mayor and the president of KSU would meet with them. Then later they were told that the two men would not meet with them. Because of this about-face, they felt that they had been double-crossed. The crowd cursed and threw rocks at the guardsmen and police; teargas was fired at the crowd. Injuries were sustained on both sides.

On Monday, May 4, I crossed the line of guardsmen at the edge of campus on the way to my office. A glass door of the building was shattered. Posted on another door was an order not to destroy any part of the campus. There was a hand-scrawled poster on the first-floor bulletin board calling for a rally on campus at noon. I asked a secretary in our office to call the provost, the chief academic officer, and ask whether or not classes had been canceled. The answer was no. My office was too cool that morning in early May to concentrate and I needed to finish grading papers for a late class, so I went back home and missed the horror in the quadrangle.

The rally took place. The students and other protestors were up against an armed military enemy. The guardsmen, some of them KSU students avoiding the military draft, tried to break up the rally. Confusion and teargas canisters followed. The guardsmen fired at the protestors: four dead and nine wounded in Ohio.

It was my job on the KSU commission and communication task force to find out how well KSU operated as a communication system during this risky and complex crisis. We found that it hardly functioned at all. The president had left town on Friday without informing anyone. The vice president and provost, who should have been in charge, did not know the president had left town. The only communications from the administration to the university community during the crisis were a statement on the campus radio station and a leaflet, placed mainly in student mailboxes in dormitories on Sunday afternoon, advising that the governor had taken control of the campus and prohibited demonstrations and rallies. The National Guard officers, on the other hand, thought the administration was still in charge, believing they and their troops were there only to maintain order.

Our interviews showed that the statement on radio and in leaflets was almost entirely ineffective. Few students check mailboxes on Sunday. Only about a third of the faculty and students knew the guardsmen had live ammunition in their weapons. Many faculty members said that if they had known the facts they would have been there to advise the students to go to classes, to stay away from the Guard. The president and the administration assumed the National Guard was in charge. The National Guard thought they there only to prevent rallies that might lead to more destruction. We found that the university qua organization disintegrated on May 4, 1970. All students and faculty members were evacuated from campus. The rest of the spring term had to be conducted by mail because students were not allowed back on campus. In addition, my interviews with administrators revealed that the disintegration during the crisis could be traced to the routine functioning of the organization. The president paid little attention to upward-directed communication; the other administrators were completely shut out of decision making. Practically nothing had been done to prepare staff, students, and faculty for this highly risky situation. It was either a stark or a vivid contrast in communication systems moving back and forth between KSU and the MSFC, depending on one's perspectival point.

A maximum sum of semantic-information distance is the best way of characterizing the vertical channels of communication at KSU, particularly pertaining to risks to students, faculty, the university, and the public. How different organizations are in their preparedness for risks, whether expected or unexpected.

A former student of mine from the seventies sent me an e-mail after the British Petroleum accident in the Caribbean, remarking on the similarity between the cases: a confusion as to which of the several organizations in the situation had authority. Shocked but not completely surprised by our research findings, I wrote a book on the sad tale: *Communication Crisis at Kent State: A Case Study*.[8] My coauthor, Elaine Anderson, became Elaine Tompkins in 1971, and we are still happily married today. Another detail I should add is that a student in one of my communication theory classes in the spring term of 1970 asked if he could give me a term paper without words.

"Well, John," I answered, "I've never seen one before."

He said he had been at the May 4 rally with his camera and thought he could tell a story about communication with photographs. I told him to go ahead, and when I received the paper I had to give it an A+. It showed the protestors gathered together, taunting the guardsmen. It showed the teargas canisters being fired at the students and other protestors, some of whom threw them back. One could see the tension building, and then there was, inevitably, the bloody student on the ground and a young woman kneeling over him with a distortedly pained look on her face as she realizes he is dead. John also sent the term paper for my class to his hometown newspaper in Pennsylvania. The newspaper staff submitted John's paper as a folio entry to the Pulitzer Committee. John Filo won the Pulitzer Prize for Photography that year. As a wedding present he drove up to Grand Rapids, Michigan, on June 12, 1971, to photograph our outdoor wedding. He also let us publish his photographs in our book.

Final Thoughts

The MSFC during the Apollo era was successful. Against the high risks of technical failure and loss of life, the Marshall Center built the rocket that took Americans to the Moon. How? By managing complexity and risk with open communication and teamwork: Dr. von Braun's risk detection system was a network of sensors placed strategically who would report back with little or no hierarchy to work through. The other practices of Monday Notes and automatic responsibility created the redundant channels so crucial to effective communication and provided an early warning system of risks consistent with the Paul-Tompkins law of risk communication. Kent State University, by contrast, lacked any kind of risk detection system in either its routine or its emergency methods of functioning. The chief administrator abandoned authority and responsibility for communicating, for warning the faculty and students about the risks posed by the loaded weapons of the National Guard.

It is difficult to find words to explain the feelings as I moved from campus to a rocket center and back to campus. I witnessed and heard rocket engine tests that were controlled explosions, and yet I felt little sense of risk from them. The hallowed university campus where one retreats to learn, read, and contemplate was far riskier and dangerous than the rocket center. It was not what I would have predicted earlier. Our rocket center director anticipated risks and planned for them while our university president was neither trained nor able to think of administering an organization of that many people during a time of riot and National Guard incursion. Nor did he learn from the many other campuses that had experienced much more protest and violence. We were helpless against the risks of protest and an attempted military enforcement of the peace.

As forecast in the Introduction, the next chapter will present and closely examine studies testing theoretical ideas—drawn in part from the MSFC communication practices—about managing complexity and risk.

Notes

1. George Cheney, Lars T. Christensen, Theodore E. Zorn Jr., and Shiv Ganesh, *Organizational Communication in an Age of Globalization: Issues, Reflections, Practices* (Prospect Heights, IL: Waveland Press, 2004), 151.

2. Karl Weick and Susan J. Ashford, "Learning in Organizations," in *The New Handbook of Organizational Communication: Advances in Theory, Research, and Methods*, ed. Fredric M. Jablin and Linda L. Putnam (Thousand Oaks, CA: Sage, 2001), 726.

3. H. L. Nieburg, *In the Name of Science* (Chicago: Quadrangle Books, 1966), 89.

4. Ibid.

5. Weick and Ashford, "Learning in Organizations," 726.

6. Atul Gawande, *Being Mortal: Medicine and What Matters in the End* (New York: Metropolitan Books, 2014), 33.

7. W. Charles Redding, *Communication within the Organization* (New York: Industrial Communication Council, 1972).

8. Phillip K. Tompkins and Elaine Vanden Bout Anderson, *Communication Crisis at Kent State: A Case Study* (New York: Gordon and Breach Science Publishers, 1971).

3

Studies of Open Communication and Teamwork

"The concept of Identification begins in a problem of this sort: Aristotle's *Rhetoric* centers in the speaker's explicit designs with regard to the confronting of an audience. But there are also ways in which we spontaneously, intuitively, even unconsciously persuade ourselves."

—Kenneth Burke, *Language as Symbolic Action: Essays on Life, Literature, and Method*

This chapter begins with an atheoretical, purely objective and quantitative study of a highly complex phenomenon, perhaps the most complex of all human endeavors: the production of knowledge, *new* knowledge I hasten to stress, even if the phrase is redundant. I shall attempt to define *complexity,* not easy to do; many writers avoid doing so because, I have inferred, it is too complex to define. Here goes:

> Complexity is a system of variables or units whose number and relationships are difficult to comprehend in their totality. Problems attacked by today's organizations are thought to be increasingly complex because the number of variables related to problems and solutions are increasing, partly because of subdivision into smaller entities and their specializations, and also because new technologies and cultural differences among workers produce additional variables and relationships among them.

If the findings in the first study we will consider in this chapter, an examination of knowledge production, turn out to be consistent with the theory of open communication and teamwork, then it should be considered all the stronger as support for the theory because, theoretically speaking, the researchers were relatively disinterested in organizations and the data are concrete and objective, not at all subjective. That is, their concern was with understanding the reaction to the increasing complexity of the world of knowledge production, not organizational theories. We shall then consider three classic case studies of open communication and teamwork: the first, a manufacturing organization in the United States; the second, a bank in Bangladesh; and the third, an important U.S. aerospace contractor. We shall also consider at least one more recent data point on each case study.

A Survey of the Production of Knowledge

The three authors of a very large research project on knowledge production—Wuchty, Jones, and Uzzi—were associated with the Institute on Complex Systems at Northwestern University. That such an institute exists is a commentary on our times. The authors begin their article, published in the journal *Science,* by mentioning that the "acclaimed tradition in the history and sociology of science emphasizes the role of the individual genius in scientific discovery"[1]; they also ironically quote F. Scott Fitzgerald, the American novelist, to the effect that "no grand idea was ever born in a conference."[2] The authors cite some rather small studies that found a modest trend toward collaboration in some scientific academic fields, then take a much larger and broader sample of published articles in all of the sciences, engineering disciplines, social sciences, arts and humanities, and patents. They also quantified the citations of each publication—the number of times the article was later quoted by others—a well-accepted measure of quality. The opening abstract of their article is a low-key summary of a truly massive and conclusive study:

> We have used 19.9 million papers over 5 decades and 2.1 million patents to demonstrate that teams increasingly dominate solo authors in the production of knowledge. Research is increasingly done in teams across nearly all fields. Teams typically produce more frequently cited research than individuals do, and this advantage has been increasing over time. Teams now also produce the exceptionally high-impact research, even where that distinction was once the domain of solo authors. These results are detailed for sciences and engineering, social sciences, arts and humanities, and patents, suggesting that the process of knowledge creation has fundamentally changed.[3]

Almost 20 million papers plus 2 million patents over a period of five decades is a persuasive sample. To repeat, the data include publications and the citations of them, thus establishing both the higher quantity and *quality* of the teams' work in comparison to that produced by solo scholars. (The more citations a publication has, the higher its quality. Some administrators have been known to consult an individual scholar's citation index while making a personnel decision.)

The closest the authors come to a theoretical explanation is the observation that the "steady growth in knowledge may have driven scholars toward more specialization, prompting larger and more diverse teams."[4] This means that to understand a problem it is necessary to gather together people who collectively have knowledge of all the new and different specializations relevant to the problem.

The hypothesis is quite similar to the observation I made in 1967 and 1968 when I discovered the ad hoc working groups appointed by Dr. Wernher von Braun to deal with risks—technical problems so complex that experts from the Marshall Space Flight Center's (MSFC's) different engineering disciplines and specializations had to work together to solve them by means of argument, rhetoric. And no supervisor, no manager could have had the combined and detailed knowledge with which to override those group decisions. Those rocket engineers and scientists were creating knowledge by finding ways to reduce the new risks, even though they usually did not publish their results. This study of knowledge production provides disinterested support for the theory of open communication and teamwork.

Barker and ISE

In 2009 Montoya, Candrian, and I published a summary of all the research on concertive control that readers may wish to consult,[5] but here I present three particularly important studies to consider at this point. The first of these was conducted by a graduate student working with George Cheney and me at the University of Colorado Boulder, James R. Barker, who was steeped in the theory of concertive control. While attending an alumni reception sponsored by the local chapter of his social fraternity, Barker found himself seated next to the man he calls "Jack Tackett," the vice president of manufacturing for a company Barker would later call "ISE," located in the metropolitan area of Denver. Barker told the man he was interested in work teams and organizational culture, to which Tackett responded by inviting him to visit ISE because it was undergoing a transformation to the teamwork approach for manufacturing electronic circuit boards. Barker spent half of a workday visiting the site and learning about this company with a workforce of about 150 people going through significant changes. Then Barker negotiated a research contract with Tackett that gave Barker rights to write a dissertation and publish his findings in return for promising to create a fictional name for the company.

Barker used an ethnographic approach with the workers, operating as if he were an anthropologist studying tribes in a foreign country. He observed them in their teams at work making circuit boards, had conversations with them, and conducted informal and formal interviews for three years, a long time for a dissertation field study. Before he defended his dissertation on this organization, he submitted an article to *Administrative Science Quarterly* that was published in 1993. The title of the article was "Tightening the Iron Cage: Concertive Control in Self-Managing Work Teams,"[6] and it won the Outstanding Publication in Organizational Behavior Award for 1993, given by the Academy of Management. This article and the award made the theory of concertive control known to students of organization and communication around the world.

The title of the article had multiple meanings. One was an allusion to a metaphor used by the German sociologist and student of communication, Max Weber, who had created an abstract description of bureaucratic control that could be used in comparative studies of this phenomenon. Weber had referred to bureaucratic control, rules applied by trained and salaried experts, as an "iron cage."[7] Barker's title also confirmed the prediction made by Cheney and me that moving from the traditional form of control to the concertive form would increase the total amount of control in the organization. Thus the cage would be even tighter than before. To paraphrase a comment made to Barker by a worker, it used to be that we could relax when the boss left the work area, but now everybody is a boss. Six years later Barker would write a book about the study: *The Discipline of Teamwork: Participation and Concertive Control*,[8] the premise of which is that discipline increases power, control, and organizational effectiveness.

It is not unimportant to this story that ISE had been struggling to stay in business when the vice president of manufacturing made the switch to teams. He was a firm believer in participative management up and down the line; he was also a consultant who coached other companies on how to make the transformation. The effect of the change to participatory communication and decision making at ISE was dramatic: it cut costs by 25 percent, mainly by flattening the organization, as Henry Ford had done with the conveyor belt, by eliminating an entire layer of supervisors who were no longer needed because the self-managing teams now did their own supervisory work. Two years later, in 1990, the company began to turn a profit. So by the first criterion stated in the Introduction—do organizations prosper by employing the theory?—it is quite clear that ISE benefited from the change in control. But what about the individual workers and their larger community? There is not much evidence one way or the other about the community, but it surely did no harm to that suburb of Denver to have a company right itself by changing its mode of control. Moreover, it is no doubt good for the democratic political system in a country when its citizens participate in decision making and self-governance at work, the reason being that the employee-citizens will be more likely to participate in the political system by staying up on issues, fighting for what they believe is right, learning the skills of participation, and voting rather than being apathetic.

As for the second criterion about the effect of the theory on workers, Barker deliberates it at great length in his book. On one hand, he was concerned about what he saw during his observations of workers disciplining others. There were now financial incentives for the workers to do their best, and they were overheard scolding each other for tardiness, absence from work, and avoidable mistakes. It also caused stress for workers who had to cancel important appointments with family members because they had to work overtime for the good of the team. There was also pressure in the disciplining of other workers, in electing their own coordinators, and making decisions. On top of all that was the social norm that teaches us to look down on people who point out our mistakes to the group.

Would the workers have preferred that ISE go back to its old system of control? In his book, Barker is adamant, emphatic that they did not want to go back to the old system, for many reasons. I had suggested to him during the time he still had access to the work group that we give them a questionnaire that measures identification to determine whether they identified more with the team or the company. He jumped at the chance because he had readily accepted the rhetorical dimension of the theory, particularly Kenneth Burke's theory of the "new rhetoric"—that is, identification as self-persuasion. Barker had discussed identification as a component of concertive control at some length, showing that the workers had persuaded themselves to accept their own, self-selected decision premises. The quantitative results showed that the workers had a higher degree of identification with their team than with ISE, the organization that had hired them and was paying them.[9] Thus, if hegemony by identification was at work, it was now happening more by the teams of workers than by management. This was actually a second data point on ISE because Barker's and my study was done by means of a quantitative questionnaire of identification created and tested by George Cheney. True, it was not long after Barker's ethnographic data gathering, but it did show that the objective and subjective data agreed.

The workers at ISE had achieved a communal-rational system in which they planned the work, elected their team coordinators, and set aside time to criticize the team's methods and decisions, and as a result they felt a sense of dignity. In rereading these descriptions years later, I detected some effects similar to those of the concept of automatic responsibility I had observed at NASA's MSFC. The team members sought and accepted responsibility for their actions. I conclude it was *healthy* for these workers, far healthier to work in self-managed teams, being heard and exercising concertive control over themselves, than to work under either bureaucratic or technical control.

The main title of Barker's book, *The Discipline of Teamwork*, gives the impression that concertive control was developed solely for teams, or small groups. Barker did not intend to create that misunderstanding; he refers to ISE after its transformation as a "new concertive organization," an expression consistent with the original expression of the theory.[10] Both the managers and the workers at ISE had to be trained in participatory management.

Can we go back for a third data point? Unfortunately, no. I heard through the grapevine that ISE met its demise. Why? Did the teamwork and open communication cause it to go out of business? Barker answered the questions via e-mail on January 26, 2014: "ISE's demise had nothing to do with concertive control or the VP [the man who introduced the system]. The company was bought out by a larger . . . board maker that wanted the circuit board IP [intellectual property] and patents, not the manufacturing capability. They already had the circuit board manufacturing capability. . . . [They] just incorporated ISE's boards into their product line and then they shut the ISE production side down." Barker has not written more about it because it is "too depressing," the "cold, hard capitalist system—bought out by the big guy."

The Grameen Bank

Barker took notice of prior studies of concertive control in the review of previous research in his dissertation, article, and book; one was a study of the U.S. Forest Service conducted by Connie Bullis that we shall consider in a later chapter. The other study Barker was fascinated by was conducted by Papa, Auwal, and Singhal: "Organizing for Social Change within Social Control Systems: Member Identification, Empowerment, and the Making of Discipline."[11] The abstract of the study is reproduced here:

In recent years, the Grameen (rural) Bank of Bangladesh gained international fame for successfully organizing grassroots micro-enterprises for productive self-employment and social change. The Grameen Bank provides collateral-free loans and various social services for the poor, charging 29% interest on capital loans and yet maintaining a 99% recovery rate. Many of the bank's 1.9 million members, of whom 94% are women, attribute their present well-being to its ameliorative qualities. Using multiple theories (coorientation, concertive control, and critical feminist theories), we analyze the Grameen Bank's programs to explicate the dialectic between control and emancipation in organizing for social change. By examining the Grameen Bank's organizational process from multiple perspectives, we draw insights about theory and praxis in organizing for social change.[12]

Papa, Auwal, and Singhal used concertive control theory as a theoretical approach to the bank study because the members, mainly women, who get the loans are the poorest of the poor in a poor country; they are assigned to groups of five in which to monitor, advise, and control each other's actions related to the loan. In addition to their collective advice, they pressure each other to repay the loans because failure to do so would jeopardize the credit opportunities for others. A principle is at work here, not unlike the one inspiring the Manned Flight Awareness program, by making borrowers understand that there would be negative consequences for the other poor women like themselves who desire loans if they are delinquent in paying off their own loans. Even though the groups of five members can be thought of as teams, the application is of the concertive organizational theory; the bank workers who in turn monitor the teams also employ concertive control. Acting collectively, they pressure each other to maintain the miraculous loan recovery rate of 99 percent mentioned in the abstract. Their recovery is generated by the bank workers, who also recognize the importance of getting loans repaid, acting in concert, not by pressure from upper management.

Making the outcome of the loans more miraculous is the fact that women generally experience discrimination in Bangladeshi society, particularly those who are among the poorest. Getting loans and experiencing the equality and teamwork of concertive control is a transformative experience for them. The loans and the advice they get from their groups is uplifting, raising them up out of dire poverty and into a form of emancipation. Women who become financially independent in Bangladesh attain a greater sense of equality, increasing their chances of being treated with respect.

Organizational identification also gets attention in this study. The members so identified with the bank and its loan program that, as mentioned, they were willing to participate in teams that advised them, thus helping them pay back their loans. The authors say that their survey showed that some of the bank workers identified so much with the organization that they might have lost objectivity about some of the organization's activities, working long overtime hours.

Michael Papa, Arvind Singhal, and Wendy H. Papa return to the Grameen Bank in their 2006 book, *Organizing for Social Change: A Dialectical Journey of Theory and Praxis.*[13] Notice the subtitle—a dialectic between theory and praxis. This book is highly recommended for people interested in both organizational communication and positive social change.

In the Introduction of the present book on complexity and risk, I write that organizational theories ought to be accountable to the organization, of course, but also to its workers, customers, and society. The Papa, Singhal, and Papa book tries to answer those questions and was published in 2006, 16 years after their research into the Grameen Bank began. We therefore can have considerable confidence that they have enough data points so that their findings are not atypical or in error because of bad timing (e.g., getting a glimpse of a passing fad).

Papa, Singhal, and Papa combine concertive control theory, including identification, with the theory of dialectical relationships. They propose four dialectics in their book on organizing and social change: emancipation and control, empowerment and oppression, dissemination and dialogue, and unity and fragmentation. The first of these dialectics, emancipation and control, is of primary interest here, but a similar idea was put forth back in 1969—the theory of the dialectical organization—that we shall take up in chapters 5 and 6 of this book. Papa, Singhal, and Papa use their dialectics well and also stress the team metaphor in their research. But to get back to the update, by early 2005, the Grameen Bank had lent the equivalent of nearly five billion U.S. dollars to 4.2 million poor people, 95 percent of whom were women, in over 50,000 Bangladeshi villages, and it still maintained that remarkable loan recovery rate of 99 percent.[14]

The idea of the Grameen Bank was conceived by Muhammad Yunus and put into practice in 1976 after he returned to Bangladesh from the United States with a doctorate in economics from Vanderbilt University.

In 1997, Dr. Yunus helped organize the global Microcredit Summit in Washington, DC, to mobilize resources to help the poor in the rest of the world. By December 31, 2003, "seven years after the campaign got underway, microcredit was disbursed to 81 million poor people, of which 55 million represent the poorest-of-the-poor. Of these poorest clients, 45 million are women."[15] The great achievements of the Grameen Bank and the Summit were recognized when Dr. Yunus received the Nobel Peace Prize in 2006. In this complex Age of Globalization, it is reassuring to know that teamwork and open communication have been validated in the most difficult of situations by the highest of awards.

Has the Grameen Bank been good for the people of Bangladash? Despite the overwhelming positive evidence, Papa, Singhal, and Papa quote from an exploration of a "paradox of control" by Stohl and Cheney"[16] that "surfaces when workers appreciate the perceived freedom that comes with creating their own control system, yet they actually experience less freedom within the work group because they must all keep an eye on one another to reach codetermined goals."[17] This idea had emerged from Barker's research on ISE, when he found that real teamwork increased the total amount of control in the system. In the case of the Grameen Bank workers, Papa, Singhal, and Papa feel that their conditions are oppressive, as they compete with each other to maintain the high loan repayment rate, working long overtime hours. They conclude their book chapter on the Grameen Bank by asking, "How can control systems be created in which members retain a voice in establishing their own path to individual and collective empowerment?"[18]

To repeat the question, was concertive control in the Grameen Bank good for Bangladeshi society? Few would dispute the positive answer to that question. There can be no doubt that concertive control was good for the women of Bangladesh: it was a participative, transformative, emancipating process for them, making explicit the feminist assumptions of the original concertive control. It seems possible, however, that the participatory, open communication was designed for the customers, not the bank workers. The workers seem to have experienced some form of communicative closure: they did not seem to participate in decision making to reduce their own stress. More research is needed on this question because it has implications for both the idiographic and nomothetic goals of organizational communication research. This work does teach us that Grameen Bank members and customers had to submit to a control system before they could be liberated—and that in self-control they paradoxically produced more control than that imposed from above. We should not, however, leave this organization for another without expressing gratitude to the researchers for showing us how communication has emancipated so many women in such a profound way.

Concertive Control in an Aerospace Contractor

Our final case study in this chapter was completed for a doctoral dissertation at the University of Colorado Boulder by Gregory Larson. This summary is based on a subsequent article by Larson and me (I was the director of the dissertation) published in 2005 under the title "Ambivalence and Resistance: A Study of Management in a Concertive Control System."[19] The organization researched was found to practice concertive control: it had a flattened hierarchy, organized its employees in teams, and its employees identified with core value premises for decisions, in this case high technical standards. The theory adopted is communicative in nature, involving direction, monitoring, and the dispensing of rewards and punishment—these three communicative acts adding up to what has been called the "double interact of control."

This is an in-depth, qualitative study of JAR Technologies (fictitious name), an aerospace company located in the Rocky Mountain region of the United States. JAR had been forced to make substantial changes in its business practices and its value decision premises. These changes at the company, tracked over the course of 11 months by Gregory Larson, provided a serendipitous moment in which to study the processes of the dialectic of control and resistance in an attempt to change basic value decision premises. Approximately 2,500 employees of the company, at the time of the study, work primarily in JAR's Rocky Mountain Headquarters, designing and manufacturing satellites for NASA and commercial customers. It is a matrix organization, with standing laboratories and project or program offices that interact with the technical units. Most of the employees are engineers and other professionals who are distinctive because of their high levels of education and professional affiliations that give them mobility. They are attracted to JAR because of the reputation of its unobtrusive, participatory management system and high technical standards. The engineers are collectively powerful, and some of them have been promoted into the top management staff.

The company had a strong reputation for solving difficult technical problems and for building reliable hardware. In the 1990s, however, JAR's biggest customer, NASA, adopted a new culture based on a different weighting of the decision premises of cost, reliability, and time. Reliability had been the first among equals during the Apollo period, but 25 years later, "Faster, Better, Cheaper" was the slogan preached by NASA administrator Daniel Goldin. It was clear that time also meant money as well as being on schedule in the aerospace business, so the slogan actually meant "Cheaper, Better, Cheaper on Time"—something of a contradiction.

This study of JAR provides a circular coincidence in that the concepts of organizational identification and concertive control were discovered and examined during my empirical studies of NASA's MSFC in 1997 and 1998. Larson chose JAR in large part because of its location, its easy access facilitating frequent research visits. Once he entered and understood the dynamics of JAR, he realized that by coincidence it provided the opportunity to test those theoretical ideas in an empirical study of a NASA contractor. It is not unimportant that the earlier and later studies have found that NASA has changed profoundly over the past 30 years, creating the strained conditions at JAR. JAR had long ago adopted the original technical culture, or OTC, that had served NASA and the MSFC so well during the Apollo Program but was now being abandoned. Larson attended meetings, conducted interviews, had access to important documents, and provided the organization with an opportunity to react to his findings. He presented his findings and conclusions to a group of two dozen JAR employees and managers, including the chief executive officer.

The two-hour briefing and discussion confirmed that the themes discovered in the research were consistent with the understanding of the JAR participants, validating the research.

Managers at JAR decided to adapt to the change in the weighting of the decision premises so that the company, like its competitors, would benefit financially. During the course of Larson's research project, the engineers who participated in concertive or collective control resisted the efforts of management to make the change. As the resistance became apparent, the managers "*subtly undermined their own change efforts*."[20] Many of the managers, as engineers who came up from the concertive technical culture, still identified strongly with the value premise of high reliability. One manager stated proudly that JAR's reputation with others in the industry was one of being "technically arrogant." The managers began to experience ambivalence about the reasons they gave for adapting to what they thought the customer wanted. Their attitude became ambivalent and their discourse at times was thereby ambiguous, calling for the change in culture while praising their past. "Finally, despite pushing for change, some managers expressed hope that the environment of the past would someday return."[21]

Larson and I concluded our article by noting that at times management may subtly support the resistance of employees. Tight teamwork might be an iron cage not only for workers but for the managers who once functioned within it. It occurred to me after we wrote that article that over time the engineers at JAR had learned the skills of concertive control: how to argue rationally for and against technical solutions to problems that were risks to their projects. Such skills are not easy to stow, out of mind and use, when management wants to change the weighting of values, their very decision premises. Finally, the researchers in this study concluded that the case should not be read as a failure of management, but rather as an episode of the dialectic of control, and a reflection of the material, value, and discursive differences that management and employees must negotiate.

Our article appeared in *Communication Monographs* in 2005, the same year my book *Apollo, Challenger, Columbia: The Decline of the Space Program* was published. As we shall see in chapter 7, Faster, Better, Cheaper did not work well for either NASA or for its contractors, making JAR's recalcitrance all the wiser and more admirable. Did concertive control work well for JAR? I say yes. The engineers' resistance produced ambivalence in the managers trying to change the value premises. It seems that the engineers, the resistors, have prevailed up to this point.

Partly because of JAR's proximity to my home and partly because it is an important aerospace company, I have kept track of its business since Larson did his research, and I report that JAR has achieved some splendid accomplishments since then. The promise made to protect the company's identity prevents me from itemizing those deeds—deeds that could not have been achieved had JAR gone too far in reducing its historic cultural stress on the premise of reliability. The dialectic of control did not diminish the quality of the company's work; the resistance by engineers could not have damaged this process. In regard to the balance among cost, reliability, and time, JAR's management did not commit what von Braun had called a "foul compromise." Open communication and teamwork worked for JAR. The resistance to the change and its effect on the company is a sign of its dialectical strength.

Procedural Clarification and Summary Comments

Before making tentative conclusions about the studies, I must make a procedural statement important to the goals of this book. Because we have considered these studies in considerable detail, including more than one data point in time, it is not possible for this to be an encyclopedia of all the studies relevant to open communication, participation, and teamwork. In addition to close readings of some studies, the book relies on the conclusions of excellent scholars who have surveyed all available research. In addition, I have decided to include accounts of teamwork and open communication from medical doctors, consultants to business, and some business leaders who have discovered and presented their own kind of data about the themes of this book. I think the analysis benefits from this type of epistemological complexity and relativity.

As the Wuchty, Jones, and Uzzi study of scholarly publications shows, in a span of 50 years the practice of open communication and teamwork has grown more and more prevalent in the production of knowledge—in both its quantity and its quality—across all academic disciplines. Complexity demands that people break up into arcane specializations and then come back together as a team with other specialists to combine their insights into the creation of knowledge. In the case studies in this chapter, we saw first in Barker's study of ISE something close to the ideal abstraction of concertive control or teamwork. Workers first were trained in the skills of participatory decision making, as were their managers, a point to remember in assessing such approaches. Duly trained, they elected their coordinators, planned their work, gave directions, and corrected mistakes: the collective, double interact of control. They worked for the benefit of the team, and the organization began to show a profit, even though the workers identified more with the former than with the latter. They also increased the total amount of control in the system, benefiting themselves, the organization, and the community.

In the Grameen Bank study, we saw an inspirational story of how an open system of teamwork could allow the poorest of the poor women in a struggling society to achieve independence, success, and emancipation. This study shows that open and supportive communication can produce profound and beneficial social change as well as good business outcomes.

In the study of JAR, we saw the power of open communication, teamwork, and identification with the decision premise of high reliability: value consensus that also equals the reduction of risk. We saw that just like simple and bureaucratic control, concertive control can manifest a strong claim on the part of the workers for the "contested terrain" between them and the managers. And it can produce resistance against management's attempt to change the traditional value consensus of reliability in order to control technical decisions in a different way. (In chapter 9 we shall take a look at a company in the Norwegian oil and gas industry in which a pseudo-participatory safety scheme imposed by management produced resistance among workers in the form of clever informal teamwork.) It takes a strong organization to function effectively while experiencing a highly dynamic dialectic of control. Altogether, the studies in this chapter show strong support for the theory of open communication and teamwork. The organizations and workers functioned in different cultures even at the global level. Yet they all seemed to agree that the results were good for their organization, the employees or workers, and their communities. The studies also strongly suggest that teamwork reduces risks in the products of their work.

Open communication, teamwork, and participation in organizations have other, far-reaching aspects. Think of the improved self-respect and reduced risk of the Grameen Bank members and the workers at ISE and JAR. Think also of the benefits to society. The workers and members may well have become better citizens, better able to participate in public affairs because of the new skills they acquired through their active participation. Think back to the ideal communication situation described by Rorty in the epigraph to chapter 1: the reduction of barriers to human communication created by levels of organizational hierarchy. We can safely say that these practices improve the quality of individual and collective existence, even elevate being.

Although risk was not a variable measured in these case studies, I am willing to assume that the participation reduced it. What industries care most fervently about reducing risk in their work? Certainly one of them must be medicine. Quality control in diagnosing our banes and prescribing antidotes for them affects nearly everyone on the planet. Chapter 4 looks at the importance of open communication and teamwork in the practice of medicine. We shall look at some astonishing data gathered in an international experiment of surgery. The answers to managing risks and increasing complexity in the realm of practicing medicine are there for us to adopt—today.

Notes

1. Stefan Wuchty, Benjamin F. Jones, and Brian Uzzi, "The Increasing Dominance of Teams in Production of Knowledge," *Science* 316 (May 18, 2007): 1036.

2. Ibid.

3. Ibid.

4. Ibid., 1038.

5. Phillip K. Tompkins, Yvonne J. Montoya, and Carey Candrian, "Watch Your Neighbor Watching You: Applying Concertive Control in Changing Organizational Environments," in *An Integrated Approach to Communication Theory and Research*, 2nd ed., ed. Don W. Stacks and Michael B. Salwen (New York: Routledge, 2009), 370–86.

6. James R. Barker, "Tightening the Iron Cage: Concertive Control in Self-Managing Work Teams," *Administrative Science Quarterly* 38 (1993): 408–37.

7. Ibid., 437.

8. James R. Barker, *The Discipline of Teamwork: Participation and Concertive Control* (Thousand Oaks, CA: Sage, 1999).

9. James R. Barker and Phillip K. Tompkins. "Identification in the Self-Managing Organization: Characteristics of Target and Tenure," *Human Communication Research* 21 (1994): 223–40. Our theory of organizational identification drew heavily from the work of Kenneth Burke, e.g., *A Rhetoric of Motives* (New York: Prentice-Hall, 1950).

10. Barker, *The Discipline of Teamwork,* 70.

11. Michael J. Papa, Mohammad A. Auwal, and Arvind Singhal, "Dialectic of Control and Emancipation in Organizing for Social Change: A Multitheoretical Study of the Grameen Bank in Bangladesh," *Communication Theory* 5 (1995): 189–223. See also Michael J. Papa, Mohammed A. Auwal, and Arvind Singhal, "Organizing for Social Change within Concertive Control Systems: Member Empowerment, and the Masking of Discipline," *Communication Monographs* 64 (1997): 189–223.

12. Ibid., 189.

13. Michael J. Papa, Arvind Singhal, and Wendy H. Papa, *Organizing for Social Change: A Dialectic Journey of Theory and Praxis* (Thousand Oaks, CA: Sage, 2006).

14. Ibid., 72.

15. Ibid., 69.

16. Cynthia Stohl and George Cheney, "Participatory Practices/Paradoxical Practices: Communication and the Dilemmas of Organizational Democracy," *Management Communication Quarterly* 14 (2001): 349–407.

17. Papa, Singhal, Papa, *Organizing for Social Change,* 89.

18. Ibid., 107.

19. Gregory Larson and Phillip K. Tompkins, "Ambivalence and Resistance: A Study of Management in a Concertive Control System," *Communication Monographs* 72 (2005): 1–21.

20. Ibid., 11. Emphasis in original.

21. Ibid., 13.

4

Operating as a Team with Checklists: Reducing Complexity and Risks in Health Care

"If anger, fear, and outrage were triggered solely by numbers of deaths, news coverage and conversation would be focused on pedestrian traffic deaths caused by drivers travelling at excessive speed—not on Ebola."

—Katherine E. Rowan, "Why Some Health Risks Upset Us and Others Do Not: Risk Perception and Risk Communication"

"Throughout I've sought to show not just the ideas but also the people in the middle of it all—the patients and the doctors alike. In the end, it is practical, everyday medicine that most interests me—what happens when the simplicities of science come up against the complexities of individual lives. As pervasive as medicine has become in modern life, it remains mostly hidden and often misunderstood. We have taken it to be both more perfect than it is and less extraordinary than it can be."

—Atul Gawande, *Complications: A Surgeon's Notes on an Imperfect Science*

This chapter on the U.S. health care system relies heavily on the work of the two most eminent reform advocates in U.S. medicine, the first of whom is the son of a mother and father who were both immigrants from India and both medical doctors.[1] Their son became a medical doctor and is now a surgeon at Brigham and Women's Hospital in Boston and professor in the Department of Health Policy and Management at Harvard School of Public Health and in the Department of Surgery at Harvard Medical School. He has written three best-selling books and since 1998 has been a staff writer for *The New Yorker*. One of his articles for that magazine, later quoted in a speech given by President Barack Obama, was about the findings of a study contrasting the most and least expensive medical care in the United States. He looked first at McAllen, Texas, one of the most costly health care markets in this country even though it is located in Hidalgo County, which has the "lowest household income in the country."[2] Dr. Atul Gawande decided to pay a housecall on McAllen.

McAllen vs. Grand Junction

When he sat down to dinner with six local physicians, Dr. Gawande asked why McAllen had the most expensive health care in the country. Some seemed dubious about the assessment, but they began to give him reasons such as "better service" and the "threat of malpractice suits" until a surgeon put a stop to the pretense by saying, "We all know these arguments are bullshit. There is overutilization here." The surgeon continued by declaring that doctors "were racking up charges with extra tests, services, and procedures."[3] Then it began to come out: many doctors in McAllen owned their own imaging offices in shopping malls where nearly every patient was sent for X-rays and other more expensive imagery, whether needed or not. A hospital administrator told Gawande in an interview that the local doctors seemed to cross over into *fraud* when they demanded $100,000 per year to send patients to the administrator's hospital. One doctor had asked for $500,000. The hospitals were forced to pass these "expenses" along to their patients. There was no evidence that the health care was any better there than in other cities in Texas.

While delving into the medical statistics to find a positive contrast to McAllen, Gawande found that one of the lowest priced health care markets in the country was in Grand Junction, Colorado, a city which also has one of the highest quality-of-care scores. Medical expenses in McAllen are nearly threefold more than in Grand Junction. Gawande learned that the doctors in Grand Junction had gotten together some years before to make decisions collectively, in *concert*. They had agreed to a fee schedule they would all follow, charging the same amount to their patients whether they were backed by personal financial funds, Medicare, Medicaid, or insurance companies, thus eliminating the temptation for individual doctors to cherry-pick patients with the best insurance or financial resources. They also decided to rely on open communication and teamwork by setting up committees to review each doctor's record, patient charts, fees, and prescriptions to root our poor practices and over-utilization, such as unnecessary imagery and operations. Unnecessary operations, of course, pose the same risks, both medical and financial, to patients as necessary ones.

This medical collective also created a shared electronic practice of interorganizational communication for the entire community of Grand Junction. All doctors now have access to the electronic medical files of all patients in the community. This has enabled them to slash their overhead costs deeply by reducing the number of office staff and filing cabinets—and to reduce the number of redundant medical examinations. As the costs went down to a level lower than almost all other cities in the country, the quality of care went up. (In the same article, Gawande observed that both the Mayo Clinic and Kaiser Permanente use the principle of teamwork by having a general provider consult with specialists to help coordinate patient care.[4] In addition, because their doctors are all salaried, there is no motive to cherry-pick lucrative patients or commit the sin of overutilization. The high quality of care provided by those organizations is well known.)

Getting Things Right

One of Gawande's books is highly relevant to the themes of complexity, risk, open communication, and quality control: *The Checklist Manifesto: How to Get Things Right,* published in 2009. In this dramatic, first-person narrative, Dr. Gawande confesses that medical science is constantly creating a condition of increasing complexity for him and other doctors. At the time the book was published, the World Health Organization (WHO) classification system had grown to more than 13,000 diseases and types of injuries, 6,000 drugs, and 4,000 medical and surgical procedures. Those numbers have presumably increased since 2009.

In his book, Gawande states that he had begun to think, *maybe it's just me;* so he asked the people in Harvard Vanguard's medical records department if they could find out for him how many different kinds of patient problems their average doctor sees in a year. He states he was "flabbergasted" by the answer that came back. Over a year's time of office practice—which excludes patients seen in the hospital—physicians encountered an average of 250 different diseases; their patients had 900 other medical problems that had to be considered; and the average doctor prescribed 300 medications, ordered more than 100 lab tests, "and performed an average of forty different kinds of office procedures—from vaccinations to setting fractures."[5] In addition to the complexities of the average doctor's practice, some areas of medicine have become so super-specialized, says Gawande, that doctors joke about right-ear and left-ear surgeons, and he worries that there might actually *be* such specialists. He states that he began to look around for other industries that had faced periods of increasing complexity in the hope of finding new ways to cope.

After the first chapter of *The Checklist Manifesto,* which is full of medical statistics demonstrating increasing complexity and risk, the reader is transported in chapter 2 to Wright Airfield in Dayton, Ohio. The date is October 30, 1935, and the U.S. Army Air Corps is holding a flight competition for airplane manufacturers, each of whom wants to build the Army's next generation of long-range bombers. The design of one of the airplanes in the competition, the Boeing Model 299, stood out in the early evaluations and was favored to win. A small crowd of Army Air Force officers and airplane executives had gathered to watch. The Model 299 tax-ied onto the runway, a gleaming aluminum-alloy bomber with a 103-foot wingspan; the pilot revved up its four engines and took off, climbing to 300 feet when it stalled and "crashed in a fiery explosion. Two of the five crew members died, including the pilot, Major Ployer P. Hill."[6]

A smaller plane designed by Martin won the competition, and Boeing nearly went bankrupt trying to figure out what caused them to lose the contract they had been confident of winning. The investigators finally came to the conclusion that the cause of the crash was pilot error. Because the Model 299 was substantially more complex than any airplane built to date, at takeoff pilot Plover had had to concentrate on all four engines, retract-ing the landing gear, adjusting wing flaps, and regulating propellers—and unfortunately he forgot to release a mechanism on the elevator and rudder controls. Although after the crash it was labeled as "too much airplane" to be handled by a human pilot, there were some people at Boeing who did not give up on the Model 299. A group of test pilots got together and came up with a checklist. Voilà! They made it simple—short enough for an index card—a step-by-step approach to takeoff, flight, and landings. The crew was now able to fly the plane with the checklist, and the rest is history. The Model 299 flew so well that the Army Air Force ordered almost 13,000 of what became known as the B-17, the famous "flying fortress" that played a significant role in helping the Allies win World War II. Checklists have been used to reduce risks in flying airplanes and in handling complex or-ganizational operations ever since.

It was a professor of organizational communication, Larry Browning of the University of Texas at Austin, who saw the importance of checklists to organizational functioning back in 1992.[7] I had taken checklists for granted back in my Marshall Space Flight Center (MSFC) days because I assumed it was necessary in that complex environment, a bit like the necessity of making a course syllabus for students, but it took people like Browning and Gawande to recognize the importance of using this seem-ingly simple yet powerful device in many different situations. Gawande helps us to understand this by observing that in a complex environment experts have to avoid falling into two different traps. The first trap is the fallibility of memory and attention: we forget to complete one of the steps in a process, or we are distracted by some noise in the system and as a result miss the step. Gawande credits engineers with an expression, "all-or-none processes"[8] that denotes situations in which missing one key thing makes the whole effort useless—or worse.

The second trap is skipping a step that we remember but think we can usually get by without. It never has been a problem to skip this step—until today. An example he gives is that Western hospitals did not start recording the four vital signs until a checklist was developed for their patients in the 1960s. (Nurses have since added a fifth vital sign to their checklist, a subjective pain rating on a scale of 1 to 10.) Skipping one of the signs on the checklist might not affect any patients on my ward today, but as for tomorrow—we might lose a patient. Gawande calls it the "discipline of higher performance,"[9] which made me think of the main title of Barker's book: *The Discipline of Teamwork*. In *The Checklist Manifesto*, Gawande goes out of his way to point out that the doctors deserve no credit for creating this new disciplined medical routine: all the credit goes to the nurses—teams of nurses.

"Charts and checklists, that's nursing stuff—boring stuff. They are nothing that we doctors, with our extra years of training and specialization, would ever need or use."[10] Although that was the attitude of most doctors, a critical care specialist at The Johns Hopkins Hospital, Peter Pronovost, decided to prescribe a checklist for those same skeptical doctors who worked in the ICU teams. He started with only one of the hundreds of potential tasks they face and plotted the steps to take to avoid infections when putting in a central line:

> Doctors are supposed to (1) wash their hands with soap, (2) clean the patient's skin with chlorhexidine antiseptic, (3) put sterile drapes over the entire patient, (4) wear a mask, hat, sterile gown, and gloves, and (5) put a sterile dressing over the insertion site once the line is in. Check, check, check, check, check. These steps are no-brainers; they have been known and taught for years. So it seemed silly to

make a checklist for something so obvious. Still, Pronovost asked the nurses in his ICU to observe the doctors for a month as they put lines into patients and record how often they carried out each step. In more than a third of patients, they skipped at least one.[11]

Pronovost did not stop there; he asked the Johns Hopkins Hospital administration to authorize nurses to step in and stop doctors from putting in a line if they skipped a step on the checklist. He got that authorization, and Gawande calls it revolutionary. Some nurses traditionally have nudged doctors when they saw them skip a step, but many have wondered whether it is within their authority to do anything. If a nurse in this one hospital saw a doctor fail to follow a single step, she or he could intervene *with the approval of the administration.* They tracked the effects over one year and could not believe the data: the infection rate went from 11 percent to zero. They followed the patients for another 15 months and counted two line infections in the entire period. The checklist, they projected, had prevented 43 infections and 8 deaths and had saved two million dollars in costs.

Gawande says Pronovost, who holds an MD and a PhD in public health, is described by his colleagues as a "genius" and by similar laudatory terms. He went on to create other checklists and got similar results. He then began to lecture around the country about his checklists, but there were few adoptions. Why? Gawande's first reason or explanation is that most doctors were offended by the suggestion that they need checklists. Others doubted the reliability and validity of Pronovost's data. And so far the evidence had come from only one hospital, a prestigious one at that, where the intensive care units (ICUs) probably had plenty of money, nurses, and doctors to bother with checklists.

In 2003 things began to change. The Michigan Health and Hospital Association approached Provonost about testing his central line checklist in the ICUs of hospitals all over the state. Gawande visited a hospital in the inner city of Detroit during the experiment. The redbrick hospital buildings were located among abandoned houses on the west side of the city. The staff cared for a population with the lowest median income of any city in the United States. More than 250,000 were uninsured. Gawande accompanied a team making its 7:00 a.m. rounds through one of the surgical ICUs. Of the 11 patients, 4 had gunshot wounds, 5 had cerebral hemorrhaging, a man's skull and left temporal lobe had been damaged by blows from a blunt instrument, and so on. But through it all, the teams were filling out their checklists, and the job usually fell to one of the nurses. In December 2006 a landmark article in the *New England Journal of Medicine* reported that the infection rate had decreased by 66 percent in the ICUs of the state of Michigan in the past three years.[12] In 2009 Gawande would write that during the first 18 months of this experiment "the hospitals saved an estimated $175 million in costs and more than fifteen hundred lives. The successes have been sustained for several years now—all because of a stupid little checklist."[13]

No More Master Builders

It was on a bright January morning in 2007 when Gawande was walking to work that he noticed the new hospital wing under construction. It would have 3 floors underground and 11 above. Although he looked forward to having new operating rooms, he wondered how they could be sure the new building wouldn't fall down and paid a visit to Joe Salvia, the structural engineer. Salvia told Gawande that his firm's specialty was designing and engineering complex buildings all over the United States, and that the tallest building the firm had under construction at that time was an 80-story tower in Miami.

After Salvia related his education and experience, he drew an analogy between a building and a body: each has a skin, a skeleton, a vascular system or plumbing, a breathing or ventilation system, and a nervous system (the wiring). He explained that complex buildings today require 16 different specialized trades, which makes their construction so complicated that there is no longer a Master Builder, the person who designed them, engineered them, and oversaw the construction from start to finish. The Master Builders of St. Peter's Basilica, Notre Dame, and the U.S. Capitol would be out of work today because the variety and sophistication of advancements in every stage of the construction process—and the 16 trades involved—have exceeded the ability of any individual to master them. "Yet we in medicine continue to exist in a system created in the Master Builder era—a system in which a lone Master Physician with a prescription pad, an operating room, and a few people to follow his lead plans and executes the entirety of care for a patient, from diagnosis through treatment."[14] Gawande pursued the building analogy and then found an answer in the main conference room: the checklists. High-rise buildings are built by checklists.

During one of the speeches I gave on this topic, at the University of Montana in 2010, some students reacted with skepticism to the suggestion that they use checklists, expressing the attitude that checklists are too rigid. (A possible explanation for this attitude is that they had attended classes taught by Gregory Larson and therefore knew about the Fire Orders of the U.S. Forest Service, a highly dysfunctional list we shall encounter in chapter 5.) So I asked the students if they thought difficulties might exist that a checklist could not anticipate. Gawande must have had the same concern because he dropped in on Finn O'Sullivan, the project manager for the building, to get the answer:

> That was when O'Sullivan showed me a different piece of paper hanging in his conference room. Pinned to the left-hand wall opposite the construction schedule was . . . a "submittal schedule." It was also a checklist but it didn't specify construction tasks; it specified *communication* tasks. For the way the project managers dealt with the unexpected and the uncertain was by making sure the experts spoke to one another—on X date about Y process. The experts could make their individual judgments, but they had to do so as part of a *team* [emphasis added] that took one another's concerns into account, discussed unplanned developments, and agreed on the way forward.[15]

This is the answer to experts who advise us that we can never anticipate everything in a modern world. Of course we can't. But it is possible to anticipate our lack of ability to anticipate by calling for communication among team members at intervals over time.

Readers of *The Checklist Manifesto* can feel the excitement of Gawande's prose as he begins to think seriously about checklists, and to experiment with them. He sees a way of bringing to an end the tradition that surgery is an individual performance, and performing is the "surgeon as virtuoso, like the concert pianist" and the case when other members of the team "are commonly not all aware of a given patient's risks, or the problems they need to be ready for, or why the surgeon is doing the operation."[16] Often, he continues, the members of the team do not even know each other's name. As he begins to understand by analogy why the checklist worked for flight crews and construction teams, he understands at an emotional level the concept of "teamness." I could have chosen the title of the present book from the pages of his book. There is no index in his book, but "extreme complexity" is part of the title of the first chapter. The words *risk* and *risks* appear in the book, as we see in one paragraph alone. On pages 102–3, some variation of the word *team* (e.g., *effective teams, teamwork*, and *team* itself) appears *eight* times. And *extreme complexity* appears as well.

Before he adopted a checklist, Gawande faced an extremely difficult intestinal operation on a man with a clot blocking blood to his bowel. He knew two of the persons in the surgical unit helping him and it went so well that Gawande is moved to give us this esthetic and emotional description:

> Because we'd worked as a single unit, not as separate technicians, the man survived. We were done with the operation in little more than two hours: his vital signs were stable; and he would leave the hospital just a few days later. The family gave me the credit, and I wish I could have taken it. But the operation had been symphonic, a thing of orchestral beauty.[17]

Gawande now thinks of the checklists he will be receiving from several sources as devices that will help him create another work of art. He sees that having a checklist forces surgical staff to talk to each other about each case before surgery. It becomes in his mind "basically a strategy to foster teamwork—a kind of team huddle as it were."[18] The checklist has become a *means* of achieving teamwork.

As he gained more experience with and respect for checklists as a way to create teamwork, Gawande was able to persuade the World Health Organization (WHO) to let his team create and test a surgical checklist for experimentation. After some doubts and additional research, the WHO agreed to let Gawande's team create and test a surgical checklist across the world, in eight hospitals in Seattle, Toronto, London, New Zealand, Manila, Amman, Jordan, New Delhi, and Tanzania. Before introducing the checklist the WHO agreed upon, Gawande's team helped gather baseline data for four months. Of the nearly four thousand surgical patients Gawande and his committee tracked before the checklists were introduced, "more than four hundred developed major complications resulting from surgery. Fifty-six of them died. About half the complications involved infections."[19]

Starting in the spring of 2008, personnel around the world began preparing to implement the two-minute, 19-step checklist to be used by surgical teams in each of the eight hospitals. They included such steps as making sure antibiotics were injected before an incision was begun. The data were analyzed in October of 2008. Working on the data were two of Gawande's research fellows and a retired surgeon. "'You've got to see this,' said the surgeon. He laid a sheaf of statistical printouts in front of me," wrote Gawande,

> and walked me through the tables. The final results showed that the rate of major complications for surgical patients in all eight hospitals fell by 36 percent after the introduction of the checklist. Deaths fell 47 percent. The results had far outstripped what we'd dared to hope for, and all were statistically highly significant. Infections fell by almost half. . . . Using the checklists had spared more than 150 people from harm—and 27 of them from death.[20]

Throughout *The Checklist Manifesto*, in which he reports this remarkable experiment, Gawande laments that organizations, mainly hospitals, have developed norms of communication that cause harm to patients. As he tried to promote the use of checklists and teamwork in the United States, some surgeons resisted the changes despite the international data that support their use. Surgeons who resist seem not to want a nurse or other person they consider to be of lower status pointing out that they have skipped an important step. They seem to be using a model of decision making that is based on what is best for the individual (themselves), not the team, and thus are resisting the idea of open communication, teamwork, and concertive control. The title of the chapter in which Gawande concentrates on the problem is "The Hero in the Age of Checklists." It seems clear that hospitals and the medical profession have long tolerated these "heroes," and it is time for this to stop. The ability to listen to others ought to be a criterion in selecting candidates for medical school.

For years I taught courses in organizational communication and enjoyed teaching the lesson of a sociological study I read in graduate school in the early 1960s. The authors and title are long forgotten, but it was a study of a restaurant in which there was a considerable strain between the cooks and the waiters. It seems that the waiters came to the kitchen window and barked out the diners' orders to the cooks. The cooks did not like being ordered around in such a fashion and punished the waiters by giving them cold food that would discourage tips. The lesson was, of course, that the hierarchy was at work; there is a norm that persons of lower status or rank should not give orders to persons of higher status or rank, nor should they criticize them or point out their mistakes. The solution in this particular restaurant was the spindle. The waiters were told to write out their order on a check and place it on a spindle. The cooks could take the orders off the spindle without a loss of status or dignity. I have chosen to call the spindle a "status-leveling device." The checklists should also serve as status-leveling devices.

Almost as a footnote I offer an important observation made by Gawande in his most recent book, *Being Mortal: Medicine and What Matters in the End,* about the changes in doctor-patient communication patterns tracked over time by medical ethicists. There are three of these relationships, the first of which is the traditional model or "paternalistic relationship": doctor knows best. The second is "informative": here are the facts and figures, the rest is up to you. The third is now called "shared decision making," and readers of this book will comprehend this readily. This is the desired relationship in today's practice of medicine.[21]

Another Reformer

The other major medical reformer is Donald M. Berwick, MD, a founder and long-time president of the Institute for Healthcare Improvement (IHI) and professor of pediatrics and health care policy at Harvard University. Berwick was nominated to speak in London on July 1, 2008, on the 60th anniversary of the National Health Service. An inveterate list maker, he gave the Brits a list of ten things they could do better, but toward his peroration he softened his criticism by praising their system, saying he loved it. This got him in trouble when President Obama nominated him to be administrator of the Centers for Medicare and Medicaid Services. Senate Republicans threatened to filibuster his confirmation. So the president gave him a "recess" appointment—so-called because he did it while Congress was in recess—in July of 2010. Berwick served in the job for 15 months.

Although he admired the British system, Berwick believed the solution to American health care problems would have to be an American solution—or series of measures. He published a collection of 11 keynote speeches he gave at the annual National Forum on Quality Improvement in Health Care from 1992 to 2002. The audience for the speeches grew from 1,600 to 4,000 10 years later. The title of the book is *Escape Fire: Designs for the Future of Heath Care*. In an earlier book, *Curing Health Care: New Strategies for Quality Improvement*, Berwick and two coauthors used an analogical method in which they told a story about successful American organizations in other areas of endeavor. They described the companies' key procedures such as quality control and quality circles. They then made a list of suggestions for their professional colleagues and sat back to watch the medical community try to implement these rules and suggestions.[22]

When *Curing Health Care* came out in paperback in 2002, the authors titled their new preface "Ten Things We Know Now That We Wish We Had Known Then."[23] The first lesson is "quality improvement tools can work in health care." It is clear that flow charts, Pareto diagrams, and other tools used by manufacturers to improve quality also work in the health care setting. Lesson 2 is central to this book and this chapter: "cross-functional teams are valuable in improving health care processes." Medical units that tried cross-functional teams found that they produced solutions that were much better than any one individual or a single-discipline team could come up with.

Berwick's most well-known book, *Escape Fire: Designs for the Future of Health Care*, gets its main title from a book written by Norman Maclean, *Young Men and Fire*, which refers to a backfire purposely set so that a wildfire would jump over it, thus protecting those in the path of moving fire. (We shall return to Maclean's book and its lessons in chapter 5.) Reasoning again by analogy from one kind of organization to another, Berwick concentrates on dropping old and outdated tools and approaches to medicine. The theme of the book is open interaction and teamwork: "To perfect care, we must perfect interactions."[24] He then lists four properties of interaction among medical providers and their patients that ought to be objects of investment and continual improvement.

The first property is *"to regard information transfer as a key form of care and to increase the accessibility, openness, reliability, and completeness of information for patients and families."*[25] The fact that *open communication* is part of the title of this book means that I strongly agree with this means to achieve better health care. Berwick even gets into the idea of *ideal interaction*: "'Nothing about me without me' is a formula for idealized interaction just as it is for idealized access,"[26] not inconsistent with the epigraph Richard Rorty supplied for this book. Don't make decisions about me without me, without my participation, in other words.

Second, all interactions should be tailored to the needs of the patients. Berwick tells about a friend who is the chief executive officer of a small hospital with a sign over the entrance that reads, "Every patient is the only patient." Each patient is a unique human being with a unique set of needs that require unique responses from providers. States Berwick: "The overall list of such qualities may be familiar: comfort, dignity, communication, privacy, involvement of loved ones, respect for cultural and ethnic differences, need for control and sharing in decisions. . . ."[27] He is not afraid to talk about control and how it should be distributed in the doctor-patient dyad.

Consider the third property of Berwick's prescribed interactions: "*The patient is the source of all control.* We act only when the patient grants that privilege, each time. The current system . . . often behaves as if control over decisions . . . begins in the hands of the caregivers."[28] He relates a story about his wife as a hospital patient. When she awoke in the recovery room after a surgical procedure, she began asking for him. "I was not permitted to join her for almost ninety minutes, even though she repeatedly asked that I be allowed to comfort her. Why did that staff and that institution willfully separate a man and his wife at a time when they could have offered support to one another? . . . Control begins in the hands of the people we serve."[29] Berwick is comfortable once again about such control in medical interactions.

Berwick's fourth property is that "*the interactions we nurture should be transparent.*"[30] Berwick abhors the secrecy and confidentiality that have "mutated into a monstrous system of closed doors and locked cabinets." He further states: "I cannot imagine a future health care system in which we do not work in daylight, study openly what we do, and offer patients any windows they want onto the work that affects them. 'No secrets' is the new rule in my escape fire."[31]

These are the four elements of Dr. Berwick's escape fire. It is a medical sermon, rich in experience and well-reasoned in its call for more cross-functional teamwork and open communication.

Cutting Costs and Increasing Communication and Teamwork

I want to mention something I learned about that promotes open communication in medical care and saves considerable money for patients: the *Carte Vitale,* France's national health insurance card. Author T. R. Reid discusses the *Carte Vitale* in his *New York Times* best-selling book, *The Healing of America: A Global Quest for Better, Cheaper, and Fairer Health Care*, published in 2010.[32] Reid served as a foreign correspondent for the *Washington Post* for many years, acting as its bureau chief in Tokyo and London. He has also served as reporter and commentator for National Public Radio. While serving in the U.S. Navy, Reid badly bashed his right shoulder. He received an operation at the time, but over the years his shoulder worsened. Eventually he checked in with an American surgeon who recommended a total shoulder arthroplasty that would cost tens of thousands of dollars. When he asked the doctor about risks, the answer included disease, paralysis, and death.

Reid took his aching shoulder on the road to have it diagnosed by doctors around the world, thus obtaining comparative data on costs and risks for most national health systems. He got support from the Kaiser Family Foundation and other sources while searching for prescriptions for the sick U.S. system. The basic problem his research diagnosed was this: "Among the world's developed nations, the United States stands at or near the bottom in most important rankings of access and quality of medical care."[33] The one area where the United States leads the world is spending: 17 percent—I repeat, 17 percent—of its gross domestic product. By comparison, Germany has the second most expensive system, and among the best in quality, by spending less than 11 percent of its gross domestic product.

This is where the *Carte Vitale* comes in: It picks up where the doctors in Grand Junction, Colorado, left off with their open sharing of electronic data that so reduced medical costs in that American city. At the beginning of each medical consultation, the French patient hands the doctor his or her *Carte Vitale*, which contains a digital record of every "doctor visit, referral, injection, operation, X-ray, diagnostic test, prescription, warning, etc. . . . It is the secret weapon that makes French medical care so much more efficient than anything Americans are used to."[34] In addition, billings are done on the *Carte Vitale*, and the digitized data are sent to the insurance companies. Doctors do not need cabinets full of files and a crew of paper pushers; thus, they have reduced the administrative personnel in the

French health care system by 67 percent. It is surprising that such a card was not invented by the technological sector of the U.S. economy.

In his book *The Checklist Manifesto: How to Get Things Right,* Dr. Gawande rightly emphasizes the checklist, but he does not do so at the expense of the team. Therefore, the words *team* and *teamwork* appear frequently in his discourse. It is clear that in most cases a team has to put the checklist together, and a team is needed for its satisfactory application. In preparation for the colloquium held in the Department of Communication at the University of Montana on April 30, 2012, I came up with a new expression in the title of my talk to emphasize how the two concepts must merge: "The Theory of Concertive Checklists for Organizations of High Complexity." The term *concertive checklist* stresses teamwork in the preparation, application, and adjustment of the checklist to cope with increasing complexity. Gawande's checklists proved to be so powerful that I feel the need to repeat that the surgically related deaths dropped by 47 percent in the experiment conducted by Dr. Gawande and the World Health Organization.

In *The Checklist Manifesto,* Dr. Gawande also stresses the need to have all of the specialties implicated in the patient's diagnosis included in the team. This is analogous to von Braun's composition of his working groups—all relevant engineering and scientific specialties had to be included. Dr. Berwick provides an ideal type for open communication in all interactions between providers and patients and strongly recommends the use of cross-functional teams in medical care. T. R. Reid teaches us that the *Carte Vitale* could provide more openness and cut costs dramatically in health care. Taken together, they do prove emphatically how open communication and teamwork help us to manage increasing complexity in the field of medicine while at the same time reducing both risks *and* costs.

The Veterans Administration and Whistleblowing

While I was writing this book, a national scandal exploded in the media involving a system of organizational communication that evolved into giving bonuses to administrators for inattention to their clients and lying about secret lists of veterans who did not get care—lying that killed Americans already at risk. I refer of course to the VA hospital scandal, which we learned more about when a hero was given attention in an article in the *AARP Bulletin* of September 2014 by Brian Mockenhaupt: "Confessions of a Whistleblower: Dr. Sam Foote Reveals how He Went to War with the VA."[35] Sam Foote played with erector sets as a boy and studied calculus and physics in college because he wanted to be like his father, an aerospace engineer. His father advised him to get a medical degree. Sam followed his father's advice.

After receiving his medical degree a quarter-century ago, Dr. Foote went to work for the VA health care system in Phoenix, Arizona. He and his colleagues struggled to take care of the rising demand created by the wars in Iraq and Afghanistan. The problem: not enough providers. According to Mockenhaupt, in 2013 "Foote examined the Phoenix VA health care system as he might a patient, and he arrived at a troubling diagnosis: The system itself was sick, and was killing veterans it was supposed to heal."[36] Foote wrote letters to the Office of the Inspector General in the VA with charges that veterans were dying while waiting for care in Phoenix and that, moreover, their identity was hidden by a secret waiting list. He then spoke to the media.

Whistleblowers at other VA facilities around the country took courage from Foote's lead and said they had observed the same phenomenon. Here is a summary of damage done: "57,000 veterans had been waiting more than three months for an initial appointment, and another 64,000 veterans had requested an appointment over the past decade but weren't on the wait list. They had fallen through the cracks or been kept on secret lists to make the facilities appear more efficient."[37] This kind of treatment after they had served their country faithfully. We also learned that VA administrators lied in their reports about their service. Why? To keep their bonuses. Nothing but good news went up the line. A friend of mine who is a registered nurse recently told me that she also saw how bonuses provided an incentive to such behavior some years ago when she worked for the VA. We have here a phenomenon we shall revisit in later chapters: government agencies that age and drift into practices that undermine their very reason for being. There is more to say about aging government bureaucracies in subsequent chapters.

There is also more to say about whistleblowing, which so many naively assume is a dependable safety mechanism. The prevarication in the reports had been going on for years, so why did Foote come out when he did? Foote says health concerns, including lingering asthma problems, and retaliation from the VA forced his retirement a year earlier than he'd hoped. But being near retirement age also made it easier for him to be a whistleblower. "It's a huge risk," Foote says, "I was one of the few people who knew enough about it, and if they retaliated I could retire a little early."[38]

Retaliation came, as it nearly always does, and Foote retired after taking the "risk" he referred to. Others waited until he had made the first report before they came forward, no doubt also fearful of being the first to blow the whistle. Dr. Foote says he blew the whistle on the VA, the VA retaliated, and he retired.[39]

What is the legal status of whistleblowers? Unfortunately, it is almost hopelessly tangled and messy. I consulted with a lawyer friend, who told me there are two relevant federal statutes—Sarbanes-Oxley (SOX for short) and Dodd-Frank—that govern people who are employed by public organizations. The statutes penalize improper conduct that would violate the securities laws or constitute fraud. What that means is open to debate. Other federal statutes give employees, like Dr. Foote, some rights, but they are not enough to protect them from retaliation.

Whistleblowing is important to both the public and private sectors. As organizations grow old and forget their original mission, they ignore messages that would wake them up and correct egregious errors. Some organizations decide for financial reasons to ignore risks they are selling to an innocent public. I submit that it is in the national and international public interest to encourage and protect whistleblowers who report organizational actions they have observed that pose a risk to the health and property of fellow employees, stakeholders, customers, clients, or foreign or domestic citizens. Congress revised the whistleblower law for government workers two years ago, although it did not seem to make things any easier for Dr. Foote. We do need reform to help prevent, for example, dozens of deaths from an automobile ignition system problem that had been identified by workers years earlier. Whistleblowing should be taught in the academy as a courageous, patriotic duty of all qualified people.

Final Thoughts

In this chapter we saw that the concern for human health and its complexities inspired some brilliant analogies with the tools of a flight crew and high-rise construction workers and the physiology of a building compared to that of a human body, all suggesting that analogical thinking may be a crucial inventive-rhetorical skill in dealing with problems of increasing complexity. Had not Kenneth Burke seen that analogical or metaphorical thinking provides us with more than a fine figure of speech? In the first paragraph of appendix D, "Four Master Tropes," in *A Grammar of Motives*, he lists them—metaphor, metonymy, synecdoche, and irony—stating, "my primary concern with them here will not be with their purely figurative usage, but with their role in the discovery and description of 'the truth.'"[40] This thought provides a transition from chapter 4 to chapter 5 because another medical reformer quoted in chapter 4, Dr. Berwick, found an analogy between fighting disease and fighting fires that produced basic lessons he passed along to his medical colleagues. Chapter 5 takes an idiographic look at the U.S. Forest Service, which employs those courageous men and women fighting risky wildfires in the United States and who supplied the other part of Berwick's analogy as well as the bridge between two chapters.

Notes

1. This chapter also draws on Phillip K. Tompkins and Carey Candrian, "Organizing Health: Communication Cures" (unpublished manuscript in progress).

2. Atul Gawande, "The Cost Conundrum: Expensive Health Care Can Be Harmful," *The New Yorker*, June 1, 2009, 36.

3. Ibid., 38.

4. Ibid., 36.

5. Atul Gawande, *The Checklist Manifesto: How to Get Things Right* (New York: Picador, 2009), 21.

6. Ibid., 33.

7. Larry Browning, "Lists and Stories as Organizational Communication," *Communication Theory* 2 (1992): 281–302.

8. Gawande, Checklist Manifesto, 36.

9. Ibid.

10. Ibid., 37.

11. Ibid., 37–38.

12. Peter Pronovost, et al., "An Intervention to Decrease Catheter-Related Bloodstream Infections in the ICU," *New England Journal of Medicine* 355 (2006): 2725–32. doi:10.1056/NEJMoa061115.

13. Gawande, *The Checklist Manifesto,* 44.

14. Ibid., 59.

15. Ibid., 65.

16. Ibid., 102.

17. Ibid., 106.

18. Ibid., 107.

19. Ibid., 144.

20. Ibid., 154.

21. Atul Gawande, *Being Mortal: Medicine and What Matters in the End* (New York: Metropolitan Books, 2014), 200–201.

22. Donald M. Berwick, *Escape Fire: Designs for the Future of Health Care* (San Francisco, CA: Jossey-Bass, 2004); Donald M. Berwick, A. Blanton Godfrey, and Jane Roessner, *Curing Health Care: New Strategies for Quality Improvement* (San Francisco, CA: Jossey-Bass, 1990).

23. Berwick, Godfrey, and Roessner, *Curing Health Care,* xiii–xvi. References in this book are to the 2002 paperback edition by the same publisher.

24. Berwick, *Escape Fire,* 208.

25. Ibid. Emphasis in original.

26. Ibid.

27. Ibid.

28. Ibid. Emphasis in original.

29. Ibid., 208–9.

30. Ibid., 209. Emphasis in original.

31. Ibid.

32. T. R. Reid, *The Healing of America: A Global Quest for Better, Cheaper, and Fairer Health Care* (New York: Penguin, 2010).

33. Ibid., 9.

34. Ibid., 57–58.

35. Brian Mockenhaupt, "Confessions of a Whistleblower: Dr. Sam Foote Reveals How He Went to War with the VA," *AARP Bulletin* 4 (Sept. 2014): 26–27, 40.

36. Ibid., 26.

37. Ibid.

38. Ibid.

39. Ibid., 27.

40. Kenneth Burke, *A Grammar of Motives* (New York: Prentice-Hall, 1945), 503.

5

Fighting Fires
with Smart Risks

"This is the truth in Aristotle's doctrine of courage as the right mean between cowardice and temerity. Biological self-affirmation needs a balance between courage and fear. Such a balance is present in all living things which are able to preserve and increase their being. If the warnings of fear no longer have an effect or if the dynamics of courage have lost their power, life vanishes. The drive for security, perfection, and certitude to which we have referred is biologically necessary. But it becomes biologically destructive if the risk of insecurity, imperfection, and uncertainty is avoided. Conversely, a risk which has a realistic foundation in our self and in our world is biologically demanded, while it is self-destructive without such a foundation. Life, in consequence, includes both fear and courage as elements of a life process in a changing but essentially established balance. As long as life has such a balance it is able to resist nonbeing. Unbalanced fear and unbalanced courage destroy the life whose preservation and increase are the function of the balance of fear and courage."

—Paul Tillich, *The Courage to Be*

While we were corresponding about the effect of organizational identification on decision making, Herbert A. Simon, the Nobel Prize winner in economics, strongly recommended that I read Herbert Kaufman's book *The Forest Ranger: A Study in Administrative Behavior*.[1] I did, and Kaufman's book turned out to be an important reference in the first expression of concertive control theory by George Cheney and me. It is an important study, one that needed to be replicated for a number of reasons. First is that Kaufman, a professor of political science at Yale University when he first published the study in 1960, tested Simon's complete theory of administrative behavior. He studied the structure and processes of a large and important organization. He looked at communication and identification as they influenced decision making. Even today the study's thoroughness reminds organizational scholars that they should be pursuing *both* idiographic and nomothetic aims, the former being those unique characteristics of *this* organization over time, the latter being the universal truths of *all* organizations. *The Forest Ranger* is accepted as a classic study by scholars in public administration, as well as many others, including me.

Cheney and I drew on the Kaufman study and the U.S. Forest Service (USFS) as exemplars of what we were trying to express with the theory of concertive control. The word *control* itself appears frequently in Kaufman's book, an honest expression of what organizations must accomplish to meet their goals. He begins with decisions made in the USFS, a large organization with personnel located all over the country, some in dense forests far away from the purview of Headquarters at the Department of Agriculture in Washington, DC. And yet these personnel were controlled from Washington despite the powerful regional forces trying to pull the organization apart and make the pieces captives of local interests instead of pursuing national policy.

Unlike many students of organization at that time, Kaufman saw the need to study the whole hierarchy and history of the organization, not just a variable or two. In *The Forest Ranger,* he gives us a brief history of the USFS and the influence of its charismatic first leader, Gifford Pinchot. He examines the forces toward disunity caused by the geographic differences and local desires to influence decisions about forests and public lands. He then explains how unity can be maintained by both the careful selection and the training of rangers and their employees; these two, plus fostering organizational identification, allowed the organization to "preform" decisions later made by those on the ground far away.

The Forest Ranger should appeal particularly to students of communication as well as public administration. The opening line of the book is this: "Policy is enunciated in rhetoric; it is realized in action." Rhetoric was the first academic discipline of ancient Greece, the management theory of the Roman Empire, and forerunner of the modern discipline of communication. Kaufman uses Simon's theory of decision making, drawing conclusions from premises in a manner consistent, as Cheney and I pointed out, with the rhetorical syllogism discovered by Aristotle and called by him the "enthymeme." Kaufman sets out to test Simon's theory that an organization can control decisions made by the rangers and their workers on the ground and in the forests, can preform their choices in a number of ways, including identification, a form of self-persuasion. *Identification* is the key term that Kenneth Burke gave to the new or contemporary rhetoric, as opposed to the old, more didactic rhetoric of Aristotle and those theories that came after.

Kaufman also gives the reader a thorough description and analysis of the organization, encouraging and almost inviting other researchers to return to the USFS to look for both permanence and change. Kaufman's esteemed book was published in 1960. Hall, Schneider, and Nygren performed another identification study on the USFS in 1970,[2] and in 1984 Connie A. Bullis completed a dissertation under my direction devoted to providing answers to those questions of universality and individuality.

The Forest Ranger Revisited

Bullis later published an article with me as second author; the following discussion draws on that *Communication Monographs* article but refers to it as the Bullis study. She conducted her study for the purposes of

(1) describing current control practices in the U.S. Forest Service, an organization frequently cited as an excellent organization due to a dated but classic study [Kaufman's], and (2) field testing three claims made in Tompkins and Cheney's theory of unobtrusive control, including: (a) unobtrusive control practices are associated with organizational identification, (b) members who report higher organizational identification scores use organizational premises in their decision making, (c) members who report higher organizational identification consider the organization as they consider the consequences of decisions.[3]

Bullis thus wanted first to make an idiographic study of an important organization to see whether there had been any significant changes, and second to test the nomothetic or general claims of the theory of unobtrusive or concertive control. Longitudinal data on organizations in general have long been sorely needed. Bullis introduced her summary of the theory of concertive control by quoting its reframing of Weick's double interact by Cheney and me as the "double interact of control," to wit

(1) commands, directions, rules, goals and decision premises are communicated to the ultimate contributors; (2) contributor's responses, whether in the form of messages, productive output, or decisions are monitored by a feedback loop; (3) the organization either rewards compliance or corrects deviation."[4]

Bullis reviewed other aspects of concertive control, such as its much more democratic nature than, say, bureaucratic or simple control by a supervisor; it is also unobtrusive and creates higher morale, self-respect, and dignity because of that. Kaufman's study is reviewed and reframed by Bullis to explain his ironic finding that "it was concertive control [i.e., teamwork or decentralization] which allowed the rangers to feel free and independent at the same time that their decisions were predetermined."[5] For historical reasons, Bullis anticipated reaching findings different from Kaufman's because during the 1970s, two prominent court decisions were made that went against the USFS, bringing about changes relevant to the way the organization functioned. The USFS was indicted for the practice of clear-cutting, the harvesting of all trees on a plot of land before replanting. In losing this case brought by people outside the agency, the USFS lost its status as the sole arbiter of such policies for our national forests.

In pursuing her research questions, Bullis visited the Washington, DC, Headquarters of the USFS, three regional offices, two national forest headquarters, and two ranger stations. She conducted 40 interviews for general information, then 15 more with officers for whom she had specific questions. She discussed her findings with one of the five forest rangers previously interviewed by Kaufman. In addition to conducting the interviews, Bullis mailed out 800 questionnaires, of which 704 were returned. Of those, 341 were completed by foresters, 126 by engineers, 112 by wildlife and fisheries biologists, and 125 by other specialists and technicians. The questionnaire included a quantitative instrument measuring organizational identification used in the 1970 study by Hall, Schneider, and Nygren, for comparative purposes, and another highly reliable and valid organizational identification-measuring instrument developed by George Cheney.

Bullis's study revealed that people who reported higher identification also reported employing organizationally appropriate decision premises more than those who reported low identification. Employees who reported higher identification also reported considering the organization in their decision making more than those who reported low identification. However, Bullis found that identification in general had decreased since 1970.

Over time, and no doubt due to the court decision on clear-cutting, the USFS was strongly relying on more obtrusive, or what Kaufman, as quoted by Bullis, dubbed "relatively crude," control practices and less on unobtrusive control through identification.[6] The stress had shifted from concertive-bureaucratic control to bureaucratic-concertive control. Bullis found that the USFS, after having been captured in an exemplary study, had changed in an important way.

Bullis makes it clear that the rangers and other workers were unhappy with the changes in the field. They looked back fondly on the past, when they were able to make decisions in the field and had identified more highly with the organization and its mission. Now, "dealing with the bureaucracy is like wading through molasses on a cold winter morning."[7] The last words of the last sentence of the Bullis article are quotations from Tocqueville on the threat of a strong culture to the individual, perhaps so far as constraining "the exercise of the free agency of man."

Young Men and Fire

In 1992 my son, an employee of the USFS, gave me a book for Father's Day: *Young Men and Fire* by Norman Maclean.[8] I quickly devoured this magnificently written tragic drama composed by a University of Chicago Shakespeare scholar. Maclean was a native of Montana and had been studying a fire at Mann Gulch ever since it occurred on August 5, 1949. On that day a crew of 15 young men, smokejumpers, jumped on a fire. Less than an hour later they were hit by a blowup, an incendiary explosion of the fire that drove them up a steep mountain climb. Although the fire was gaining on them, the smokejumpers so identified with their heavy firefighting tools, called Pulaskis, that instead of dropping them so that they could more easily outrun the fire, they carried them as they raced up the grade. Maclean was so haunted by the fire and its effects that he began writing about it much later in life.

The smokejumpers' leader for the jump was a supervisor named Wag Dodge, who was unknown to them. Because this was the first time they had worked with him, they were not used to his ways of communicating. As Dodge stood at the top of the mountain watching the fire chase the young men up the slope, he got an idea. He took out a match and set fire to the grass at his level, hoping that it would burn up the fuel before the larger fire reached that point, and thus the larger fire would either stop or jump over the burned grass. As the young men reached the point where Dodge was creating what is now called an "escape fire," they saw him walk into the fire, beckon them to follow him, and then lie down. Nonplussed, they all disobeyed him and kept running until the fire caught them. Twelve of the 15 young men were either killed or mortally burned, later dying in the hospital. Wag Dodge was not seriously injured.

Two lessons emerged from this narrative: throw away useless tools, and reverse the words *escape fire* to make a *fire escape*.

Escape Fire

Maclean's book became a critically praised best seller, and it was the first item on the reading list in both a graduate and an undergraduate seminar I taught at the University of Colorado Boulder. Karl Weick, a social psychologist well known for his theories of organization, wrote a stimulating essay about it.[9] Readers of chapter 4 of this book will recall that one of the expert reformers in the U.S. health service sector, Donald M. Berwick, MD, gave this title to an important book he wrote: *Escape Fire: Designs for the Future of Health Care.* Where did he get this title? Berwick explains:

> When I first read *Young Men and Fire*, the story gripped me. I didn't understand why until I read a paper by Professor Karl Weick. . . . His paper is called "The Collapse of Sensemaking in Organizations." I want to review some of Weick's main points here, and then I will find my way—though you probably think I can't—back to health care.[10]

Berwick then derives a list of five lessons learned from Maclean and Weick about how to reduce risks while fighting fires and providing health care, among others.

Lesson one: We must face reality. Weick thinks the firefighting team lost its ability to face reality during the crisis because the threat was too big for them to process. Berwick says the problems of health care in the United States have become so large that "our challenge is to have the courage to name clearly and boldly the problems we have—many—and their size—immense. We must find ways to do this without either marginalizing the truth-teller or demoralizing the good people working in these bad systems."[11]

Lesson two: We all need to learn to drop our tools. The Pulaskis slowed the smokejumpers as they ran up a 76 percent slope. Likewise, medical doctors are using tools that are no longer useful in new situations. Using both the old tools and the new ones is a case of overutilization. The smokejumpers failed to drop their backpacks as well. In another characteristic analogy, Berwick says: "Healthcare's backpack is full of useless assumptions that are so old and so often repeated that they become wisdom from the mouth of Hippocrates himself, and one questions them at grave risk to one's professional relationships."[12]

Lesson three: Stay in formation. "Successful sensemaking can't leave anyone out."[13] Readers learned in chapter 4 that Berwick wants groups or teams to include everyone, including the patient, in decision making. No one at Mann Gulch remembered that Wag Dodge was the most experienced member of the crew, forgetting that they could learn a lot from him. In relating this to health care, Berwick creates his own critical theory, stating that it is impossible for most people to avoid assuming that financial stability in thriving organizations and great medical care are mutually exclusive; no, he says, those goals must become aligned if progress is to be achieved.

Lesson four is procedural: "To achieve sense, we have to *talk to one another, and listen.* Sensemaking is fundamentally an enterprise of interdependence, and the currency of interdependence is conversation."[14] Even in the heat, smoke, and noise of the fire, we must maintain a civil, open dialogue.

The fifth and final lesson: Leadership. The kind of leadership needed to avoid risks comes from people who can exhibit certain skills: "clearly defining tasks, demonstrating their own competence, disavowing perfection so as to encourage openness, and engaging and building the team." Dr. Berwick summarizes the five lessons as "facing reality, dropping the old tools, staying in formation, communicating, and having capable leadership—set[ting] the stage for making sense as the fire blows up."[15] He goes on to describe the escape fire for medicine as involving three attributes: access—24/7/365—of patients to medical help; reliance on medical science in an age of increasing complexity; and, finally, "cooperation, communication, teamwork, and knowledge."[16]

The Fire Seminar

My apparent diversion from fighting fires to Dr. Berwick's medical reforms for reducing risk and costs is not aimless; it is intended to show the *analogous*, similar risks and complexities that are relevant to both of these causes: fighting fires and providing medical care. Indeed, one of the purposes of this book is *to show the similarities, the interconnections across a wide range of modern complex and risky situations.* I organized the fire seminar at the University of Colorado in this way: The first assignment was to read *Young Men and Fire*, and it invariably captured students' attention like no textbook ever will. The students then wrote a paper about how the smoke-jumpers could have performed to increase their chances of surviving the fire at Mann Gulch. They had some original ideas, but we then moved into the theory and empirical research pertaining to organizational communication. (As educators, we usually believe we must begin at the abstract level and move to the particular, the examples; reversing the process can produce great success, particularly when beginning with a gripping and eloquent narrative of a case, such as Maclean's *Young Men and Fire*.)

The students then wrote a term paper with the same assignment: how to improve on the performance of the firefighters. This time their analysis was deeper and their papers presented new communicative and organizational insights. After the course was offered one time, tragedy struck closer to home: the South Canyon Fire on Storm King Mountain in Colorado, seven miles west of Glenwood Springs. The accident investigation team issued its report on August 18, 1994. The group found that 8 of the 10 Standard Firefighting Orders—the Rules—were compromised during the four-day firefight from July 3 through July 6, 1994, which involved firefighters from the Prineville Hotshots, the Bureau of Land Management/

USFS, smokejumpers, and a Helitack group. Fourteen of them were killed, both men and women, by a blowup similar to the one at Mann Gulch. A graduate student at the University of Colorado named Craig Melville, who was assisting me with the teaching of the fire seminar, photographed for us the burned out slope and gravesites where firefighters had again been overtaken by a blowup. With the various reports about the two fires, the students could now make *comparative* studies of them, looking at the effect the changes in policies and practices had made, if any, on the behavior of firefighters. They began to have success with their term papers, revising them into convention papers and academic journal articles.

The fire seminar became so well known on campus that even after retirement I was invited to a meeting of a selection group from the university's Center of the American West, headed by the eminent historian of the U.S. West, Professor Patricia Nelson Limerick. They were planning the 2001 Wurth Forum with this title: Facing Fire: Lessons from the Ashes. It was to be held in the Old Main Chapel on Saturday, February 17, 2001. I had retired by then, but they invited me to help make plans and mention the research and papers of the graduate students who had taken the fire seminar. They picked two, one by Craig Melville and me. They also wanted someone from the USFS and invited a paper by my son Terry and me.

Craig Melville's paper was "Fighting the Mundane Fire, Smartly! Training for Smart Risk, Organizing for Effective Firefighting."[17] Craig was already at work on his paper when I found the relevant passage in Paul Tillich's *The Courage to Be*,[18] a book on existential philosophy and theology. We used it as an epigraph, the same one used at the head of this chapter. My name was listed as second author because I persuaded Craig to write his observations and prepare for an oral presentation at the Forum. In addition, I composed an introduction about the fire seminar and introduced Craig. I said that he took the first seminar about the Mann Gulch and then the South Canyon fire occurred in Colorado:

To help us understand the South Canyon Fire better, Craig hiked the area and provided us with photographs. . . . It helped, but I neither directed nor suggested that he apply to the Helena Hotshots.

But he did. And he was accepted. He fought some major fires. The crews he worked with realized he was taking notes for a purpose, for a doctoral dissertation. They nicknamed him the "professor." He will tell you about his experiences with these crews, but I want you to know that at the ritual beer party at the end of the fire season, the leader of the crew said publicly he had as much respect for Craig as he had for anyone in the crew. I now turn to a true Hotshot.[19]

Craig began his talk at the Wurth Forum by referring to the title of his paper: "Fighting the Mundane Fire, Smartly!" He continued:

I use the term mundane with great liberty; few would refer today to a fire as ordinary. Indeed, if the typical fire was run-of-the mill, the men and women who fight fire would seek elsewhere for employment, for when firefighters err on Tillich's fear-courage continuum, it is on the side of risk. There is a thrill, a rush when the fire call comes.[20]

Craig told the audience he became a firefighter by calling Terry Tompkins in the Black Hills National Forest. Terry gave him the name and number of Larry Edwards, who was the superintendent of the Helena Hotshots. They were interested in research and improving firefighting training so they welcomed him. Melville was also a long-distance runner in great physical shape. He started at the bottom of the squad, but graduated to the Pulaski and fought 10 fires in two months. Craig described a mundane, highly ordinary firefight on July 4, 1996, that involved a falling tree that nearly killed the crew. As the crew was making a fire line—an open pathway in the woods free of trees and other fuels created with chainsaws to make a space the fire cannot burn across—a grapefruit-sized rock whizzed by Craig's head. That night their camp in the woods had no food other than Meals Ready-to-Eat, and the Hotshots slept with only a space blanket during a cold night at high altitude. His point is that beings cannot fight even ordinary fires without considerable courage to face the risk and discomfort. His recommendation had two parts:

(1) First we will emphasize smart risk in training firefighters rather than making safety a separate component of training, and thus a separate component of practice. (2) The second suggestion is to mandate . . . that individual crews be organized as cohesive yet flexible groups."[21]

After Craig finished his talk, I introduced Terry, who gave me permission to mention that as a boy he was "always at home in the outdoors. He also had a profound interest in matches, kindling, and fire. He started all of our campfires, and attended them carefully, almost obsessively. He tells me his colleagues in the USFS frequently admit to such youthful preoccupations."[22] Terry began his remarks by talking about the Jasper fire of 2004 that took place near his home in Rapid City, South Dakota, saying that it "is one of the 104 fires I have fought for the U.S. Forest Service in the past ten years,"[23] before listing some of the more prominent ones. Then he delivered his stern, predictive thesis: *"Because of ninety years of fire suppression, fuels have accumulated in certain forests (ponderosa pines) to the point that blowup fires are inevitable; moreover, we have not adequately prepared people for these catastrophic fires. Finally, we need to accept fire the way we accept hurricanes and tornadoes, and help people prepare for them."*[24] He discussed the Idaho Blowup of August 20 and 21, 1910, when the temperature in Denver dropped almost 20 degrees and a 40-mile-an-hour wind covered the capital of Colorado with ashes. Since then we have suppressed fires, letting people move into areas impossible to protect, and then had to send firefighting crews in to try to save their homes. The suppression of fires since then has made for more than an analogous amount of fuels that blew up in 1910. He sticks to his thesis to this day.

Another student who took the fire seminar, Gregory Larson, is today a professor of communication studies at the University of Montana at Missoula. He teaches an up-to-date version of the fire seminar in which the students in the class read, among many more recent studies, *Young Men and Fire.* The Maclean family typically invites the seminar members to their cabins to honor the late author.

Although Craig Melville did not explicitly define smart risk, he, Aristotle, Tillich, and my son left enough clues for me to hazard an attempt:

Smart risk is *the willing and courageous acceptance of the probability of threat because it is balanced by the ability and resources to resist nonbeing*. That is, those who accept facing risk will do so smartly if they figure that the individual *and* collective knowledge, skill, and flexibility of their participatory teammates will make the odds worth taking. In the case of firefighters, training with team members can provide some if not most of the resources to give confidence that a flexible, well-trained team can resist and avoid nonbeing. This would also apply, in the most obvious cases, to police teams and military groups in all of the services. It would apply to others as well, and the compensation for accepting the smart risk are the "thrill, rush" of a challenge and for some, financial reward and fame. Come to think of it, this definition comes close to describing the top managers of a corporation who are willing to take a chance on buying or selling bad mortgages, and to the top managers of an automobile manufacturer who are willing together to take the risk that a faulty design that is known to workers will not harm buyers and come to the light of the media and the law. We shall return to the problem of these antisocial cabals in the Epilogue.

Discursive Closings and Openings: The Fire Orders

Another student who took the fire seminar at the University of Colorado is today one of the current experts on the USFS and its Fire Orders: Jennifer Ziegler (née Thackaberry). One of her first significant studies has a title relevant to the title of this book: "'Discursive Opening' and Closing in Organizational Self-Study: Culture as Trap and Tool in Wildland Firefighting Safety," published in *Management Communication Quarterly* in 2004, 10 years after the South Canyon fire. Reviewing the work called "critical theory," mentioned in chapter 1 as having been drawn from Karl Marx, Jürgen Habermas, and others by communication scholars such as Stanley Deetz and Dennis Mumby,[25] Ziegler invokes the concept of "discursive closure." In terms of an organization, discursive closure refers to the "suppression of a particular conflict" and, of course, any discourse by the parties to it. The theoretical basis for the concept is Habermas's ideal speech situation, which Ziegler acknowledges as having been criticized for its reliance on philosophic or intellectual reasoning and a universal ideal. Nonetheless, she finds it a useful heuristic. She could have used the ideal communication situation by Richard Rorty quoted in this book had it been available then.

From "discursive closing," or stifling of all discussion on a topic or event, it is a short dialectical step to "discursive opening" and to the term used in this book—*open communication*—and defined this way by Ziegler: "'Open' communication in organizations, then, refers to the ability of organizational stakeholders to question sedimented procedures, meanings, rights of participation, and even preferred ways of being."[26] Ziegler states that the critical theorists believe that discursive closures are ineluctable, given that they take place within the ubiquitous universe of the "discourse of managerialism," but she believes it is important to search for moments of discursive opening that could lead to productive changes. Ziegler then examines the possibilities of discursive opening in a then-recent self-study contracted by an interagency task force and sponsored by the five main federal fire agencies, including the USFS.

Ziegler traces attitudes toward safety rules expressed by the 300 firefighters who were interviewed by a contractor individually and in focus groups in 1995. She finds that the firefighters placed the following suggestion, an echo of Melville's "smart risk" idea, among their top five choices more often than any other solution considered: "Develop a safety culture that encourages people to think rather than just obey the rules."[27] In addition, the firefighters complained that it was not currently acceptable to point out violations of the safety rules made by supervisors. "This is consistent with statements made by firefighters who were interviewed for the Storm King Mountain investigation, who complained about having to follow orders that actually violated safety rules...."[28] This clearly indicates that the firefighters knew that they had lost their voice and the openness experienced earlier in the organization's history. By including these points in their self-study, the participants appeared to create a discursive opening for firefighters to express a new and different vision of how to manage safety in wildland firefighting. The self-study was released in 1998, and Ziegler was writing in 2004. Intervening was the Thirtymile Fire in Washington State.

In 2001, four firefighters were killed during a routine mop-up of a fire in the Okanogan National Forest in Washington State. Despite the statement that the 10 Fire Orders should not be used as a yardstick, the accident investigators came to the conclusion that all 10 had been broken. Similarly, the investigators found that the firefighters broke the intent of the Watchouts, the list of 18 cautions for firefighters, even though the self-study had warned not to use them as a punitive checklist. Parents of the fallen firefighters and others were angered that despite the hope of change afforded by the self-study, the firefighters were once again being blamed for their own death by official statements about rule violations. After summarizing techniques of discursive closure outlined by Deetz, Ziegler comes to the following conclusion:

> These findings reinforce Bullis and Tompkins's observations about increased reliance on bureaucratic controls at the Forest Service. . . . Whereas bureaucratically managed rules offer a ready discourse of evaluation, fire-fighters have difficulty talking back to rule-based determinations of blame in the wake of tragedy.[29]

Ziegler writes that the study had both encouraging and discouraging implications: the "trap" and the "tool" in her article title. Calling the internal communication at USFS "systematically distorted," she nonetheless sees the potential for self-studies to provide discursive openings.[30]

After Ziegler wrote that article, she was asked by Gregory Larson of the University of Montana and a fellow graduate of the fire seminar to participate in the Wildland Safety Summit that was to take place in Missoula, Montana, in April 2005. By that time she was on the faculty of the Brian Lamb School of Communication at Purdue University, where she introduced an updated version of the fire seminar. She was concerned about how the fire community would receive her at the Summit because of her article on discursive closings and openings, and she was pleasantly surprised when members of the community became a welcoming committee. The paper she presented at the Summit, "Wisdom in the Lessons Learned Library: Work Ethics and Firefighter Identities in the Fire Orders,"[31] was well received, was printed in the proceedings, and 10 years later is still cited by the fire community.

A Genealogy of the Fire Orders

At the 2005 Wildland Safety Summit, Jennifer Ziegler met Dr. Ted Putnam and Dick Mangan, both of whom were members of the accident investigation team for the South Canyon fire, and both of whom had refused to sign the investigation report because it blamed the dead. Ziegler interviewed them during the conference for a case study later published in a collection of readings on communication ethics edited by Steve May.[32] Jennifer Thackaberry had become Jennifer Ziegler in 2005, and she continued her work on the history of, and controversy about, the Fire Orders. In an article published in *Communication Monographs* in 2007, she presented the results of her study of the genealogy of the 10 Standard Firefighting Orders, reproduced here:[33]

Standard Firefighting Orders (1957–1986)

1. Keep informed on FIRE WEATHER conditions and forecasts.
2. Know what your FIRE is DOING at all times—observe personally, use scouts.
3. Base all actions on current and expected BEHAVIOR of FIRE.
4. Have ESCAPE ROUTES for everyone and make them known.
5. Post a LOOKOUT when there is possible danger.
6. Be ALERT, keep CALM, THINK clearly, ACT decisively.
7. Maintain prompt COMMUNICATION with your men, your boss, and adjoining forces.
8. Give clear INSTRUCTIONS and be sure they are understood.
9. Maintain CONTROL of your men at all times.
10. Fight fire aggressively but provide for SAFETY first.

Every Forest Service employee who will have firefighting duties will learn these orders and follow each order when it applies to his assignment.

The Firefighting Orders have been revised twice since being introduced in 1957; the first revision came in 1987, when the first letter of each order collectively spelled FIREORDERS, so that the men (only men fought fires then) could memorize them more easily. They were changed back to the original list in 2003 in order to "get back to basics." But the apparent constructive move, returning to the original list, belied the meaning of the orders expressed in the discourse about them. Ziegler again begins with Kaufman's description of the USFS, and with Bullis's conclusion that bureaucratization had increased significantly because of outside pressures and court decisions.

What are we to make of this list of Fire Orders? They do not resemble the checklists that Dr. Gawande developed for surgery. Take number 6: "Be ALERT, keep CALM, THINK clearly, ACT decisively." Great general advice, but nothing like an instruction to "inject antibiotics before beginning an incision." Ziegler uses Larry Browning's idea that lists and stories serve as a dialectical pair in organizational communication. Although he advocated the value of lists, Browning would not deny that there are *bad* lists as well as good ones. Ziegler mentions that Barker found that a list developed "concertively by team members can exert more power than any manager could by enforcing a bureaucratic code."[34] This helps to provide the context of searching for theoretical explanations of the Fire Orders by appealing to the discourse of Habermas and his followers.

Ziegler's method in this study was to follow Foucault in studying the history of the Fire Orders and texts related to them. But despite the controversy, the list had changed very little over the course of its 50-year history at the time of the study. At that time those who defended the Fire Orders said they were now, and always had been, a tool for risk management. Ziegler finds support for Bullis's conclusion that the USFS had a history of moving from *concertive*-bureaucratic control to *bureaucratic*-concertive control, and this may have "reached its absurdist limits in the Fire Orders."[35] As a list, she continues, it may have done well in capturing organizational memory about things that got firefighters into trouble, but those who composed it did not take into account how difficult it is to translate the list into total situational awareness when one is threatened by smoke inhalation, fatigue, lack of sleep, fear, and the fire itself.

Ziegler has continued to research discourses relevant to fire operations and safety in the wildland fire community, such as the community's move to redefine leadership as "communicating intent" and to assess organizational learning from more open reviews of prescribed fires that escaped control. In addition, in 2008 she was prepped as an expert witness by the crew boss in the Thirtymile Fire case from 2001. Her role was to explain to the jury the origin of the Fire Orders and the evolution of their use in accident investigations over time. But the case pleaded out before trial.

Assessment of Orders and Watchouts

It appears to me that the Fire Orders and Watchouts, whatever their original purpose, have been translated into a defense mechanism for the management of the USFS. The administrators seem to want the men and women in their service to put down wildland fires, but they do not want to be blamed for their death or injury while on the lines. The rules are impossible to obey—if that was their purpose in the beginning—because no one can hold 28 thou shalts and shalt nots in the conscious mind while fighting a fearsome fire, nor can anyone perform all of those actions simultaneously; this is especially true of such general, abstract statements as opposed to specific strategies. This appears to be an example of a dangerous neurosis created by Ulrich Beck's concept of risk society, discussed in chapter 1. That the rangers fight them at all anticipates a concept the reader will meet in chapter 6: the normalization of risk. If all of us had the everyday equivalent of the 10/18 lists memorized, we might never leave our home, walk across the street, drive to work, or eat or drink anything we had not sanitized or filtered. We would be a paralyzed risk-aversive society without courage. And if we did get killed by a hit-and-run driver running a red light, our obituary would also have to blame us for breaking several orders and watchouts.

It is also clear that it is time for an organizational communication researcher to replicate the Kaufman and Bullis studies of the USFS. We have seen that the lists of Fire Orders and Watchouts have been tracked since those important studies, but we need to know how the rest of the system has functioned, where it stands on what has been shown originally by Bullis to be on a scale moving from a *concertive*-bureaucratic to a *bureaucratic*-concertive organization, how communication and the level of identification function in a world that produced even greater tendencies toward fragmentation. It is a bit ironic that Bullis anticipated the changes she found because of external forces on the service—including the lawsuits to force changes. The external forces today appear to be sympathetic to the firefighters and their families, while it appears that the USFS blames the victims via the versatile Fire Orders and Watchouts, or did so up to the time of the Thirtymile Fire.

Another idiographic study is needed, and it would be interesting indeed if the researcher conducting it would at least tentatively apply the communicative theory of the firm developed by Timothy Kuhn after Ziegler conducted her major studies. In 2008, Kuhn published his theoretical development of the approach to organizational communication known as the Montreal School.[36] That emphasis on texts and conversations would seem to be a natural way of trying to sort through the relationships of the USFS, using lists-as-texts and the conversations about applying them in decision making about firefighting. I think it would work despite the fact that the USFS is definitely not a "firm."

Reality Check

Academics have a reputation for producing so much fog at times that we can't see the forest for the trees. I e-mailed my son on March 8, 2014, saying I had some questions about the USFS. He called me back the next day to answer my questions to him as an interviewee in his role as Terry Tompkins, then a 24-year veteran of the USFS who has fought fires in Los Angeles, Québec, and many points between. He is currently the fire management officer for the Mystic District of the Black Hills National Forest and was called upon during the summer of 2011 to serve as the incident commander of the Coal Canyon Fire in the Black Hills of South Dakota, a fire that had claimed the life of a South Dakota firefighter only a few hours earlier. I sent him a copy of my notes and he made some corrections, additions, and deletions.

His impression was that things in the USFS have gotten better, with the exception of a possible setback last summer, 2013, in Arizona. He emphasized that he was only one person speaking, but that something happened after the Thirtymile and Cramer Fires. He mentioned the Cramer Fire of 2003 more than once as a turning point. The pendulum seemed to change direction after that as the USFS tried to adopt a learning culture. People were no longer penalized for talking openly. "If you are involved in a fire that goes bad, you will be okay as long as you're honest." He continued to say that following the Thirtymile Fire (that occurred in 2001) and Cramer Fire, many incident commanders began to feel that assuming the role of incident commander was too risky, that the USFS wouldn't support them if something happened or, worse yet, would bring them up on charges of involuntary manslaughter, like it did with the incident commander of the Cramer Fire in 2003.

My son made it clear that it is nearly impossible to have complete control of firefighting resources as an incident commander, especially on transition fires—fires that have escaped from the initial action and are growing and becoming destructive. "You're juggling different roles. You can't control the fire, and you must delegate authority and hope they do the right thing." After 2003, good strides were made toward becoming a learning organization—"it was not so punitive after that. But," he continued,

> there was a fire in Arizona last year at Yarnell Hill in which 19 Hotshots were killed. The Arizona State Forester delegated authority to an interagency team to conduct a serious accident investigation. The investigation didn't come up with causal factors, but tried to get the reader to gain the perspective of what might have been going through the minds of the firefighters prior to the entrapment. Arizona's equivalent of OSHA (ADOSH) got a second report that was a throwback to the pre-Cramer era by going down the list and finding things wrong.

The second investigating group was mostly made up of retired fire managers, and they were more critical than other recent investigators had been. He repeated, however, that although the USFS had made some good strides, fighting fires can still be an impossible situation. The USFS is compelled to protect values at risk, which ultimately means homes on private property. My son told me that about 98% of the time the USFS is successful at suppressing fires during initial attack. "Eventually the fuels accumulate in a given area to the point that suppression becomes impossible," he said, "during hot, dry conditions when the wind can turn unpredictably. Because of our success, we have essentially been saving up large areas of the West for the grand finale. Those areas will burn eventually. There is little we can do." And things are more dangerous now because of the "100-plus years of fire suppression. We do the best we can."

I recalled the presentation Terry gave at the Center for the Study of the West at the University of Colorado Boulder in 2001. He mentioned how the USFS had advised people not to build residences in mountainous areas that could not be easily defended. But many went ahead, built their homes without regard for risk and then expected, even demanded, that the firefighters of the USFS come in the face of grave danger to save their homes. Television and other media report fires as threatening mountain homes in a way that creates the expectation that the firefighters should defend all of them. The problem has spread throughout the Rocky Mountain West region. That problem, plus fire suppression in general, has produced enough kindling throughout this country to produce the coming "grand inferno."

Terry wanted to leave me with the conclusion that things had improved since the Cramer Fire, that the USFS has become "a learning organization."

I asked him about that phrase: *a learning organization.*

"Yes," he said, "High Reliability Organizations, HROs, by Karl Weick. You probably know him. I still remember reading about the aircraft carrier, and the mechanics were taught that if they left a wrench on the flight deck, it might be sucked into a jet engine and destroy the plane. They found that by rewarding, instead of punishing, people were more apt to report unsafe acts or conditions." (Terry was referring to the book, *Managing the*

Unexpected: Assuring High Performance in an Age of Complexity, by Karl E. Weick and Kathleen M. Sutcliffe.[37]) HROs include such entities as aircraft carriers, nuclear power plants, and, yes, firefighting crews, and the authors say they have five hallmarks: preoccupation with failure; reluctance to simplify interpretations; sensitivity to operations; commitment to resilience; and deference to expertise. (Weick and Sutcliffe might have added the *Saturn V* because those traits were manifested by NASA's Marshall Space Flight Center during the race to the Moon.)

Terry also sent me the study "Best Places to Work [U.S. Government] Agency Index Scores" for 2012 and 2013, based on "employee satisfaction and commitment."[38] Commitment is a behavioral manifestation of identification, so this gives us another data point for identification in the USFS. With a satisfaction-commitment score of 49, the USFS was ranked at 260 out of 300 units listed. This means that if discursive opening is correlated to morale, commitment, and identification, the recent increase has not begun to be enough.

There is still another reason for a replication of the Kaufman and Bullis studies. In 1969 a public administration researcher, Orion F. White Jr., wrote an essay on the dialectical organization in which he mentioned that over time people at the top of bureaucracies seek forms of "blamability" that they can impose on people at the bottom. He also observed that as organizations age, they become much less flexible.[39]

In the next chapter about NASA and the space shuttles *Challenger* and *Columbia,* the aging effect on a government agency, communication, and risk will come to center stage.

NOTES

1. Herbert Kaufman, *The Forest Ranger: A Study in Administrative Behavior* (Baltimore: The Johns Hopkins Press, 1960). References in this book are to the 1967 paperback edition by the same publisher.

2. Douglas T. Hall, Benjamin Schneider, and Harold T. Nygren, "Personal Factors in Organizational Identification," *Administrative Science Quarterly* 15 (1970): 176–90.

3. Connie A. Bullis and Phillip K. Tompkins, "The Forest Ranger Revisited: A Study of Control Practices and Identification," *Communication Monographs* 56 (December 1989), 287.

4. Ibid., 288.

5. Ibid., 291.

6. Ibid.

7. Ibid., 301.

8. Norman Maclean, *Young Men and Fire* (Chicago: University of Chicago, 1992).

9. Karl E. Weick, "The Collapse of Sensemaking in Organizations: The Mann Gulch Disaster," *Administrative Science Quarterly* 38 (1993): 628–52.

10. Donald M. Berwick, *Escape Fire: Designs for the Future of Health Care* (San Francisco: Jossey-Bass, 2004), 188.

11. Ibid., 197–98.

12. Ibid., 200.

13. Ibid., 201.

14. Ibid. Emphasis in original.

15. Ibid., 202

16. Ibid., 207.

17. Craig Melville and Phillip K. Tompkins, "Fighting the Mundane Fire, Smartly! Training for Smart Risk, Organizing for Effective Firefighting" (paper presented at the Wurth Forum: Center of the American West, University of Colorado at Boulder, February 17, 2001).

18. Paul Tillich, *The Courage to Be* (New Haven: Yale University Press, 1952/1980), 78–79.

19. Melville and Tompkins, "Fighting the Mundane Fire, Smartly!" 1

20. Ibid.

21. Ibid., 2.

22. Terry Tompkins and Phillip K. Tompkins, "The Next Catastrophic Fire in the American West Will Be of Our Own Making" (paper presented at the Wurth Forum: Center of the American West, University of Colorado at Boulder, February 17, 2001).

23. Ibid.

24. Ibid., 6.

25. Stanley Deetz and Dennis Mumby, "Power, Discourse, and the Workplace:

Reclaiming the Critical Tradition," in *Communication Yearbook 13,* ed. James A. Anderson (Newbury Park, CA: Sage Publications, 1990): 18–47.

26. Jennifer A. Thackaberry [Ziegler], "'Discursive Opening' and Closing in Organizational Self-Study: Culture as Trap and Tool in Wildland Firefighting Safety," *Management Communication Quarterly* 17 (February 2004): 323. doi:10.1177/0893318903259402.

27. Ibid., 333.

28. Ibid., 335.

29. Ibid., 351.

30. Ibid.

31. Jennifer A. Thackaberry [Ziegler], "Wisdom in the Lessons Learned Library: Work Ethics and Firefighter Identities in the Fire Orders," in *Proceedings of the 8th International Wildland Fire Safety Summit, April 26-28, 2005 Missoula, Montana,* ed. Bret W. Butler and Marty E. Alexander (Hot Springs, SD: International Assembly of Wildland Fires, 2005).

32. Jennifer A. Thackaberry [Ziegler], "Blaming the Dead: The Ethics of Accident Investigations in Wildland Firefighting," in *Case Studies in Organizational Communication: Ethical Perspectives and Practices,* ed. Steve K. May (Thousand Oaks, CA: Sage, 2006), 265–86.

33. Jennifer Anne Ziegler. "The Story Behind an Organizational List: A Genealogy of Wildland Firefighters' 10 Standard Fire Orders." *Communication Monographs* 74, no. 4 (2007): 415–42. doi:10.1080/03637750701716594.

34. Ibid., 421.

35. Ibid., 431.

36. Timothy Kuhn, "A Communicative Theory of the Firm: Developing an Alternative Perspective on Intra-organizational Power and Stakeholder Relationships," *Organization Studies* 29 (2008): 1227–54.

37. Karl E. Weick and Kathleen M. Sutcliffe, *Managing the Unexpected: Assuring High Performance in an Age of Complexity* (San Francisco: Jossey-Bass, 2001).

38. Recent Best Places to Work Agency Rankings are available at http://bestplacestowork.org/BPTW/rankings/overall/%20%20.

39. Orion F. White Jr., "The Dialectical Organization: An Alternative to Bureaucracy," *Public Administration Review* 29 (1969): 32–42.

6

Challenger, Columbia, and Risk Communication

"Quality improvement teams help in several ways. First, they facilitate dialogue, understanding, and knowledge of processes that cross formal departmental boundaries. Understanding a process often requires that people from different staff areas, and people from different hierarchical levels, think together—people who, without a team, might never meet each other. These special opportunities to work together are necessary simply because no single person occupies a perch from which the whole process is visible, and yet it is precisely the whole process that is the object of improvement. When people work hard at improving only their own, visible, local segment of a process, the result may be that, while their segment is made better, the process as a whole is made worse."

—Donald M. Berwick, A. Blanton Godfrey, and Jane Roessner,
Curing Health Care: New Strategies for Quality Improvement

CHALLENGER

We had seen the expectant profile of a space shuttle ready to launch some two dozen times, but it was different on the morning of January 28, 1986—this time there was a schoolteacher on board. The rest of the teachers around the country were trying to keep their students' attention focused on the television set after the delays. At last they heard the disembodied voice intone the final countdown: "T-minus ten. Nine. Eight. Seven. Six. Five. Four. Three. Two. One. And lift-off of the twenty-fifth shuttle mission, and it has cleared the tower."[1]

Roger Boisjoly, an engineer working for Morton Thiokol in Brigham City, Utah, was greatly relieved. Morton Thiokol, a Utah firm, was the prime contractor for the two solid-fuel boosters blasting the shuttle into space. The night before, Boisjoly had strongly recommended against the launch of the *Challenger* on the grounds that the O-rings—rubber gaskets that prevent the escape of explosive gases—had never been tested under freezing conditions. The ambient temperature at Cape Canaveral, Florida, was 36 degrees Fahrenheit, but icicles still hung from the tower scaffolding due to freezing temperatures the night before. Boisjoly was relieved because he had been advised by his technical team that the greatest risk would be at the moment of liftoff.

A Major Malfunction

The families of the *Challenger's* crew (Greg Jarvis, schoolteacher Christa McAulliffe, Ron McNair, Ellison Onizuka, Judy Resnik, Dick Scobee, and Mike Smith) watched what appeared to be another routinely successful launch. Then some saw a puff of smoke. Objects seemed to break away from the spacecraft. Then came the fearful, shattering message over the loudspeakers:

> "Flight controllers here looking very carefully at the situation. Obviously a major malfunction. We have no downlink. We have a report from the Flight Dynamics Officer that the vehicle has exploded."

The cries rose to a keening wail. Children sobbed for their fathers and for their mother. The adults were helpless to comfort them. As the escorts led the families from the roof, the cloud spread and softened the sky. Feathery vapor trails descended, distant streaming debris.[2]

I was walking across the campus of Purdue University when I got the word. *What happened? What went wrong? Why did it happen?* These are only some of the questions that ran through my mind. I felt a personal sense of loss and some anger because of my past experience with NASA and the Marshall Space Flight Center (MSFC). I had been part of that organization, it was part of me, and I had a vague sense of responsibility. At the time I was a professor in the Department of Communication and associate dean of the School of Liberal Arts at Purdue, which claimed to have produced more astronauts than any other university, save one of the military academies. Neil Armstrong, the first man to walk on the Moon, was a Purdue graduate. We at Purdue identified with NASA and the space program and agonized over the accident.

Christa McAuliffe was a singular personification of the *Challenger* tragedy. Teachers had put bumper stickers on their cars quoting her as saying, "I touch the future. I teach." President Ronald Reagan promised there would be more teachers in space.

The Rogers Commission

President Reagan appointed a Presidential Commission, the Rogers Commission, to investigate the accident because of the deep response of the American people. I followed the proceedings and the media coverage of testimony given to the Commission and its investigators. I soon noticed that descriptions of certain communication events leading up to the accident didn't jibe with the practices I had observed and studied by interviewing the participants at the MSFC in the late 1960s. One example was the highly publicized teleconference held on Monday, January 27, 1986, the night before the ill-fated launch, between representatives of the MSFC, the Kennedy Space Center in Florida, and Morton Thiokol.

Testimony about this telephone conversation described MSFC representatives as reversing their traditional approach to dealing with a contractor. Instead of *penetrating* Morton Thiokol (the concept explained in chapter 2 of entering the organization's communication system) and demanding evidence that the spacecraft would fly, they pressed Morton Thiokol's representatives to prove that it would *not* fly. During the Apollo era when Wernher von Braun was the director at the MSFC, not asking them to prove that it *would* fly would have been the equivalent of breaking one of the Ten Commandments. Reversing the Commandment by demanding that they prove it would not fly would have been considered doubly sacrilegious to the organization's culture and history.

Under von Braun's management, the MSFC operated under the assumption that the contractor had the burden of proof, a concept originally defined by the English rhetorical theorist Richard Whately (1787–1863). *Burden of proof* is a dialectical term whose meaning is made clear by its opposite, the presumption. To define by illustration, in the United States a person is presumed to be innocent (the presumption) until proved guilty (the burden of proof). The presumption at the MSFC, if not NASA as a whole, had been that the contractor had to prove that its part of the spacecraft would fly safely because the other presumption was that in this high-risk endeavor, there was a high probability that some components might be flawed.

Recall that von Braun had been summoned to a congressional investigation into why contractors performed better for his organization than for the U.S. Navy. His answer was in a word: *penetration*. Penetration was an external extension of the buyer's presumption in asking the seller to demonstrate that the product it was selling was made correctly and would function properly.

Organizational Forgetting?

I began thinking about this sacrilegious change of policy at the MSFC. *How could it have happened?* After the success of the Apollo Program, the inferiority complex suffered by the rest of NASA involved in man-rated programs had led to the early retirement of most of the German team. Von

Braun had been kicked upstairs in 1970 to become NASA's associate deputy administrator for future planning in Washington, DC. He was bored with the job and resigned from NASA two years later to take a job with Fairchild Industries at Germantown, Maryland. He died in 1977 after a long bout with cancer. His successor at the MSFC was Rocco Petrone, transferred from NASA Headquarters to serve as director of the MSFC in Huntsville. My sources at the MSFC told me that Petrone's main concern was to execute a RIF, a reduction in force, and to get rid of the remaining Germans. It seemed to me it was highly likely that the RIF and changes at the top meant that the exemplary communication practices I had discovered and praised in print and lectures might have gone the way of "organizational forgetting" and been replaced by more traditionally bureaucratic ways. I was pressed by the media to give opinions about the shuttle accident; I resisted but finally talked to a local affiliate of CBS News when someone called me at home. I was more than a bit uncomfortable, as I explained, because the only evidence to which I had access was circumstantial and slender.

Return to Marshall Space Flight Center

On October 26, 1989, I wrote a letter to the director of the MSFC, T. J. "Jack" Lee, introducing myself and recalling my previous association with the center. I enclosed copies of two articles I had published in a journal in my field, *Communication Monographs*,[3] based on my research during the Apollo era. I proposed returning to the MSFC between late October of 1989 and April of 1990. My plan was to interview Lee and other management personnel about the then-current communication practices and also pose questions concerning events leading up to the *Challenger* accident. I got the approval and on January 8, 1990, I flew into Huntsville, now even more a bustling, sprawling metropolis with countless new hotels and restaurants. I invited Walter Wiesman, the youngest of the Germans on von Braun's team and the man who in 1967 had recruited me to work as a summer faculty consultant, and his wife to join me for dinner. We had a lovely reunion. Walt had written me a sad letter about the *Challenger* disaster not long after it happened, saying that although he was in retirement what he had heard through the grapevine made him think the problem was with "communication."

I interviewed 16 people from the top three layers of the MSFC organization. Although I had feared they might not open up to me, they did. Some remembered me, and newer people knew me by reputation. They knew that I would maintain their anonymity with regard to the quotations I would use from the interviews—including highly negative comments about the hierarchy that existed leading up to the accident. (Much of that top management had been replaced immediately after the *Challenger* accident.) Although I had not promised them a report after the interviews, they asked for one and I obliged. I had intended to put the interview notes together for another *Communication Monographs* article, but a young writer named Claude Teweles, who had recently founded a new publishing company, Roxbury, had heard about my study and persuaded me to write a book for him.

I signed the contract and delivered the manuscript. Roxbury's attorneys read it and decided that for legal reasons everything attributed to my interviewees had to be fact-checked. I had to write a formal letter to every interviewee, indicating what quotations I wanted to use from his or her interview—even though no names were identified with quotations. Virtually everything I wanted to quote was verified on a legal form, making it the most thorough attempt to establish the validity and reliability of data of any social scientific study I have heard of, particularly one using so-called qualitative data. The reader who wants to pursue this in detail can do so by reading pages 157–58 in the book *Organizational Communication Imperatives: Lessons of the Space Program.*[4]

Findings

Yes, there had been organizational forgetting. Although interviewees praised the old Monday Notes, now called Weekly Notes, they were now transmitted via e-mail. There was no feedback from the boss, no marginal notes coming back to the senders. What about automatic responsibility? About this exemplary practice I wrote: "In short, automatic responsibility had been forgotten by most managers in the best position to remember it, and the practice had thus fallen into disuse."[5] Only 6 interviewees could define *penetration,* 3 of 16 knew it had been a communication practice. Some who did not understand its past practice said that the reductions in force had left them too thin in personnel to maintain it as they had in the past. No one, however, defended reversing the burden of proof with the contractor.

Damning indeed were the criticisms of the director at the time, William Lucas. Here is a sample from the interviews:

"Dr. Lucas lost touch. We were not being effective in downward communication and he did not make people comfortable coming up the line."

"I feel bad about saying this, but people were afraid to bring bad news [to Lucas] for fear they would be treated harshly. . . . It was kill the messenger."

"Lucas was a dead fish. Cold, vindictive, he would embarrass people publicly. It was very hard to go to him with a problem."

"The messenger gets shot, in other words. It takes a strong messenger under those circumstances."

"Communication for a year or two before *Challenger* was a problem."

"Lucas wanted information filtered. His communication style was intimidation."

"The pre-*Challenger* period was the worst we've seen in communication. There was a fear on the part of people to surface problems at a high level: kill the messenger. I'm at fault for not surfacing problems. I saw it in meetings with Dr. Lucas—people humiliated in front of peers and contractors."[6]

In contrast with von Braun, Lucas did not instill trust in people so that they would bring risks forward, which had worked so well at the MSFC during the Apollo period. People were not responsible about reporting the risks. And they asked Morton Thiokol to prove *Challenger* would not fly. These were communication transgressions. And other changes had taken place at the Marshall Center. People who would soon move into positions of authority told me the MSFC had not tested the shuttle sufficiently on the ground.

Reconciling Different Explanations

In 1998, 12 years after the accident, the international journal *Organization* invited me to review two books: *No Downlink: A Dramatic Narrative about the Challenger Accident and Our Time* by Claus Jensen and *The Challenger Launch Decision: Risky Technology, Culture, and Deviance at NASA* by Diane Vaughan.[7]

"The tenth anniversary of the *Challenger* tragedy was 28 January 1996. Two very different books about the accident were published on that occasion," began the essay-review.[8] The first book, written by a Danish professor of literature, is a long-distance philosophic discussion of American technology and tragedy, told with elegantly translated prose. He would also call attention to a particular question and answer in the investigation that is important to an understanding of the teleconference the night before the launch. The second book, by Diane Vaughan, is hard-nosed sociology. Another book not assigned to me by the journal editor nonetheless rose to the surface, one written by Howard E. McCurdy, *Inside NASA: High Technology and Organizational Change in the U.S. Space Program.*[9] McCurdy was a professor of public affairs at American University who mailed a culture questionnaire to NASA's employees in 1988. This allowed him in 1993 to describe in detail the premises of what McCurdy calls

> the original technical culture [OTC] of NASA: a commitment to research, testing and verification; to an in-depth, in-house technical capability (the old Army Arsenal concept); to the belief that engineers had to keep their hands dirty, or a hands-on discipline; to the

"normalization of risk, the acceptance of failure, and the anticipation of trouble [which] led to an atmosphere in which these things could be discussed openly" (or wide-open communiction); to the belief that NASA recruited exceptional people; and to a "frontier" mentality.[10]

McCurdy believes the OTC, including its emphasis on open communication, is what produced the early and spectacular successes of NASA; he describes it in much the same way I had. He goes on to argue that the OTC had given way to a much weaker culture in the second and third decade of NASA's life, and that this weakened culture, including less open communication and little attempt to discover risks early in the development process, explains the failure of NASA in the *Challenger* tragedy.

The title of my book about *Challenger* is *Organizational Communication Imperatives: Lessons of the Space Program;* it came out at the same time as McCurdy's book. Neither of us was aware the other was working on the same problem, but we came to roughly the same conclusion. I argue that the MSFC forgot its open communication culture, its exemplary communication practices described in chapter 2 of this book; that culture also included high technical standards. Vaughn, however, in her 1996 book, rejects the explanations offered by the Rogers Commission, McCurdy, and me to argue the sociological thesis of the "normalization of deviance," a phrase strikingly similar to McCurdy's OTC expression, the "normalization of risk." Let's look at them one at a time.

The Normalization of Risk . . . and Deviance

By *normalization of risk,* McCurdy means the willingness to fail, the action of striving for goals so difficult that odds are against complete success. He states: "The normalization of risk, the acceptance of failure, and the anticipation of trouble led to an atmosphere in which these things could be discussed openly."[11] Notice his use of the expression "could be discussed openly," which is repeated throughout his book. (*Open communication* is a term included in the index of McCurdy's book, with eight entries.) The normalization of risk means that taking risks is normal—but risks are to be avoided or reduced as much as possible by open communication about potential problems.

By *normalization of deviance,* Vaughan means that "behavior the work group first identified as technical deviation was subsequently reinterpreted as within the norm for acceptable joint performance, then finally officially being labeled an acceptable risk. They redefined evidence that deviated from an acceptable standard so that it *became* the standard."[12] Vaughan's term is derivative of McCurdy's in this sense: Both are referring to cultural change about standards. McCurdy is referring to the aging problems of NASA, that the second generation at NASA had much weaker central control in terms of standards and far more bureaucracy. Vaughan sees an incremental descent into bad technical decisions, again a normalizing process. Both practices are at odds with Melville's notion of "smart risk" and the definition of it I offered in chapter 5.

McCurdy and I agree that cultures and communication practices had changed as the organization aged. The wide open or concertive discourse of the OTC was gone, and in its place was a culture of discursive closure, meaning that issues were not always discussed. For my part, the failure to penetrate the contractor and do early testing was risky to say the least. Vaughan does not think communication was a problem and takes a unique position on the teleconference the night before the launch. Morton Thiokol, represented by Roger Boisjoly and others, recommended against launching the *Challenger* the next morning. George Hardy, the MSFC's deputy director for science and engineering, was "appalled" to hear their decision, based as it was on a lack of experience with the suspect O-rings at such low temperatures. The MSFC's managers demanded that the Morton Thiokol engineers prove that they were not ready to launch. Morton Thiokol's managers forced their engineers to reverse their recommendation. Because the O-rings hadn't been tested at temperatures below freezing, *they couldn't prove they would fail.* The reversal of the OTC led to the shaky conclusion that *Challenger* was ready to go.

No contractor had ever made a no-launch recommendation. The contractor always had the burden of proof in regard to the readiness and reliability of its equipment, thus making potential problems clear long before a launch. This is Vaughan's interpretation of the episode that turns everything upside down:

> The Thiokol engineers believed that the burden of proof was different than in the past because *they had never come forward with a no-launch recommendation in an FRR before.* Marshall's managers and Thiokol's proponents of the no-launch recommendation were both partially correct: managers did not behave differently, but the burden of proof did shift. It shifted because the contractor position shifted.... Since their position deviated from the norm, the burden of proof deviated from the norm.[13]

This highly original interpretation is wrong. Vaughan confused *social* role expectations with *logical* responsibilities in argument, thus eliminating any examination of evidence. This was not a case of the normalization of deviance. The Danish writer Claus Jensen understood how "unnormal" this deviation was in quoting an exchange between the Commission chairman Rogers and NASA official Larry Mulloy:

> *Rogers:* Do you remember any other occasion when the contractor recommended against launch and you persuaded them they were wrong and had them change their mind?
> *Mulloy:* No, sir.[14]

This exchange, from the values of the OTC as epitomized by the MSFC, records the ultimate sacrilege.

COLUMBIA

I was hopeful that my book about *Challenger* would be of help to NASA. I did see that NASA had summarized my findings and conclusions in an e-mail circulated throughout the agency. I had also seen hope for reforms during my interviews and in the Rogers Report. Then the sky fell. *Columbia* broke up on February 1, 2003; seven astronauts were killed. Although I was again depressed, I decided not to pursue the case. And yet I could not stop reading about the accident and the investigations of it. A good friend, Gregory Desilet, said I would have to write another book. I disagreed. But then in April I was invited to talk to an organizational communication class at Michigan State University. As I prepared for this talk, I heard that Dr. Sally Ride had called the accident an "echo" of the *Challenger* accident. What I had said in my book about the first shuttle accident seemed to fit the evidence in the second shuttle accident. Claude Teweles, who had persuaded me to publish the first book, made me an offer I found hard to resist. But I did. Until the day I was walking along the 16th Street Mall in downtown Denver and in my head appeared the title of the book and the title of each chapter. I signed Teweles's contract and wrote the book.

There was no need for another trip to Huntsville. I would have to concentrate on NASA as a whole, not on a field center. The evidence this time would come from the report of the Columbia Accident Investigation Board (CAIB) and from press reports. My daughter Emily, much more skilled in using the Internet than I, agreed to become my research assistant, and she gathered for me everything I asked for, and then a lot more. I was no longer an insider, and in the end that became a positive factor because it gave me some needed perspective by distance.

My friend and neighbor Gregory Williams, a graduate of Michigan State University with a degree in civil engineering, had been vacationing in Florida and decided to watch the landing of the space shuttle *Columbia* with his cousin. While waiting at the Visitors Center at the Kennedy Space Center in Cape Canaveral, they heard the announcement at 8:45 a.m. that the shuttle had reached California at about 20,000 miles per hour at 200,000 feet. Five minutes later it was flying at 18,000 miles per hour over Texas, and it was to be landing in Florida in about 15 minutes. That was the last official announcement Williams and the others heard. Thus began the mystery. When he returned to his hotel he heard the shocking news.

While Williams and the others were experiencing shock, two reporters were filing a story for the *New York Times* with a dateline of Nacodoches, Tex., Feb. 1, and this headline: "LOSS OF THE SHUTTLE: ON THE GROUND; First the Air Shook with Sound, and Then Debris Rained Down." The article appeared in the *Times* the next day.[15] Texans in the area were unhurt physically by the lethal rain, but a hospital worker in Hemphill was horrified to find the charred torso and skull of an astronaut near some pieces of debris on a rural road. Human remains were also found in Sabine County. I followed the daily round of new evidence and hypotheses about the accident in the press and online—with Emily's help. In my mind's eye, I could see the style of the book: it would be written like a nonfiction mystery novel, a true police procedural, in which I would approach a "crime" by examining the evidence day by day and come to my own conclusions.

Possible Causes of the Disaster

An article in the *New York Times* on February 2, written by William J. Broad and James Glanz, listed six possible causes of the space shuttle *Columbia* disaster in order of decreasing likelihood:

1. Damage to the protective tiles on the left wing.
2. An explosion of the ship's fuels and oxidizers, which were kept under high pressure.
3. Collapse in the shuttle's structure, which was aged.
4. Faulty navigation setup for the fiery re-entry, caused perhaps by a computer problem.
5. A collision with a speeding meteoroid or piece of space debris.
6. Terrorism, perhaps by a technician at the launching site.

Research and analysis would proceed by an attempt to reject faulty hypotheses and seize upon the one that would explain most of the facts. Although my mystery novel would be factual, it would rely on quotations from a fictional character, perhaps the best-known sleuth of all time, such as this one: "But we are bound to exhaust all other hypotheses before falling back on this one"—Sherlock Holmes in *The Hound of the Baskervilles* by Sir Arthur Conan Doyle.

Part of the detective story was procedural. The NASA administrator had appointed members of the Air Force, Navy, and, yes, NASA, to the CAIB. An outcry was that the government was investigating itself. Additional members were appointed from business, the academic world, and, notably, Dr. Sally Ride, professor of physics, astronaut, and member of the Rogers Commission that investigated the *Challenger* accident.

Columbia Accident Investigation Board Report

Within seven months, on Tuesday August 26, 2003, the CAIB issued its report. I got a copy the next day. It was the basis for the last chapter of the mystery, when the case is solved. The CAIB had concluded that either (1) the shuttle had sustained structural damage that undermined the altitude or angle of re-entry, or (2) the shuttle maneuvered to an altitude for which it was not designed. The data strongly indicated that improper maneuvering was not the problem, dictating that most of the fault tree analysis be concentrated on structural damage. (A fault tree is a method for examining possible hypotheses, called "branches," by slowly eliminating each one for lack of evidence until there is only one explanation left. In this fault tree there were 10 branches.) It was just as Sherlock Holmes had done, except that he had done it all in his head without any deadwood.

I climbed down the branches as they were eliminated, 1 through 9. Number 10 remained: Foreign Object Damage Prevention. There was damage to the left wing of the shuttle caused by a piece of foam which had separated from the external tank at 82.7 seconds after launch. This had been seen at the time, but few could believe that a piece of foam (!) could have damaged a space-rated material. Even the experts were saying that the piece of foam was falling at a very slow rate of speed. It turns out that what was thought to be soft foam was actually as hard as a rock, and a later experiment showed that the orbiter hit this foam with a relative velocity of about 545 miles per hour. Although the foam was falling slowly, the accelerating shuttle was speeding up, and ultimately it ran into a "brick" of foam.

The Mystery of NASA'S Culture

There was still some suspense from the other mystery—what would the CAIB find and recommend about NASA and its management? One of the NASA groups, the Debris Assessment Team (DAT), had made a request up through the channels right after the launch for better images. The DAT team subsequently learned that the managers of this particular flight had declined to image *Columbia*. The CAIB reported that *three requests* for imaging had been denied by management. The managers had decided that this was a mere "turnaround" issue, a mere matter of maintenance that could be done before *Columbia's* next flight, and thus did not pursue a request for more imagery. This was crucial, and I quote from my nonfiction novel: ". . . the Board later determined that there was a possibility that the shuttle *Atlantis* could have *rescued the seven astronauts on Columbia had NASA known about the damage to the left wing.*"[16]

Sally Ride was correct about the echo of the *Challenger* in this second shuttle accident. The CAIB found that the managers this time put the engineers of NASA in "the unusual position of having to prove that the situation was *unsafe*—a reversal of the usual requirement that a situation is *safe*."[17] This is a repetition of the problem I called "the reversal of the burden of proof" in my analysis of the *Challenger* tragedy. The DAT wanted more pictures of the shuttle in flight—in the hope of saving the astronauts on board—and they were put in the place of having to prove an argument about risk *before* they had the evidence to back it up. Some managers later claimed that they didn't know about the requests for more imagery, another serious communication problem if true. Other astronauts volunteered to go up in another shuttle to rescue their colleagues in orbit.

Faster, Better, Cheaper

Although the CAIB did not know the jargon of the field of organizational communication, they managed in their own terms to indict the NASA management for communication failures. They found fault with managers who did not create viable routes for the engineers to express their opinions and receive information. The CAIB then took a look at the organizational culture of NASA, focusing on NASA administrator Daniel S. Goldin, who had been appointed by the first President Bush in 1992. They found Goldin to be a man from outside the NASA culture, someone who proved to be more receptive to White House views than his predecessors. He had been a robotics expert at TRW, an important contractor at the time. In his frequent pep talks to employees, Goldin said they would have to do more with less money. His slogan was "Faster, Better, Cheaper," a rhetorical contradiction discussed in chapter 2. Faster, Better, Cheaper is a badly warped version of time, reliability, and cost, the three *topoi* or premises for arguing solutions to technical problems I had identified at NASA's MSFC during the OTC established by von Braun. In fairness to Goldin, the term did originate in the White House and was supposed to refer to the launching of satellites in large numbers, not to flights with astronauts, but slogans can become pervasive and persuasive.

Goldin cut the personnel at NASA by 25 percent, adopted questionable business practices, and *outsourced the shuttle.* This is an important, drastic historical change. The personnel at the MSFC at its founding had come over with von Braun from the U.S. Army, which as mentioned earlier had an arsenal concept, which von Braun brought with him to the MSFC. This meant that the MSFC in von Braun's time had enough in-house technical personnel to do the research and development of the *Saturn V;* contractors were allowed to bid only on the construction, not the R&D. The MSFC had the technical ability to do the R&D and was able to effectively penetrate its contractors. This guaranteed that the MSFC would be a better buyer than, say, the Air Force, and it established what McCurdy called the "original technical culture" (OTC) at NASA.

Goldin moved to have more and more work done by contractor organizations, those folks the astronauts in the Manned Flight Awareness program used to refer to as the lowest bidders. The CAIB understood this change in the history of the agency and its effect on communication, stating in its report that "the Space Shuttle Program had altered its structure by outsourcing to contractors, which added to communication problems," and concluded that NASA suffered from a "broken culture."[18]

Although I was sympathetic to and in agreement with the CAIB's analysis, I disliked its metaphor. It seemed a brittle figure of speech to speak of breaking a culture. Culture is organic, a living thing. I decided, by quoting the CAIB's own findings, to argue that the culture I knew during the Apollo era had been subdued, defeated by a competing culture imposed from the top down which sought low costs at the expense of reliability—a two-culture dialectical explanation.

There is another factor observed by Howard McCurdy: as government agencies go through the aging process they change. In his book *Inside NASA: High Technology and Organizational Change in the U.S. Space Program,* he mentions the Tennessee Valley Authority, the U.S. Forest Service, and NASA at various points, emphasizing that after early periods of expansion, growth is a severe challenge. Organizations must try to substitute qualitative growth for quantitative, and only a few institutions are capable of that—well-respected universities are his prime example. NASA's great successes, its qualitative achievements, were accomplished in its first decade or so of existence, a period McCurdy characterizes as having a norm of wide-open communication. We need more nomothetic and idiographic studies of NASA to test this theory of bureaucratic life cycles, as argued in chapter 5 about the USFS.

SHUTTLE FAILURES, COMMUNICATION, AND RISK

In considering shuttle failures, communication, and risk, the reader may want to consult Figure 2 in chapter 1 of this book. The intersecting curves, as we saw, greatly favor discovering and diagnosing a risk early, as early as possible. Von Braun had to understand that relationship, as demonstrated by his practice of *penetration* and the *earliest possible* testing of components. In addition, the Monday Notes, automatic responsibility, and penetration served to shorten the scalar chain from engineer in the lab to the director. Layers could be bypassed with a technical problem, thus saving time (and money) by solving problems early. The semantic-information distance in the organization had been collapsed by von Braun, and then *lengthened* by his successor and the other members of the new management culture. It is even clearer to me now that von Braun's communication practices probably would have prevented both shuttle disasters. But then they could only have been kept in practice with in-house technical depth, a greater value on reliability, and a culture of open communication.

As soon as my second space shuttle book was published, I was besieged with requests to speak about my analysis. There were so many that I could not accept them all, even though I was by then retired from teaching. Because of the subtitle I had given that book—*The Decline of the Space Program*—and my criticisms of its performance, I never expected to hear from NASA again. But the space agency surprised me by inviting me to speak at an international conference to be held in Washington, DC, in 2005. *What do they want me to talk about and why?* That question haunted me.

The answers will be provided in the next chapter, in which I relate NASA's explanation for its invitation, and my response. In that chapter I also discuss other reactions to the book, ones that indicate that people have a great interest in how communication can be a means of managing complexity and risks, as well as a way to meet other challenges.

Notes

1. Malcolm McConnell, *Challenger: A Major Malfunction: A True Story of Politics, Greed, and The Wrong Stuff* (Garden City, NY: Doubleday & Co., 1987), 239.

2. Ibid., 247.

3. Phillip K. Tompkins, "Management Qua Communication in Rocket Research and Development," *Communication Monographs* 44 (1977): 1–26; Phillip K. Tompkins, "Organizational Metamorphosis in Space Research and Development," *Communication Monographs* 45 (1978): 110–18.

4. Phillip K. Tompkins, *Organizational Communication Imperatives: Lessons of the Space Program* (Los Angeles: Roxbury Publishing Company, 1993).

5. Ibid., 173.

6. Ibid., 164–65.

7. Claus Jensen, *No Downlink: A Dramatic Narrative about the Challenger Accident and Our Time,* trans. Barbara Haveland (New York: Farrar Straus & Giroux, 1996); Diane Vaughan, *The Challenger Launch Decision: Risky Technology, Culture, and Deviance at NASA* (Chicago: The University of Chicago Press, 1996).

8. Phillip K. Tompkins, Kurt Heppard, and Craig Melville, "Review Article: Deviance from Normality or Normalization of Deviance? Making Sense of the *Challenger* Launch Decision," *Organization* 5 (November 1998): 620–29.

9. Howard E. McCurdy, *Inside NASA: High Technology and Organizational Change in the U.S. Space Program* (Baltimore: The Johns Hopkins University Press, 1993).

10. Tompkins, Heppard, and Melville, "Review Article," 623.

11. McCurdy, *Inside NASA,* 65.

12. Vaughan, *The Challenger Launch Decision,* 65. Emphasis in original.

13. Ibid., 343. Emphasis in original.

14. Jensen, *No Downlink,* 625.

15. David M. Halbfinger and Richard A. Oppel Jr., "Loss of the Shuttle: On the Ground; First the Air Shook with Sound, and Then Debris Rained Down," *New York Times,* February 2, 2003, 27.

16. Phillip K. Tompkins, *Apollo, Challenger, Columbia: The Decline of the Space Program* (Los Angeles: Roxbury Publishing Company, 2005), 173. Emphasis in original.

17. NASA, *Columbia Accident Investigation Board Report, Volume 1* (Washington, DC: Government Printing Office, 2003), 169.

18. Ibid., 198.

7

Responses to *Apollo, Challenger, Columbia: The Decline of the Space Program*

"*Man is the symbol-using (symbol-making, symbol-misusing) animal, inventor of the negative (or moralized by the negative), separated from his natural condition by instruments of his own making, goaded by the spirit of hierarchy (or moved by the sense of order), and rotten with perfection.*"

—Kenneth Burke, *Language as Symbolic Action: Essays on Life, Literature, and Method*

Writers like to hear from readers, particularly when they have praise for, or questions about, what they have read. *Apollo, Challenger, Columbia: The Decline of the Space Program*[1] was written only after persuasion by friends and a publisher. The subtitle was bound to alienate my former employer, an organization I had been proud to be part of during the glory days of Apollo. We did go to the Moon, after all, and return safely.

I did not expect to hear from NASA ever again and assumed that if I did, it would be a negative exchange. But I did hope to hear from others, so I included my e-mail address (tompkinp@colorado.edu) in the book.

It was fun to receive e-mails from students with comments and questions. In some cases we connected via a conference call with a class. I also heard from a rocket scientist in South Korea who was full of praise for the book. He said it "proved" many ideas and principles he had come up with from his own experience. I replied, and he then asked for permission to translate the book into Korean. Eager to see how the book would look in Korean, I sought permission from Oxford University Press, who had acquired the small original publisher, but before that could come to pass, the e-mail correspondence with the South Korean rocket scientist came to an end, perhaps because I had asked too many questions about the rocketry capabilities of his neighbor, North Korea.

A Visit to Embry-Riddle Aeronautical University

Another e-mail message arrived from a young professor, Dr. Joanne Detore-Nakamura, at Embry-Riddle Aeronautical University, known locally as ERAU, in Daytona Beach, Florida. She had read *Apollo, Challenger, Columbia,* was going to use it in a class in organizational communication, and invited me to visit ERAU's campus, meet with a class reading the book, and give a public lecture about my findings and advice for the students. I had never heard of ERAU but it sounded like a fascinating institution. There was a generous honorarium, but part of the allure was getting my wife and me out of the Colorado winter and in Daytona Beach in January of 2006. I accepted the offer and began preparations for the trip.

Dr. Detore-Nakamura's students impressed me favorably. All the students at ERAU were being educated for some kind of career in aeronautics: pilots, engineers, and some even wanted to be astronauts. They had not yet finished reading my book but peppered me with questions about what they had read. They were intrigued by the Monday Notes and were projecting themselves into a future time and place where a version of those notes might be useful. As I walked around the campus I could see the posters announcing the speech, and I could sense there was great interest in the topic. The title, chosen by Dr. Detore-Nakamura, was "NASA's *Challenger* and *Columbia:* Averting Disasters by Means of Better Communication." I was a bit nervous when I showed up early to sign copies of the book sold at the campus bookstore. My nerves got worse because, as the student newspaper later correctly reported, the speech was delayed for 15 minutes while workers brought in many more extra folding chairs. The person in charge of setup volunteered to me that it was the largest audience ever in the Miller Center Auditorium.

I have a good idea of what I said because my address was published in *Vital Speeches of the Day* for February 15, 2006. I began by thanking Dr. Detore-Nakamura for making the arrangements, adding, "I'm still wondering how she got NASA to launch the Pluto Probe this afternoon so I could watch it from campus." I then paid tribute to Walter Wiesman of NASA and W. Charles Redding of Purdue University. I narrated my experience with NASA as the technicians flashed huge slides of Wernher von Braun, various rockets, and the shuttles as I signaled them. Wanting to end the speech on a positive note, I drew on my research into the Aviation Safety Reporting System (ASRS; considered in chapter 9 of this book) and ended with some practical advice that pertains to more in life than just piloting an aircraft.

Pilots are trained, I continued, so that when they sense trouble, or a serious *risk,* they should climb in altitude while they learn more about the problem and in case they have to glide without power to a safe place; then they should speak up—communicate with the flight crew and air traffic controllers at the first sign of a risk—and they should also be ready to admit error, either at that moment or in a later report to ASRS. My last, alliterative words were these: "I leave you with the 3 "C's" of aviation safety, and with the assurance that they apply to people other than pilots and to situations other than a crisis in the air: climb, communicate, confess."

I was later invited to join the advisory board for the communication program at ERAU and accepted. I enjoyed serving with representatives of airlines and other aeronautical organizations, learning much in conversation and group discussions with them. I worked for a couple of years on a long-distance basis with students and returned to campus for board meetings and other activities. I received and accepted invitations to give similar lectures and an emerging discourse of my own on communication and risk management at Western Kentucky University and the University of Maryland.

The International Conference on Systems Engineering: Risk as Communication

The phrase "out of the blue" is not a cliché when used to describe an e-mail message I received from an aeronautical engineer who was a total stranger. The message was from Dr. Stein Cass, then the risk management board chairman of Ball Aerospace. This began a long and intermittent correspondence between the two of us, one in which I learned a great deal about the mathematical approach to risk and what I shall call the rhetorical approach to risk. His message was sent from Ball Aerospace of Boulder, Colorado, on Thursday, March 24, 2005:

Dr. Tompkins,

I just finished your recent book on Communication in NASA for Apollo, Challenger, and Columbia. I found it particularly interesting how culture change and risk seem to be intertwined, especially for the change in risk perception on the Shuttle program.

We at Ball Aerospace have been dealing with the Faster Better Cheaper (FBC) mentality and impacts on our NASA program for several years. Deep Impact is one example of programs that start off

FBC and then changed to a mission success oriented philosophy. Increased costs by 1–15% to change philosophy but was worth the risk reduction.

Dr. Cass and Ball Aerospace were clearly on the side of the low-risk, high-reliability culture battle that had taken place within NASA and between it and its contractors. His e-mail message went on to say that Ball was undergoing another change, from building one spacecraft at a time to multiple, simultaneous projects. He thought and hoped Ball could learn from NASA's problems and could "manage change without losing sight of program risk." He then mentioned that he was heading up a special session on risk at the International Conference on Systems Engineering in August of 2005 in Las Vegas and was wondering if I might be interested in presenting my findings. The session was entitled "Current Trends and Best Practices in Risk Management for Aerospace Projects." The final sentence in the letter: "Thank you very much for your time—once again, I enjoyed the book, and hope to implement some of your observations of Von Braun's team in our work practices at Ball (especially automatic responsibility, and penetration of our suppliers)." Learning that an important contractor would want to penetrate *its contractors* was fascinating to me, and it was good news for taxpayers, if only they knew. In addition, I was intrigued by the invitation to present a paper about the communicative approach to risk to a bunch of scholarly engineers who approached the topic mathematically.

Dr. Cass invited me to a long working lunch in Boulder. After explaining that he and some colleagues believed they had reached the limits of the mathematical approach to risk and that he hoped the communication approach might complement it, making it stronger, he gave me a short course in the mathematical approach to risk. Using his paper "Risk Management in the Aerospace Industry: Past and Present"[2] as a textbook, we had a Socratic dialogue that continued in our e-mail correspondence, with my cross-examination of him and his patient answering of all my questions. I began working on the paper for the convention of systems engineers in Las Vegas.

An Invitation from NASA

The biggest surprise came when I received an e-mail message from someone claiming to be a NASA (!) official. The date of the message was
Tuesday, April 5, 2005. I glanced at the end of the electronic document to
learn the identity of the communicant, the source of the surprising message. I reproduce it here, beginning with his signature:

Richard B. Katz
Head Grunt, Office of Logic Design
National Aeronautics and Space Administration
Goddard Space Flight Center

With a title like that, I thought, *the guy must have a sense of humor*. I
scanned back up to the message itself:

Hi Phillip,

I'm a NASA design engineer and read your book, Apollo, Challenger, Columbia: The Decline of the Space Program. Each September
we have a conference in Washington, D.C., with a history theme
running through it. . . . I'm building up this year's program and
would like to have a talk on the history of technical management
at NASA. After consulting with some space historians, with your
name coming up several times, I am now writing you this letter.

Katz included a short description of the program and after an exchange
about my role in participating in it, I accepted his offer. This person was
real, and I enjoyed the anti-bureaucratic title "Head Grunt." Katz is an
interesting and brilliant man. He explained to me that MAPLD meant
Military and Aerospace Programmable Logic Device, whatever such a device might look like. NASA had been putting on this international conference about it for several years. The conference was about historical matters
as well as current engineering topics.

The 2005 MAPLD International Conference

The 2005 MAPLD conference was to be held at the Ronald Reagan Building and International Trade Center in Washington, DC, September 7–9. NASA's Office of Logic Design put out a flyer with biographical information and a color photograph of me with a smile on my face. The abstract of the paper said I would talk about my work at NASA's Marshall Space Flight Center (MSFC). It concluded with these two sentences:

> Taken together, the organization's [MSFC's] practices of organizational communication constitute a theory of organization and decision-making, and an effective approach to the management of risk. The author will mention well-known theories of his that were inspired by the research at MSFC and will conclude with his thesis that communication is the geometry of human organization.

Upon meeting Richard Katz, I asked him why, given the subtitle of my book, *The Decline of the Space Program*, I had been invited to the conference, along with such distinguished guest speakers as Robert C. Seamans Jr., former secretary of the U.S. Air Force and acting administrator of NASA, and professor at MIT. Katz replied, "Because we read your books and wanted the young engineers and managers to know how you did things during Apollo."

In preparation for writing this chapter I reviewed my notes for that speech, written on an eight-inch square tablet from the Ronald Reagan Building and International Trade Center. I began with the story of the "five nines," a story told to me during an interview in 1967 about director von Braun when he was at NASA Headquarters for a meeting. Someone asked, "What is the reliability figure for the second stage of the *Saturn V*?" Dr. von Braun said that he couldn't remember but would call the official with the answer as soon as he got back to the MSFC in Huntsville. When he did call back, the NASA official said that the answer he heard was "five nines," the quantification of reliability or risk factor of the second stage as .99999.

"Fine," said the official, "How did you arrive at that figure?"

"Well," answered von Braun, "I called Walter Haeusserman in the Astrionics Lab and asked him, 'Are we going to have any problems with this stage?' He answered, 'Nein.' Then I posed the same question to Karl Heimburg in the Test Lab and he also said, 'Nein.' I kept at it until I got five *neins.*" The story got a huge laugh at the NASA convention, as it always does. It may be apocryphal, but this story characterizes a basic element of von Braun's leadership: respect for his teammates and reliance on the ethos, or credibility, of his staff sensors. It is also about open communication. For the first time, however, I realized what it also means in terms of the mathematical approach to risk analysis. My reading and thinking about the mathematical approach to risk allowed me to see that the verbal or rhetorical approach comes before the mathematical approach and is the more important of the two. I wanted the NASA audience to understand how the words *discourse* and *communication* antedate and constitute the first of the two meanings of the pun. This also set up the final part of my presentation, when I talked about von Braun's theory of management qua communication, that "upward communication must be free, not tied to channels, if management is to be kept informed." There must be, however, a clear action and command channel. I mentioned how he described the Monday Notes. I confessed that it took weeks for me to understand the whole organization and his comments about the communication that constituted it. It became clear, I said, that upward-directed communication was most important to him.

Then I said, "One more quotation from von Braun" and read this:

This is like being in the earthquake prediction business. You put out your sensors. You want them to be sensitive enough, but you don't want to get drowned in noise. We have enough sensors, even in industry.

I mentioned that von Braun was a genius at creating analogies, no doubt in part because he spent a lifetime explaining rocketry, technology, and the heavens to people who did not know anything about engineering or astronomy. People in the audience were enjoying the analogies, those marvelous discursive comparisons that, to paraphrase Kenneth Burke,[3] bring out the "thisness" of that and the "thatness" of this, the sensors in this case who were human communicators located even in the contractors. But perhaps they were most interested to hear what I had to say about penetration, both internal and external, because my listeners were from industry—contractors—as well as from NASA and universities. I mentioned von Braun's testimony to a congressional committee, his answer to the question of why contractors performed better for the MSFC than they did for other agencies such as the Air Force: in a word, he said, *penetration.*

I also gave them a report on the Monday Notes and their communication benefits, emphasizing the *redundancy* of channels von Braun had created, just like the backup parts engineered into NASA's spacecraft and the extra organs we human beings carry around. I used the expression "backup channels," and went on to emphasize that the human social need is for more than is ideally necessary to communicate: "Zero redundancy produces a situation in which any 'errors in transmission, owing to disturbances and noise, will cause the receiver to make an uncorrectable and unidentifiable mistake.'"[4] I did not tell them the source of the quotation, but readers can find it in the book by Colin Cherry, *On Human Communication.* The redundant channels von Braun created not only reduced the risk of making an uncorrectable and unidentifiable mistake, but also they helped upper management know sooner rather than later about risks from problems that needed both resources and attention, as revealed by the Paul-Tompkins law of risk communication discussed in chapter 1.

I then moved into decision making and tried to boost my ethos or credibility by saying that I had been trained in what Aristotle thought of as the "universal arts of argumentation"—dialectic, rhetoric, and logic—and reminded them that the "L" in MAPLD, the title of our conference, stood for *logic.* I talked briefly about the *topoi,* or places to look for arguments, and said that the three I had found at the MSFC were reliability or safety, cost, and time or schedule, which were used as premises for arguments in decision making. I saw some nods around the room. I explained that the working groups at the MSFC would get in a room and argue openly about possible tradeoffs among the three premises, keeping in mind that von Braun wanted no foul compromises. I should have mentioned that my wife, George Cheney, and I had written an academic article about organizations as arguments,[5] a metaphor of our own. I completed that segment of the speech by relating that recently a risk manager at Ball Aerospace had used the e-mail address in my book to say that he wanted to get together and talk about the fact that he and his colleagues felt they had reached the outer limit of the effectiveness with the mathematical approach to risk, and that he thought von Braun's communication approach was the thing to complement it. I will return to this topic in the final chapter.

Turning to specific advice, I mentioned one of the most serious problems I had encountered while ferreting out communication problems for von Braun: what I called the "formalism-impersonality syndrome." I told the audience how my interviewees at the MSFC had talked at length about how their computers and management tools had become an end in themselves rather than a means to an end—that these were replacing old fashioned face-to-face communication with the maximum visual clues about the speaker's intended message. Then I brought up the Saturn V Control Center (SVCC) at the MSFC. I had researched it because a young American assistant to von Braun, Jim Shepherd, had talked to me before I set out to do my first research interviews in 1967. He had said that it was in a separate building, had displays on all four walls, and supposedly kept track of every part of every *Saturn V* and its components as they were being built. Shepherd said that he and von Braun would go over to the SVCC for a briefing and would be overwhelmed by the abundance of information in the massive displays, including Wasserfall, the German version of PERT (program evaluation and review technique, a statistical tool used in project management). It was the pride and joy of the administrator of NASA then, James E. Webb, who was neither an engineer nor a scientist and who believed his contribution for the ages to come would be management tools such as the SVCC. He brought visitors to Huntsville, it was said, mainly to see the SVCC. I had agreed to take a look at it and give Shepherd and von Braun a briefing on it.

The director of the SVCC was Arthur Rudolph, a shadowy figure I never met, who was later extradited to Germany because he had used slave labor to build the V-2 during World War II. His assistants gave me a tour of the huge, quiet room that was empty except for the three of us. The walls were meant to depict the PERT charts, but according to the assistants, Rudolph did not understand them so they were replaced by cartoon cutouts and Wasserfall, which Rudolph had used in Germany while manufacturing the V-2. I noticed that the postings were out of date and got an inspiration after they told me Rudolph visited the SVCC three times a week.

"Where does Rudolph begin and end the day?" I asked.

They took me across the hall to a room about one tenth the size of the SVCC. In contrast to the empty cavern we had just left, this room was alive with activity; people were on the telephone, talking to contractors and NASA personnel all over the country, making notes and then transferring them onto the grease-pencil charts that almost filled the room. Here I had found the beehive, the informal and *real* control center for the *Saturn V.* I was told that Rudolph also kept a chart of his own in his office. I reported back to Shepherd and von Braun and eventually the entire staff and board meeting of more than 55 people. "The Saturn V Control Center is more for show than utility." I was told that von Braun never attended another briefing in Webb's showplace, saying "You can't argue with the walls and the displays."

The SVCC was one of the best demonstrations of the waste and ineffectiveness of too much formalism and impersonality. By contrast, the informal Monday Notes were very effective: these single-page reports contained only the person's name and date in the heading, the boss provided handwritten feedback on each one, and copies of each were distributed to all 24 contributors and those in between.

Limited to 30 minutes, I had to apologize for not having time to talk about communication as the geometry of organizations and other topics advertised, but I gave the audience my e-mail address and told them I would send them a 22-page single-spaced paper with my thoughts about the subject. I then sat down in the audience to hear the other speakers on my panel. One of them was a communication specialist on Apollo 13, made more famous by the film of that name. The man, whose name I can't recall, got the biggest laugh of the day when he showed a still photograph from a scene in the film. The actor playing his part was completely bald. After we stopped laughing, the man, with a full head of hair, explained that the actor was director Ron Howard's brother. That was all he had to say, knowledge of DNA in the audience being enough to produce the laugh about the hirsute differential. He went on to disabuse us of the line, "Houston, we have a problem." He said he had listened to the tape over and over and he had no doubt that the astronaut had actually said, "Houston, we had a problem." *Ah, yes,* I thought, *Ron Howard appreciated the dramatic difference between past and present tense.*

People approached me after all the presentations had been made, pressing me about this and that, particularly about the practice of penetration. A professor from MIT said he had done some work during that period and wondered if the Institute had been penetrated. After one of the meetings later in the conference, Richard Katz, the head grunt of MAPLD, walked with me to the cafeteria, and along the way he told me that my point about redundancy of channels was new and important news to him, no doubt because of the analogy to engineering design. He then talked about his experience with Faster, Better, Cheaper and the practice of penetration, or lack of it. A contractor he mentioned had put in a bid for a satellite and did not want to supply any designs or other technical materials as part of the bid because the company's work was "proprietary." The contractor got the job anyway and the project failed, and as soon as Katz saw the designs he spotted the problem. The loss: $75 million, and it might have been saved had NASA demanded more information. When I got back home there was an e-mail message from Katz. He gave me more details about the case and ended with this message: "Oh well, $75 million down the tubes :-("

The 2006 MAPLD International Conference

Richard Katz knew my work so well that he sent me a proposed outline of what I might say as an invited speaker at the 2006 MAPLD Conference at the Ronald Reagan Building. He also gave me a title: "Lessons Learned in the Technical Management of Some Major Space Programs." In preparing for my assignment, I carefully studied No. 14 in the series Monographs in Aerospace History published by NASA: *Managing the Moon Program: Lessons Learned from Project Apollo.* This is a transcript of the collective recollections of six "key participants in Apollo's administration"[6] in a discussion moderated by John Logsdon on the 20th anniversary of the Moon landing. It was a collective history project. The discussants represented technical management from NASA Space Centers Langley and Johnson, and Headquarters.

Unfortunately no one from the MSFC had participated in this project, so I supplemented the lessons with ones I had learned there. I asked professors Gregory Larson at the University of Montana and Joanne Detore-Nakamura at ERAU for help. They were both teaching courses in which they used *Apollo, Challenger, Columbia: The Decline of the Space Program* as a textbook, so I asked them to find out from their students what lessons they had learned. Larson's class used group discussions—teamwork—to develop an outline of four main lessons learned, while Detore-Nakamura's more technically oriented students got a question on their final exam that each one had to answer.

Lessons Learned from the Apollo Program
Lesson I

In selling real estate, the most important factor is location, location, location; in managing technical projects, it is communication, communication, communication. For both the students and the Apollo managers, this was the first lesson learned. The NASA discussants heavily emphasized the matrix management structure, particularly because the project managers had to enter the traditional engineering disciplines via the laboratories, making for a new and difficult problem in horizontal or lateral communication that had to be overcome. This was also the main lesson learned from my research on MSFC for von Braun.

Lesson II

Technical management must penetrate contractor organizations with enough competent technical personnel to ensure that the products and messages submitted by contractor management are sufficiently reliable. I passed along to the NASA audience that Dr. Stein Cass, risk manager at Ball Aerospace, had told me that after reading my book he tried to penetrate his company's subcontractors, an idea I had not thought of, but one that makes eminent sense. Furthermore, Cass said he also preached penetration of the customer, NASA, as well. Again, this made sense. Dr. Cass had provided corollaries to this important axiom. It is clear that this lesson applies to more than important aerospace projects.

Under this lesson I mentioned to the audience that I had read an article written by an assistant professor, George A. Akerlof, in August of 1970: "The Market for 'Lemons': Quality Uncertainty and the Market Mechanism."[7] Thirty years later he won the Nobel Prize for some ideas expressed in the lemon article, concepts such as "asymmetry of information" and "quality uncertainty," and the idea that information is power. Asymmetry of information simply means that in transactions one party, whether an individual or an organization, knows more than the other. The party with less information is at a disadvantage, of course, and sometimes the party knowing more acts unethically, withholding or lying about what is known.

As a result of Akerlof's ideas, the latest round of corporate scandals at that time were known as "sins of information" by some, although I prefer the term *inequality of information*. The concept is highly related to the chances of being sold a lemon, whether in the form of an automobile or a spacecraft. This lesson does assume that the agency buying the hardware has sufficient technical competence—we called it "in-house technical depth" at the MSFC—to comprehend and evaluate the quality of work and information submitted by the seller, a point addressed under Lesson III.

In a conversation with an economist about trying to help NASA avoid buying lemons from contractors, we came up with the idea of offering, say, a 10 percent bonus to contractors who submit a completely transparent contract. Indeed, word should go out that transparency is a key criterion in NASA's process of evaluating bids and awarding contracts.

Lesson III

Until you really understand and have built within yourself the technical capability of knowing something very well and in-depth, you really ought not to try to manage a program. This is an exact quotation from *Managing the*

Moon Program: Lessons Learned from Project Apollo, a remark made by Dr. George Mueller, associate administrator of NASA during the Apollo Program.[8] At the MSFC there was a saying that you had to keep your hands dirty to be a good engineer. We thought we were better than the other NASA Field Centers because we had more in-house technical depth, looking down on the Johnson Center in Houston, for example, because it had too many managers, too many cooks, and not enough engineers with dirty hands. There is no doubt this was a factor in the failure of *Columbia*—the culture clash between the technical people of the original technical culture, who cherished reliability, and the managers who were obsessed with schedule and cost.

Lesson IV

Find non-quantitative ways of assessing risk-benefit questions. By way of illustrating this lesson, I quoted Dr. Chris Kraft, flight director for the Mercury Program and director of the Johnson Space Center, who said the "numbers game" of statistical risk analysis got worse and worse during his career at NASA. I repeated the story I had told at NASA's MAPLD Conference the year before: the five nines (.99999) or five *neins,* the perfect illustration of how argumentation and communication take place prior to, and are complementary to, the mathematical approach.

Lesson V

Technical managers must find the proper balance between efficiency, confidence in engineering, and redundancy in both the hardware and the channels of human communication. There were times when too much redundancy in the hardware was forced on the engineers, according to those six Apollo managers as they looked back 20 years later, but I am sure at times this helped. And then there were some components that could not have a backup. In terms of communication, there needs to be a balance. Too much redundancy—a message repeated over and over and over, for example—can put everyone to sleep. Von Braun no doubt erred in the direction of totally open communication, as facilitated by automatic responsibility.

Lesson VI

Technical managers must insist that contractors assume the burden of proof.
Because of the increasing tendency toward the inequality (asymmetry) of
information between buyer and seller, the seller must prove rigorously that
the product meets the standards of quality—must reduce uncertainty. To
reduce risks in the *Saturn V,* the MSFC assigned a sizeable number of
personnel to its contractors, to penetrate these organizations and establish
tight links with their technical counterparts. This lesson was clearly *broken*
by Marshall's managers during that teleconference about the *Challenger*
launch, when they demanded that Thiokol prove that the O-rings would
not work. That caused a major malfunction, a missing downlink, and death
to the astronauts on board. Buyer beware indeed.

Having learned that some contractors have claimed that their designs
are proprietary, NASA ought to press them to assume the *burden of proof at
every step in their interaction with them,* from beginning to end. If they resist, the space agency should find additional incentives designed to change
their behavior—or change the contractors to ones that meet the technical
and transparency requirements.

Lesson VII

*The uniqueness of the MSFC as I saw it during the Apollo Program was
such that it became an "ideal type."* Ten years after my work at Marshall, I
began to write monographs about it. As indicated in chapter 1 of this
book, my research led to a theoretical and empirical program dealing with
communication, organizational identification, and the teamwork which
my fellow theorist, George Cheney, and I decided to call *concertive control*
or *open communication and teamwork.* Max Weber, the great German social
scientist, developed a method of analysis and research he called the *ideal
type* or *pure type.* Engineers and scientists make a similar move when they
posit a concept such as a "frictionless plane" or "total vacuum" that does
not exist in reality but can be used to measure those things we can see
and measure. For example, Weber wrote that there were three ideal types
of legitimate authority: rational, traditional, and charismatic.[9] The first,

rational, derived from the rational-legal basis of bureaucracy; the second, traditional, is the authority granted royalty and other forms of authority; the third, charismatic, is that magical charm that people cannot resist. Weber did not use the word *ideal* in an evaluative sense, as in perfection, but as an abstraction, something not found in reality but which can be used to measure those things that are observable. The MSFC was very close to being an ideal type of organization in both senses, closer than most real-world organizations to Rorty's ideal type, illustrated in the epigraph in chapter 1 of this book.

Lesson VIII

The six trips to the Moon and back taught us the power of communication, cooperation, collaboration, identification, and their relationship to our infinite potential. A group of opinion leaders was polled by news magazines in 1999 about the 100 most significant events of the 20th century. Second only to the splitting of the atom and its use in World War II was the Moon landing. A popular president, not long before being assassinated, presented a stirring challenge to the people of the United States of America; government made commitments to the goal, and the nation, through NASA, its contractors, and taxpayers, made that vision come true. As mentioned in chapter 2, I saw civil service employees working overtime at salaries much less than what they could have made with contractors, and I am filled with awe when I think that over 200,000 persons collaborated, cooperated, and communicated with each other to make President Kennedy's vision come true. Infinite potential can achieve great goals when we live by what Kenneth Burke called those marvelous "co" words.

* * *

After my speech I moved into the audience to hear the next speaker. As I stood in the back of the room, a tall man with a notepad in his hand stepped up to me, shook my hand, and apologized to me. "I should have interviewed you," he said. He apologized again and repeated that he should have interviewed me, stating that his book on von Braun was at the printer. I later read his book, *Von Braun: Dreamer of Space, Engineer of War,* by Michael J. Neufeld. It is comprehensive but also the most negative biography of von Braun.

Writings about Dr. von Braun

Richard Katz had arranged for veteran astronaut Thomas D. Jones to acquire my two books about space and meet with me after my session so that I could autograph them for him. Jones also autographed for me a copy of his book, *The Complete Idiot's Guide to NASA.* He wrote:

To Phil—

With admiration for your work with "The Rocket Team"!

Best wishes—

Tom Jones
STS-59
-68
-80
-98

Katz got in touch with me again to say that I would have been invited again and again to speak at their conferences, but a legal decision had been made within the government making it impossible for NASA to sponsor such conferences in the future. I was disappointed, but I soon discovered that there were enough problems of risk and complexity to keep me busy. While I was in seclusion writing the first draft of this book, I was informed by two friends via e-mail that a new book about Nazi scientists brought to the United States had been mentioned on National Public Radio and that I should read it and discuss it in my book because von Braun was included in it.

I promptly bought the book, *Operation Paperclip: The Secret Intelligence Program that Brought Nazi Scientists to America,* by Annie Jacobsen. I gave it a cursory reading to get the drift and then made a double check on all index entries referring to von Braun and other Germans who became part of either the U.S. Army or NASA. The book uses newly released government documents to tell the story of all the German scientists brought to the United States after WWII—the good and the bad—people who conducted hideous "medical" research on captives and war prisoners, along with von Braun and the 120 persons cleared to work for the U.S. Army and NASA. Jacobsen also relies heavily on the existing biography of von Braun by Michael J. Neufeld, the man who apologized to me at the NASA MAPLD Conference, who read German and had written the most critical of the biographies of the rocket scientist.

Jacobsen does have damning evidence against Arthur Rudolph, the shadowy figure I never met at MSFC but who was later sent back to Germany when it became clear that the factory he ran while building the V-2s at Mittelwerk in the Harz Mountains was run with slave labor, people who were starved and beaten to death. Von Braun is said to have visited Mittelwerk and picked qualified technical prisoners at the Buchenwald concentration camp to send to work there. Jacobsen does acknowledge that von Braun always said in his own defense that he was coerced to join the Nazi Party and SS and did nothing more than follow orders. Jacobsen does not mention that von Braun was once sent to prison by Heinrich Himmler, the head of the SS, for talking about what he really wanted to be doing: designing rockets to explore space and go to the Moon. In fact, I heard one report that von Braun was imprisoned for saying that a V-2 came down on the wrong planet.

Jacobsen seems to fault von Braun and the Americans for making him a celebrity, for appearing on a Disneyland television program about outer space that captured the second largest television audience in history at that time. She does mention that he became an American citizen and a Christian, and seems to think he was too proud of those parts of his new identity. I was a boy in Wichita, Kansas, during WWII, and what I know about von Braun's past I read about in books and heard the other Germans talk about. What I know by observation was that he was a great, even charismatic leader, kind and supportive to his office staff and everyone else. I can say he promoted open communication and participation.

My Impressions of Dr. von Braun

During my orientation period at the MSFC, I was surprised when officials at the museum sat me down to read some of von Braun's earlier correspondence translated into English. I read his letter to Albert Schweitzer inviting the good doctor, organist, and theological scholar to visit him in Huntsville. He also explained his theory of afterlife in the letter to Schweitzer, a theory I had read in a magazine article. His basic argument was that science had taught him that nothing ever disappears, that all things are transformed into something else. Schweitzer wrote back inviting von Braun to visit his medical compound in Africa and telling him that his own theories of religion had no place for afterlife.

I was also appreciative of what von Braun did for race relations in Alabama. It was difficult if not impossible for him to recruit black engineering graduates of MIT to move to Huntsville, Alabama, but the receptionist outside his office was an African American woman. African Americans held the most visible jobs at MSFC—for example, tour guides and museum attendants. More importantly, von Braun took a stance against segregated schools. He had publicly criticized the governor of the state of Alabama, George Corley Wallace, for his segregationist practices. I happened to be in von Braun's office late one evening in 1968, briefing him about my ideas for reorganizing the MSFC in the post-Apollo period, when we were interrupted as Bonnie Holmes, his secretary, came in to report that James E. Webb, NASA administrator, had released the announcement of his resignation and sent word that von Braun was free to make a public statement. He dictated a statement which she promptly returned in typewritten form. He asked Bonnie to give it to me, asking me to check the grammar and style. I pronounced it to be good English, but questioned the statement of gratitude that alluded to "storms" through which Mr. Webb had steered NASA and the MSFC safely.

"What does that mean?"

"The 204 fire, Governor Wallace, and the Alabama environment," he replied. (The "204 fire" was a reference to the January 27, 1967, command and service module accident during a test on Earth; astronauts Gus Grissom, Edward White, and Roger Chaffee were killed in the accident.)

Getting back to Annie Jacobsen's case against von Braun, there is a paragraph that I had never read nor heard before. It is the implied charge that von Braun did not tell the truth in recruiting a German who had not come over in the first wave of 120:

Von Braun had also sold the army on hiring Walter Weisemann [*sic*], a Nazi public relations officer who had done some work in the Peenemunde valve shop. Von Braun called him an "eminent scientist." In reality, Weisemann learned engineering in America working for the army.[10]

Walter Wiesman, the name we knew him by, was not a PR man, did not learn engineering, but became the first person in NASA and any other government office to have the title coordinator of internal communication. Von Braun did fake his credentials, but at the time he was one of the few people in the world who knew that an expert in organizational communication was at least as important to managing complexity and risk as a scientist, many of whom he had already brought over.

Wiesman became a close friend of mine, but only by chance did I read his letter to the editor in the *Huntsville Times* about a censorship bill being considered by the Huntsville City Council. The bill proposed to ban artwork—paintings and sculpture—that displayed any form of nudity. Wiesman wrote a letter in opposition saying that as a boy he was a member of the Hitler Youth and burned books. He had learned his lesson and become an American citizen and an ardent champion of free speech. He urged the council to reject the measure. I called the letter to Walt's attention and congratulated him on it; he confessed that he also gave many speeches on the responsibilities we all have as citizens of a democracy.

* * *

Von Braun and the other Germans, many of whom I knew, made the transition from one homeland to another. In the many speeches he made, von Braun often began by apologizing for his accent. "I live in Alabama," he would explain and get a good laugh. We shall now make the transition from the complexity and risks of space travel to consider the people in our society at the moment who are most at risk in their mundane daily living: the homeless men, women, and children of our day.

Notes

1. Phillip K. Tompkins, *Apollo, Challenger, Columbia: The Decline of the Space Program* (Los Angeles: Roxbury Publishing Company, 2005).

2. Stein Cass, "Risk Management in the Aerospace Industry: Past and Present" (paper presented at the quarterly meeting of the Colorado Chapter of the International Council of Systems Engineering, December 2004).

3. Kenneth Burke, *A Grammar of Motives* (New York: Prentice-Hall, 1945), 503.

4. Colin Cherry, *On Human Communication*, 2nd ed. (Cambridge, MA: MIT Press, 1966), 186.

5. Elaine V. B. Tompkins, Phillip K. Tompkins, and George Cheney, "Organizations as Arguments: Discovering, Expressing, and Analyzing Premises for Decisions," *Journal of Management Systems* 1 (1989): 35–48.

6. NASA, *Managing the Moon Program: Lessons Learned from Project Apollo*, Monographs in Aerospace History Division, No. 14. (Washington, DC: NASA History Division, 1999.)

7. George A. Akerlof, "The Market for 'Lemons': Quality Uncertainty and the Market Mechanism," *Quarterly Journal of Economics* 84 (August 1970): 488–500.

8. NASA, *Managing the Moon Program*, 40.

9. Max Weber, *Economy and Society: An Outline of Interpretive Sociology*, ed. Guenther Roth and Claus Wittich (Berkeley: University of California Press, 1978), 215.

10. Annie Jacobsen, *Operation Paperclip: The Secret Intelligence Program that Brought Nazi Scientists to America* (New York: Little, Brown and Company, 2014), 221.

8

Our Homeless Neighbors: "At Risk" and "Risky" to the Domiciled

"Homeless people tend to be placed conceptually in that category usually reserved for animals. This is because the distinction between 'nature' (or the animal world) and 'culture' (the human world) rests upon such differences as animals have no permanent homes, live outdoors, roam about, void their wastes outside, do not wash, smell offensive and have little control over their actions, while humans dwell in fixed residences, void their bodily wastes privately and indoors, bathe and use deodorant to avoid smelling badly, and exert control over their actions."

—Deborah Lupton, *Risk*

"The compulsion to stereotype the homeless as dependent and deviant turns the poorest Americans into an abstract 'other,' separate and inferior from everyone else. Although their problems are more severe, however, destitute people living on the streets and in homeless shelters are not so different from the rest of us. They never have been. Any genuine effort to end homelessness must begin with a recognition of that essential truth."

—Kenneth L. Kusmer, *Down and Out, On the Road: The Homeless in American History*

A ccording to the article "The Astonishing Decline of Homeless in America" published in 2013 by Stephen Lurie,

despite a housing crisis, a great recession, rising income inequality, and elevated poverty, there is some good news among the most vulnerable segment of American society. America's homeless population—an estimated 633,000 people—has declined in the last decade.[1]

Lurie goes on to write that as incredible as it may seem, the National Alliance to End Homelessness estimates a 17 percent decrease in total homelessness from 2005 to 2012. This happened during a period in which unemployment doubled and foreclosures quadrupled. How can this be? Who is responsible? Here is an even bigger surprise to most people who have not studied this social problem: Lurie correctly gives the second President Bush credit for starting the Housing First program, which was led by the incredible efforts of a member of his administration—Philip Mangano. Bush appointed him to the position as head of the U.S. Interagency Council on Homelessness and created what may be the brightest accomplishment of his administration. The media called Mangano the "homeless czar" because of his heroic efforts to promote 10-year plans to end homelessness in all cities and states in this country and for his promotion of Housing First, which we shall discuss more later in this chapter.

Mangano was so effective in his job that President Obama asked him to stay on after the change of administrations. Mangano did serve for a few months before resigning to form a nonprofit organization, the American Roundtable to Abolish Homelessness. As I write this in early 2014, he is in California meeting with politicians, business leaders, service providers, and others to tackle the problem of homelessness in that state, particularly around Santa Barbara, where the problem has been serious since at least the early 2000s. He will work with the Central Coast Collaborative on Homelessness, or C3H. This is typical of Mangano's tireless efforts to bring together disparate yet important segments of U.S. society to act concertively in an effort to end or abolish homelessness. He stresses getting local business interests involved because of their ability to get things done when they see they have an interest in a problem.

A New Calling

I knew I would have to find a new calling after retiring from teaching in 1998. I found it almost immediately in the St. Francis Center (SFC), a daytime homeless shelter eight blocks from the loft in downtown Denver where my wife, Elaine, and I live. After applying, being accepted, and then training as a volunteer, I could walk to the shelter, work about six hours, and then walk home. The SFC is open weekdays from 6:00 a.m. to 6:00 p.m., with shorter hours on the weekend. It was created by an Episcopal priest, Father Bert Womack, in 1983 when he noticed the needs of people who were released from the sleep shelters early in the morning and had nowhere to go to get in out of the weather. In addition, there was a need for those people sleeping along Denver's Platte River, in fields, and in the alleys downtown to have a place where they could come in out of the elements, clean up, and find other services.

The year 2013 was the 30th anniversary of the SFC, and I was asked to write a short history of the shelter and homelessness for a book that would be sold at a fund-raising gala. I began by saying that it was more than an amazing coincidence that we were celebrating our 30th anniversary because research I had done showed that before 1980, there were no stories in the *New York Times* about homeless persons, only articles about "vagrants." By 1983, the year the SFC was founded, there were 82 articles about homeless persons in the *Times* and only 5 articles about vagrants. It was not that there were no homeless people before 1983; they were, however, called "vagrants," "bums," and "hobos" until then. The homeless population was growing, and a new group of people without housing needed a new name. The founders of the SFC made a timely perception and took timely action.

The Department of Housing and Urban Development (HUD) also saw the need for what it calls "drop-in shelters," places where people can get out of the weather and find other needed services. The SFC was one of the first day centers in the country. HUD later provided part of the money to run it. Baby boomers, the earliest of whom had reached the age when physical and mental illness could cause them to become homeless, added to the number of people needing a place like the SFC. HUD has cited the SFC for best practices for such a facility and has recommended that people in cities without such a service visit Denver to learn how it works.

Over the three decades since its founding, the SFC has added many services, and one way to list them is to describe the shelter itself:

Inside the front door, there is an intake office to the right that homeless guests must visit the first time they enter. HUD requires the center to gather information from newly homeless people. Guests are then given a list of general rules, which I reproduce here in part:

St. Francis Center

Welcome—General Rules

To ensure a safe, peaceful environment in which all of our guests, staff, and volunteers feel respected, we ask you to cooperate with us by following these rules:

- Identify yourself to the greeters at the front desk *each* time you enter the building and wait until they check you in to proceed. Remove sunglasses or anything covering your eyes while you check in.
- Be alcohol-free and drug-free to enter our facility. Do not use or have in your possession alcohol, drugs, or drug paraphernalia while you are on our property.
- Avoid using a loud voice or making disruptive noises (including singing and whistling). Music and video may be played using headphones.
- Treat each guest, volunteer, and staff person respectfully. Profanity, name-calling, racial remarks, sexual harassment, threats, fighting and theft are not allowed. Respect race, religion, sexual orientation, gender, gender identity and expression and variance and origin of all people.

If you are unwilling to cooperate with us by following these rules, you will be asked to leave our property and will not be able to return for a specified period of time. Our intention is to treat each person who walks through our doors with the respect and dignity that all people deserve.

Thank you for your cooperation!

After being processed at the intake office, guests are free to enter the great room after checking in with one of two greeters. The great room contains tables and chairs where other guests are seated. They might be reading, talking, playing checkers or chess, eating, thinking, writing, drawing, or snoozing. The room is not always large enough to accommodate the more than 700 people a day who come through the doors. To the right rear is the entrance to the men's showers, sinks, and toilets. A volunteer or staff member is behind the counter handing out towels, soap, and other hygienic items. A hot shower for a homeless person can be a big morale booster, and another one, at least for the men, is "smellgood." Smellgood is aftershave or cologne and pronounced as one word. I heard a smiling guest say after slapping some aftershave on his face, "I love smellgood because then they don't know you're homeless."

In the rear center of the room is a door to the women's showers, and to the right of that is the entrance to the clothing room. The women's showers are unattended—there are many fewer female guests than males—and women get soap, shampoo, and other toiletries at Mail and Storage. A guest has to have a yellow slip to enter the clothing room, which is stocked with new and clean used clothing. A yellow slip is earned by doing a 20 or so–minute chore for the staff, such as sweeping, dusting, mopping, or cleaning toilets. The clothing room has a door leading to the rear of the building, to the huge industrial-sized laundry and donations room. I heard Tom Luehrs, the director of the SFC, say that some male volunteers don't want their wife to know they know how to operate those washing machines and dryers. The towels, floor mats, and washcloths used in the showers go through the washers and dryers, as well as used clothing that has been shed and left behind in the showers by people who have earned a change of clothes.

If guests walk back into the main room from the clothing room, they can see a large counter running along the front wall to the right of the entrance. This area is called Mail and Storage, and usually there are two lines of guests waiting for service: one line for storage bags, towels, and toiletries for women; the other for mail and messages. We have spaces in the storage room for 550 30-gallon plastic garbage bags that contain most if not all of the worldly possessions our guests can claim. Most homeless people don't have a mailbox, so they get a card with the shelter's address and zip code and telephone number on it. They can give it out to friends, the Veteran's Administration, the Social Security Administration, and anyone else, and then come to the SFC to pick up their mail by showing a photo ID—a vital document we help them acquire. There is also a message board on the wall behind the counter. If they see their name on it, they can pick up their message by showing their photo ID. Without that ID, staff members and volunteers must find another way to verify their identity before giving them the messages or mail. When the phone with the number we give them rings, the staff member does not say, "Good morning, this is the St. Francis Center." It is simply "Hello," in case the caller is a potential employer trying to reach one of our guests with a job offer. The person is paged and if in the building, he or she can take the call at one of the several phones in the room provided for them. If not, the message is written down, stored alphabetically, and the name goes up on the big message board for all to see.

There are many other services in the SFC's new $12 million building next door, the Cornerstone Residences, which houses 50 persons making the transition from being homeless to being a housed human. There is also a medical clinic for guests, offices for the outreach workers who scan the city looking for homeless folks who need information about vital services, and an employment office. In the year 2012, the office found full-time jobs for 219 homeless people. All of these services, by the way, are attempts to reduce the *risks* for homeless people in Denver. Their life expectancy is much shorter than that of domiciled folks, and I have an example to illustrate one of the ways in which we try to reduce the risk of early death. In the summer of 2013, I was giving a tour of the shelter to a group of 15 women from one of Denver's downtown churches, Trinity United Methodist Church.

After the group entered the building, I took them back out on the sidewalk in front of the SFC to show them improvements in the neighborhood made since I had been volunteering there. I pointed out the nice condos across the street where there had once been a crack house. I showed them the beautiful five-story Cornerstone Residences building that we had built next door after buying and tearing down the ancient wooden Alpine Hotel, which also had been used as a crack house. I was telling the women that by cooperating with the neighborhood association, we avoided the attack of the NIMBY forces, the Not in My Back Yard people, who oppose the opening of homeless shelters near where they live. As I was explaining all of this to the group, I could see them looking off to my left. I turned to see a late middle-aged man in jeans and baseball cap who was listening to me intently. He edged closer to me and when he sensed I had finished, he asked, "May I add a few words to this?"

I nodded and said, "Sure."

"This is a great place," he said. "When I first got here from Florida I was down and out. And sick. I was told to come here, and they got a doctor to take a look at me. I had lung cancer, and they got me an operation. This is a wonderful place, and I still come here to get my mail."

A Murder Mystery

Another way of illustrating some of the risks to homeless people is by relating what happened in 1999, my first year at the St. Francis Center. We got word that a homeless man had been murdered. Then a second one, a third, a fourth, and a fifth. Most of them were reported to have been decapitated. I knew one of them by sight. A sixth man was killed, and our guests were getting nervous. Working in the men's showers, I observed an argument between some white and black men getting louder and louder. As I was about to call for help, a huge naked black man addressed his white and black "brothers," trying to calm everyone down by saying that they were all in this together, that there was someone out there who would like to kill all of them. His remarks about the unknown enemy prevailed, and we all settled down.

One guest I knew well, Joe Mendoza by name, a former prominent professional boxer from Los Angeles who was brought down by alcohol abuse, came to see me while I was working in the showers. He had been sleeping in a field near the union railroad station the night before when he woke to see a man standing near him. Joe pulled back his fists and the man walked away. "What was he doing there, Phil?" I did not know what to say to him then, but it dawned on me later that I should encourage Joe to go to the police, to relate the incident to them and describe the man who might have been the mass murderer. I went to work the next Friday and looked for Joe while working in Mail and Storage and in the men's showers, but it was a busy day and I didn't run into him.

In those days we volunteers used to gather together at the end of our shift with our director, Tom Luehrs, to discuss the events of the day. Tom informed us that the seventh victim, also headless, had been identified by his fingerprints. "His name is Joe Mendoza." My brain refused to register this for several minutes.

The police department knew we were upset by these killings, so it sent an officer to see Director Luehrs, telling him that the department had held a formal policy discussion of what had happened and had decided to treat the incidents as crimes. I repeat, *crimes.* The mayor at the time told a local television news reporter, when asked about the policy decision, that homeless people were *humans.* The assumptions he had made about his audience made me get upset again, as if I as an audience member would not think them to be humans, and the more I thought about it, the madder I became. When I cooled off, I decided to become an advocate for homeless people and ultimately I became an abolitionist. I would like to see all of us work to end homelessness.

Communication Capital

In the meantime I continued my volunteer work and found myself making scratch notes on the back of my work slip. At home I would expand them into what ethnographers, or students of cultures and subcultures, call field notes. As a professor emeritus of communication, I could not help noticing that our shelter helped provide the guests with basic communication needs—telephones, mailboxes, messages, and social interaction. The St. Francis Center is clearly a crucial communication center for these needy citizens. I continued doing research on the subject and decided that in addition to physical and mental illnesses, plus addictions, another cause of homelessness is a lack of social capital, a sociological concept I document in my book *Who Is My Neighbor? Communicating and Organizing to End Homelessness,* published in 2009.[2] No one has challenged my argument that this is a contributing cause of homelessness. In the present book, however, I prefer to call it a lack of *communication capital.* Homeless persons lack the *network* of people they can call upon who have the resources and willingness to help keep them off the streets during a tough time by giving them an empty bedroom or money enough to get an inexpensive rental place to stay.

The concept of communication capital was presaged by a standard blues song I heard while writing this chapter: "Nobody Knows You When You're Down and Out." This blues classic was composed in 1923 by Jimmy Cox. Bessie Smith made the best-received recording of it in 1929. It's a song about a millionaire who treated one and all to what they wanted till he lost his money, and then, he laments, *nobody knows him* now that he's down and out. The song and Smith's recording of it captured the times as well, coming just before the stock market crash in the United States that led to the Great Depression. How can society best help those who are down and out? By providing them with the communication capital they lack, by volunteering at and supporting homeless shelters and other projects I shall now consider.

Who Is My Neighbor? brought me invitations to speak around the country at universities and in the communities in which they are located. I shall mention two, one of which was Loyola Marymount University in Los Angeles. I was invited there in 2010 to give the keynote address for Homeless Awareness Week and a workshop for faculty and students who wanted to create a new awareness of this serious problem in their large city. Many of the students slept in tents on the campus during the week, and

it was moving to meet with the students who wanted to supply communication capital to the homeless people of Los Angeles. Central Michigan
University invited me to visit its campus and its town of Mt. Pleasant in
September of 2012 and March of 2013 to give the keynote for two con-
ventions on social justice for the homeless people of that region.

I had done my homework before my first trip to Central Michigan
University and discovered there was no homeless shelter in the city of Mt
Pleasant. The citizens were in denial, as is the case in many towns and cities, believing they had no homeless people, only drifters from other places.
Couple that with the magnet theory—that is, if you open a shelter and
provide services, even more will come from Mississippi or New York or
California or any other location. Combine those common beliefs and you
now have a city or town in total denial about its homeless community. But
some local citizens came to hear my speech on campus and asked me to
speak to them at the St. Johns Episcopal Church one morning during my
second visit six months later. I spoke to the audience of 50 or 60 people
comprising the mayor and other politicians, ministers, and good citizens.
After I finished, the organizer of the event asked members of the audience
how many of them had signed a commitment to work toward providing a
shelter and other services for the local homeless community. Virtually every person in the room held up his or her written commitment. I witnessed
concertive communication at work that morning. During the Q&A period, a woman with a concerned look on her face asked me if it is possible
that some people with jobs can't afford to pay the rent. My answer was a
sad positive, "Yes." Wages and rent no longer meet for many workers in this
country, particularly if they have developed the habit of eating and wearing
clothes. About 40 percent of the people who are homeless are also working
full- or part-time but either cannot get enough hours on a part-time job or
cannot afford the high cost of housing on the minimum wage.

In early February of 2014, I received a large brown envelope from
Professor Renz, now retired from Central Michigan University. It contained newspaper clippings about my speeches in Mount Pleasant and
work to help homeless people. Also included was a pamphlet, "Volunteer
Training Information 2014," from the Isabella County Restoration House.

The mission statement reads as follows: "To provide immediate, temporary housing to individuals of all social and cultural identities in Isabella County and to advocate for access to services needed by patrons to address their individual needs." Under the heading of HISTORY, the organization states that a "group of concerned citizens has been meeting since March of 2013 to study and work on solutions for homelessness in our area." The narrative continues to say that the same team seeks "to provide a permanent shelter and coordinate solutions to alleviate the underlying causes of homelessness." In the meantime Restoration House has organized a rotating shelter model in the city's churches, each church opening one week to keep homeless guests warm for the night. Its work is inspiring.

Open Communication and Teamwork with Discursive Closure

For the past 16 years I have witnessed open communication and teamwork at the St. Francis Center. An organization that provides services for more than 700 homeless people a day, and has seen as many as 1,000 a day during a transition period when it was open nearly 24 hours a day, the SFC does it with a small staff. There are only about two dozen people in Basic Services. Getting the job done every week requires nearly 200 volunteers. The ratio of staff members to volunteers alone would suggest a flat organization, a short hierarchy. Everyone feels free to communicate directly with Tom, the director, and it is not surprising to see him doing a tour of duty in the laundry. Each day of the week there is a different staff member who serves as the coordinator of the day, passing out work slips to the volunteers and coordinating their tasks. This person is responsible for making difficult decisions brought to him or her by volunteers and staff members, who are often asking for recommendations about problems not covered by the rules.

The current Friday coordinator, Beth Whaley, refers to the staff and volunteers who work that day as the "Friday team." She and the co-coordinator of volunteers, Susan Eddy, chair luncheon meetings with volunteers in which they report changes in the, yes, bureaucratic rules so that everyone is up to date on how to treat every guest the same way. They also ask for *suggestions for changes* that will improve the lists of rules and the services. The head of Basic Services, Lukas Sliva, also meets with groups of homeless guests, asking them for suggestions about how the Center could better serve them. As I write this, Dr. Tamla Clarke, resident psychiatrist, has plans to meet with a group of guests to discuss ways of understanding better and improving the mental health of our guests.

How proud I was years ago when I made a suggestion in one of those volunteers' meetings and it was *accepted* and then put into effect. When we help a guest get her or his storage bag, we do not want to give it to the wrong person. So when the guest gets to the head of the line, we ask for the name so we can look up his or her record in the alphabetical file. After we find it, we then ask the person for the last four digits of his or her social security number. Or in the case of a person without such a number, we ask for the maiden name of that person's mother. If everything matches, we then escort the guest into the storage room and check the name on the tag wired to the bag she or he picks out of the 500 or so 30-gallon storage bags. If the name matches what is on the form in the file, everything is fine. But this takes time. I suggested that if a guest has a photo ID, that should be good enough. And now it is. I am still proud of that suggestion. They listen to us. It is closer to a *consultative* process than a *participatory* one, but we do have voice.

Recall the St. Francis Center general rules reproduced earlier in this chapter. A copy is given to each person who enters the shelter for the first time. They are also posted on a bulletin board next to the entrance to the clothing room. Recall that one of the rules is "treat each guest, volunteer, and staff person respectfully." Informally the workers say that no one can "dis" anyone else in the SFC—if you do, you get "86'd." Elsewhere I have described the culture of SFC as the actualization of the Golden Rule: Do unto others as you would have them do unto you. The Rule is the primary major value premise for all decisions about our guests. The SFC is a *haven*. Homeless people are at risk when on the mean streets of Denver and all other cities. They are treated with disrespect by those who find them to be the Other, to be risky threats. They are beaten and, as we saw earlier, murdered, even decapitated. That is why the SFC enforces discursive closure in an organization having otherwise open communication where everyone—guests, volunteers, and staff members—have voice. To maintain that safe, peaceful haven, we insist that no one express disrespect to another human being while on our property. The hope is to promote *healing* by this strict taboo against disrespectful communication. Guests may not dis each other or volunteers or staff members; nor can the workers express disrespect to guests or others.

Although some aspects of the job may get tedious or hectic—as when the day's mail is ready to be distributed and it is the day government checks are expected, most volunteers at the SFC have something approaching a peak experience while doing the job. I have made good friends, one of whom I am still mourning some months after she died at age 94, only a few months after having to resign from volunteering. Howard Giles, a professor of communication and social psychology at the University of California, Santa Barbara, sent me an unpublished paper he had written that summarizes the social scientific research on people who volunteer at organizations such as the SFC. When compared to similar people who do not volunteer, those who do are happier, have greater self-respect, like to talk about their volunteer work, and are healthier and live longer.

That paper has now been published in the *International Journal of Communication* with a coauthor, Jessica Gasiorek. In addition to the summary of points given above, the article now has a different emphasis as is shown in the Abstract:

Americans' annual volunteer service totals over 8 billion hours and is estimated to be worth more than 100 billion dollars. Older adults perform much of this work, and being a volunteer has been identified as a predictor of successful aging.[3]

Housing First

In 2003 the St. Francis Center, in cooperation with the neighborhood homeowners association, agreed to host a political forum in the shelter for the Denver mayoral election. Most of the candidates participated. After short platform statements, they were asked by one listener what they would do about homelessness if elected. One answer stood out, marking the candidate who thoughtfully made it, a former geologist who had opened a successful brew pub in LoDo, Denver's lower downtown area not far from the SFC: "That is a problem we can do something about. That is a problem we can solve." That candidate's name was John Hickenlooper and he won the election handily.

Mayor Hickenlooper went into action immediately, announcing the creation of the Denver Commission to End Homelessness. He appointed Roxane White, his head of Human Services, as chair of the commission of 42 members, or as she called them, her "42 cats who had to be herded." One of the 42 was Tom Luehrs, executive director of the St. Francis Center. Other members included business leaders from downtown Denver and the tourist industry, homeless people, politicians, and others who, like Luehrs, were involved in providing services to the homeless population of Denver. In retrospect, when the commission passed numerous recommendations under eight broad categories—all approved *unanimously*—it was a miracle of concertive communication and teamwork. I explained it in *Who is My Neighbor? Communicating and Organizing to End Homelessness* by means of a theory of modern rhetoric published in the interdisciplinary journal *Philosophy and Rhetoric*.[4] In the days of ancient Greece, the rhetorical theories, or theories of persuasion, assumed that listeners would have similar value premises for their enthymemes, or rhetorical syllogisms. In contemporary society we experience radical heterogeneity, the differences among citizens of all races, religions, and economic status and conditions. Unlike in the days of ancient Athens and Rome, we are more likely to bring about a principled coordinated action than mass persuasion. The modern theory of persuasion by Cushman and me called "coordinated action" put it this way:

When one must act in cooperation with others who hold divergent ideologies and must as a condition for cooperation understand and respect those differences in selecting an appropriate principle for guiding collective action, then in order to do what is wanted, *one has to do things that he or she does not want to do for their own sake.*[5]

Roxane White, as a trained group facilitator, knew that her 42 cats had to understand this rhetorical principle. Downtown business leaders on the commission might not want to raise taxes to build new shelters for their own sake, but they could see that such action could be good for the sake of their business interests, who depended on tourists and citizens who view homeless people sleeping on the central 16th Street Mall as risky to them. She allowed dissenting opinions to be expressed, but she also championed compromise by encouraging people to listen and learn about what others needed. However, she was wary of the foul compromise.

Readers who want to know more about the recommendations made to Mayor Hickenlooper, which resulted in the formation of Denver's Road Home, can find more information in my book mentioned previously, *Who is My Neighbor?* But one important recommendation was the funding of the Housing First project. Researchers found that 80 percent of the money spent on homeless people goes to only 20 percent of the population, the chronically homeless people who wind up in jail, emergency rooms, and detox centers. Housing First assumes it is easier to help these people with their illnesses and addiction while housed than it is when they are sleeping on the streets. After identifying persons in need, the program first subsidizes their housing and provides a caseworker who checks in with them, encouraging them to take their meds, which may have unpleasant side effects, and helping them kick their addictions. The plan works because the rent subsidies and caseworkers cost the taxpayers significantly less money than is required to take care of them after they are picked up on the streets sick, intoxicated, or both.

An illustration may help. Denver appeared in an article in *The New Yorker* magazine in February of 2006: "Million Dollar Murray: Why Problems Like Homelessness May Be Easier to Solve Than to Manage,"[6] by Malcolm Gladwell, the best-selling author of books popularizing the findings of social scientists. After reading the article, I remembered the time Gladwell visited the SFC while doing research in Denver for his article. The Murray of his article's title was a charming, likable bear of a man who lived and died in Reno, Nevada. After his death, Reno officials calculated that he had cost the city over a million dollars, paying the bills for picking him up when he passed out drunk and for the hospitals, doctors, and nurses who took care of him in emergency rooms.

Gladwell used Murray to illustrate the findings of a graduate student at Boston College, Dennis Culhane, who had lived in a homeless shelter for seven weeks while working on his doctoral dissertation. Culhane later returned to the shelter to gather data on homelessness and discovered that this was a phenomenon that did not fit the familiar bell-shaped curve—instead, the data fell into a power law distribution shaped like a hockey stick. He found that 80 percent of the homeless people were in and out of the shelter quickly, the next 10 percent were episodic users of shelters, and the final 10 percent were the chronically homeless. And it cost cities much less money to subsidize the housing of chronically homeless people than to pay for their jail time, emergency room visits, and detox. Philip Mangano, the homeless czar, learned of this and became an abolitionist of chronic homelessness, saving money for the cities that adopt this partial solution, Housing First.

Denver's Road Home did not anticipate the 2008–2009 Great Recession that we experienced as a city and a country. The U.S. homeless population increased after the housing bubble burst, but study after study has shown that in Denver, and in other cities who invested in Housing First, the number of chronically homeless people did not increase.[7] President Obama's administration has continued the practice of Housing First, and the trend has continued since then in those cities that have put Housing First into effect. The numbers of homeless people are still down and decreasing. On the day I started writing this chapter, December 23, 2013, I worked until about 6:30 in the evening, ate some beef stew with my wife, and after dinner I sought to catch up on the news and commentary of the day. I settled in with MSNBC's Rachel Maddow, who was talking about the problems our nation encountered in 1968, "one hell of a year" as she put it. She showed a video from the Apollo 8 mission, as the astronauts orbited the Moon and sent pictures and a message back to Earth on Christmas Eve. Maddow then said that some problems that seem unsolvable are in fact solvable, and the Apollo Program proved that. She switched to a live shot of Greg Stanton, mayor of Phoenix, Arizona, who had solved an unsolvable problem: he and his city had found a place to live for all of the homeless veterans of Phoenix. When she asked Mayor Stanton how he did it, he mentioned the cooperation he received from federal programs in the stimulus package and then used the expression "housing first," and I got the impression he was talking about the program. He talked about getting the veterans a place to live *first*, and then helping them with their physical and mental illnesses and their substance abuse—then the problem becomes solvable. Having proved it would work for the veterans, Mayor Stanton said, we need "to go on from there," meaning to help find housing for the *rest* of the chronically homeless population.

I later learned that Mayor Stanton, a Democrat, had put together a concertive coalition of nonprofits and government agencies. U.S. Senator John McCain, a Republican, made it a bipartisan effort to house all the homeless vets in Phoenix by Christmas of 2013. Project H3 VETS, as the effort is called, began as a coalition of the Arizona Coalition to End Homelessness, Phoenix VA Health Care System, Arizona Department of Veteran Services, Arizona Department of Housing, Valley of the Sun United Way, Community Bridges, City of Phoenix, and others. All of these organizations, plus both Republican and Democratic elected officials, have successfully practiced concertive communication.

Thanks are due to Rachel Maddow for making the link of *solvability* between Apollo and Housing First; and thanks also are due to Mayor Stanton and Senator McCain for making the link of teamwork between the patriotism of American veterans and Housing First. Success and managing risk by means of open communication and teamwork are the themes of this book. Denver's Road Home is a special example of the successful result of concertive control and coordinated action. And I hasten to repeat the comments I made about the SFC earlier in this chapter: the value of the training I received in the basic value premise of the shelter's culture, that no one can express disrespect to any other person in the building. The two dozen staff members and the nearly 200 volunteers all practice this form of the Golden Rule and enforce it with each other as well as the guests. We thus practice concertive communication.

In the short history of the SFC I wrote for the 30th anniversary gala, I mentioned an informal poll I took of volunteers in which they told me how important it was to help out at the shelter. Many said it was more important than their career or business experience. Some compared it to a religious experience. They used the plural pronoun *we,* and clearly expressed a heightened state of organizational identification, that important phenomenon I first experienced at NASA's Marshall Space Flight Center and have formally researched. These comments were consistent with the review of research studies of volunteers done by Howard Giles, discussed earlier in this chapter. Yes, the SFC is a place where the staff and volunteers experience satisfaction, identification, open communication, and teamwork.

I need to make a couple of final points about Housing First. On Sunday, February 9, 2014, the television program *60 Minutes* presented a 17-minute segment on the reduction of chronic homelessness in Nashville, Tennessee, by means of the Housing First program. That homeless people have the "greatest risk of dying on the streets" became a priority concern for the people of Nashville. And their community's success was due to getting people who don't normally work together to solve the problem together. Anderson Cooper coordinated the segment. He listened while several citizens of Nashville in turn stressed that it saves money to subsidize housing for the chronically homeless. Housing First also works because it increases the communication capital of the homeless persons because a caseworker makes sure they take their meds and encourages them to reduce if not quit the substances demanded by their addictions.

"But is it fair?" asked Cooper—an important ethical question. A local reformer could only repeat that it saves money.

"You're rewarding people who don't deserve it," said a voice off camera. No response was given.

What is the answer to the objection to helping chronically homeless people first? Part of the answer must certainly be that they are not well and are the *most at risk.* They could easily die if not helped. The less chronically homeless do seem to find a way back to being sheltered; those who do not should become eligible for Housing First as chronically homeless persons. It is the right thing to do. In addition, the objection makes clear that we must work together to find other solutions to *prevent people from becoming homeless in the first place.*

I make the final connection to another word in the titular theme of this book by citing a book I recently read. The title is *Risk.* The author is Deborah Lupton. In it she speaks of homeless people as the "Other," beings who are seen by some as radically different from us, from one's own self. Lupton's distinction helps me emphasize that homeless persons are on both sides of the risk equation. They are at risk sleeping in the field near the union train station on a freezing December 23 night, and on other nights as well. And they are also feared as "risky," needful "of control, surveillance and discipline."[8] The ways to reduce if not eliminate the risks to them and their perceived riskiness to others are found within a concertive culture, one that practices teamwork to work with them—to help them—and that tries to discover better ways of preventing potentially homeless people from losing their place to live.

While in the last stages of writing this book, which for me means lots of rewriting, I received an e-mail from Professors Fyke, Faris, and Buzzanell of Purdue University, who were putting together a casebook to be used by students of organizational communication. They asked me for a case dealing with homeless people and our shelter qua organization. I asked Dr. Clarke, the psychiatrist on staff at the SFC, to join me in writing the case. I had in mind a project that ended up with this title: "Managing Communicative Manifestations of Psychiatric Disorders at a Homeless Shelter." For the paper, Dr. Clarke created a composite character we called "Jack" who had been diagnosed with schizophrenia, which explained some of the difficulties staff members and volunteers had with his near-mutism, disorganized behavior, and nonsensical speech ("word salad"). Some of his behaviors seemed rude, breaking the "no-dis" rule of the shelter and warranting Jack's eviction.

The case details how open communication and teamwork between the Basic Services Committee, the Wellness Committee, and the Oversight Team made an exception of Jack, "stretching the boundaries" for him. This led to research into his background and discovery that he should have been receiving disability income that would allow him to get an apartment and prescription drugs that would produce improvements in his behavior.[9]

The SFC is now following a policy that is consistent with the Paul-Tompkins law of risk communication in that we now administer an oral questionnaire to people entering the shelter for the first time called the

Homeless Vulnerability Index. The highly personal questions are designed to identify those people who are most at risk of becoming chronically homeless. The sooner we can get them into Housing First, the better for them, society, and the taxpayers.

Pot as a Homeless Magnet?

All of this put the executive director of the SFC, Tom Luehrs, on the *Today* show in September of 2014. Currently Colorado is one of three states (the other two are Washington and Alaska) that have made marijuana legal medically and socially, even though it is against federal narcotics laws. The feds looked the other way during the first year of legalized pot in Colorado, perhaps to find out just what would happen. One thing is that our homeless population began to grow. Tom Luehrs was interviewed for an article in the *Denver Post* in which he said people were coming to Colorado for jobs and marijuana.

This was picked up by a television station in Houston, Texas, who sent a crew north to do a segment for its viewers to answer this question: are homeless Texans moving there for marijuana? It filmed segments at the SFC, one of which I watched, and my daughter Kari, who lives in Houston, sent word that she had watched it. She later sent me a link to it. The spin on the story was, yes, homeless Texans were moving to Colorado. Another independent video journalist filmed the segment that he sold to *Today*. People find it fascinating that homeless people will move that far for pot, that legal marijuana is a magnet to homeless people. Luehrs, however, stressed that they come here first for jobs and second for marijuana. Many of those seeking the drug find that it is far more effective in dealing with their ailments—seizures being frequently mentioned—than their prescribed drugs. That makes their motivation even more understandable and defensible. We are now organizing a point-in-time survey of homeless people in Denver to determine to what degree marijuana might be a magnet, and *why*. The first peek at the data indicates that some but very few homeless people came to Denver for legal pot.

Summary Statement

Homeless people have the same problems many domiciled people experience in the privacy of their home—for example, addictions under the radar—but in addition, they have lost their communication capital. Homeless people lack the friends and relatives who are able and willing to reach out to them and give them the extra bedroom or help with the rent until they can make it on their own. They need help from the domiciled population, people with homes who can supply the missing communication capital by volunteering and supporting shelters, Housing First, and other programs homeless people need. A large proportion of the homeless people in our society do find housing with help or on their own.

While I was writing the first draft of this chapter, a staff colleague at SFC asked me for a list of readings on income inequality. It was implicit that we both had been thinking of this problem as a cause of the increased number of newly homeless people. I could not think of a single source to recommend. Then the March 16 issue of *The New Yorker* magazine arrived at home in the mail with an article by the distinguished Harvard historian Jill Lepore; the title of the article is "Richer and Poorer: Accounting for Inequality."[10] I leapt into its pages about the increasing income inequality in the United States, the greatest among the democratic nations of the world. Lepore reviews recent books on the subject and finds there is no doubt about the problem and that even Republicans and Democrats agree about it, if not how to deal with it. Lepore also uses a phrase used by several authors mentioned in this text, the "privatization of risk."

Lepore attributed this concept to a recent book by Jennifer M. Silva, *Coming Up Short: Working-Class Adulthood in an Age of Uncertainty*. Silva was informed by Beck's theory of the Age of Risk when she interviewed 100 young men and women between 2008 and 2010 for the book that was published in 2013. Tracing the neo-liberal ideology of individualism back to the economic views of Milton Friedman, she found that as "risks are increasingly redistributed away from the state and onto the individual, the freedom from tradition more often leaves them longing for the connections—and constraints—of the past."[11]

As if to give me verbal support for the preceding sentence, an article appeared in the March 14, 2015, *Denver Post* written by Steve Raabe:

"High rental rates spur house allure:
Denver is the 11th-most-expensive U.S. city"

The data came from a Zillow survey released earlier that week. Wages and salaries in Denver do not match those on the East or West Coast, thus adding to this city's privatization of risk.

* * *

In this chapter we saw that a shelter, an organization with open communication and cooperating teams of staff members and volunteers, has been cited as having best practices. The concept of coordinated action discussed in this chapter provides a transition to the topic of the next chapter. How can we encourage open communication about imminent risks in an entire industry—aviation—well known for its riskiness? The principles of an open risk communication system are now known and can be applied to such efforts as making nuclear power safer, the reduction of gun violence in our schools, and other risky human enterprises.

Notes

1. Stephen Lurie, "The Astonishing Decline of Homelessness in America," *The Atlantic,* August 26, 2013, http://theatlantic.com/business/archive/2013/08/the -astonishing-decline-of homelessness.

2. Phillip K. Tompkins, *Who Is My Neighbor? Communicating and Organizing to End Homelessness* (Boulder, CO: Paradigm Publishers, 2009).

3. Jessica Gasiorek and Howard Giles, "Communication, Volunteering, and Aging: A Research Agenda," *International Journal of Communication* 7 (2013): 2659.

4. Donald P. Cushman and Phillip K. Tompkins, "A Theory of Rhetoric for Contemporary Society," *Philosophy and Rhetoric* 13 (Winter 1980): 43–67.

5. Ibid., 47. Emphasis added.

6. Malcolm Gladwell, "Million Dollar Murray: Why Problems like Homelessness May be Easier to Solve than Manage," *The New Yorker*, February 13 and 20, 2006, 96–98, 161–67.

7. Pathways to Housing, "Results in 'Mental Health,'" accessed March 19, 2015, https://pathwaystohousing.org/tags/mental-health.

8. Deborah Lupton, *Risk*, 2nd ed. (London: Routledge, 2013), 202.

9. Phillip K. Tompkins and Tamla Clarke, "Managing Communicative Manifestations of Psychiatric Disorders at a Homeless Shelter," in *Stretching Boundaries: Cases in Organizational and Managerial Communication*, ed. Jeremy P. Fyke, Jeralyn Faris, and Patrice M. Buzzanell (New York: Routledge, in press).

10. Jill Lepore, "Richer and Poorer: Accounting for Inequality," *The New Yorker*, March 16, 2015, 26–32.

11. Jennifer M. Silva, *Coming Up Short: Working-Class Adulthood in an Age of Uncertainty* (New York: Oxford University Press, 2013), 145.

9

Interorganizational Risk Communication: The Aviation Safety Reporting System, STOP, and Safe2Tell

"The single biggest problem in communication is the illusion that it has happened."

—George Bernard Shaw

t was in 1986 when the German sociologist Ulrich Beck's book on the risk society was published. It was translated six years later into English as *Risk Society: Towards a New Modernity* and sparked much debate about the topic in Western societies. According to Lupton, he set out his argument that

> individuals in contemporary Western societies were living in a transitional period, in which industrial society was becoming a 'risk society'. In this transitional period, the production of wealth was accompanied by that of risks, which have proliferated as an outcome of modernization. The central problem of Western societies, therefore, was not the production and distribution of 'goods' such as wealth and employment in conditions of scarcity (as it was in early modernity and remains the case in developing countries) but the prevention or minimization of 'bads', that is, risks. Debates and conflicts over risks had begun to dominate public, political and private arenas. Individuals living in these societies had therefore moved towards a greater awareness of risk and were forced to deal with risks on an everyday basis.[1]

Could it be that the professors who made up the highly esteemed Center for Hazards Research at the University of Colorado Boulder had read Beck's book in German by the time they organized a colloquium sponsored by the National Science Foundation (NSF) on risk communication in 1987, one year after it was published? They were famous for their research on natural hazards such as floods, but they had come to realize that even human beings can contribute to floods, as in a human-made dam that will eventually give way to a basic law of science: the weakest force, gravity, always wins. They wanted to expand their coverage to include human-made risk, knew about my work with NASA's Marshall Space Flight Center, and invited me to participate. I agreed to dive into the risk communication literature and then gather some data on a new problem or topic. Only one year earlier Beck had treated "'risk' as another word for a hazard or danger," wrote Lupton, and had "demonstrate[d] anger at the ever-hazardous nature of life in late modernity."[2] One year later the experts on hazards were now asking me to talk about risks.

The literature on risk communication was new to me. It clearly was an interdisciplinary research area, and I did not recognize many names from the academic field of communication among the researchers. These researchers were from the social sciences in general and new areas—at least to me—with names such as "decision science." They seemed to know or assume what our risks were, and they were interested in getting the word out to those who might be subject to them. Even today much of this interdisciplinary research is directed to the science of discovering the most effective way of communicating the dangers of a risk taken for granted—such as global warming—to the largest possible relevant audience. My interests, in addition to climate change, were and still are in broader questions, such as how can we discover new and local risks by means of communication, and how only then can we best communicate these risks to the interested audiences, simultaneously asking them to help us complete the process of risk management?

An influential book of the 1980s was *Normal Accidents: Living with High-Risk Technologies*, published in 1984 by Charles Perrow.[3] The title of his book seems to qualify clearly as symptomatic of a risk society. It also gets attention by using two words, *normal* and *accidents*, that are not usually thought of as belonging together, thus exploiting the technique that Kenneth Burke calls "perspective by incongruity" or "planned incongruity."[4] Perrow brings two incongruous terms, *normal* and *accidents*, together in the hope of providing a new perspective, a basic argument that operations by our organizations are more complex than human operators can handle, making it inevitable that the abnormal accident will become the normal one. The results he predicted would be catastrophic. He took a dim view of risk communication and of risk analysts, calling them "a new breed of shamans."[5] I was amazed, however, that his human beings, his operators of organizations, seem to be speechless. The word *communication* does not appear in his index. Communication neither causes nor solves problems in his book. But in what must have been an *unintended* incongruity, he discusses the Aviation Safety Reporting System (ASRS),[6] and this brief description sounded so promising to me that I decided somebody had to research it carefully; this I did for my paper for the NSF risk and hazard colloquium.

THE AVIATION SAFETY REPORTING SYSTEM

The origin of ASRS is rooted in tragedy. On Sunday, December 1, 1974, at 11:09 a.m., Trans World Airlines (TWA) Flight 514 was headed to Dulles International Airport in turbulent weather. The aircraft descended below the minimum safe altitude and slammed into a Virginia mountaintop. Nearly 100 people were killed. As required by law, the National Transportation Safety Board investigated the accident as usual.

Two significant findings emerged from the investigation. The first was that a United Airlines plane had narrowly escaped the same fate in the same approach only six weeks before the crash of TWA Flight 514. If the incident involving the United flight had taken place one year earlier, the result would have been only a troublesome memory for the crew. Eleven months earlier, however, United had created an internal reporting system called the Flight Safety Awareness Program, in which crew members were strongly encouraged to report anonymously any incident they felt was a potential risk or threat to safety. The pilots reported the incident at Dulles, and the rest of the United Airlines pilots were informed of the trap. Unfortunately at that time there was no established channel of communication available for spreading the word to other airlines, and so the TWA crew was unable to benefit from the report filed by the United crew.

The second finding that emerged from the National Transportation Safety Board investigation was that both the United and TWA incidents were caused by the "ambiguous nature of the charted approach procedure and the differences in its interpretation between pilots and controllers."[7] The difference in interpretation was that the controllers and pilots assigned two different meanings to the word *clearance:* the meaning intended by controllers was that the approach plan was approved; the meaning understood by pilots was that the actual landing may now begin. In short, a misunderstanding, a breakdown in communication between pilots and controllers, created the risk in both cases. The drama of the two flights illustrates the potential importance of communication in both *creating* risks—by misunderstandings—and mitigating or *removing* risks and hazards with alerts and corrective actions, including clearer terminology.

In May of 1975 the Federal Aviation Administration established the ill-conceived Aviation Safety Reporting Program (ASRP) to encourage members of the aviation industry to provide the FAA with timely reports about critical incidents. As an incentive, the FAA offered a limited waiver of disciplinary action in case the person making the report had broken any laws. The ASRP did not work: the FAA, as both the broker and enforcer of the rules in the industry, was not viewed as a disinterested party. As a result, NASA, which still enjoyed an incomparable reputation at the time, was asked to serve as a broker, an honest third party, in receiving and processing the reports. NASA designed and to this day administers the Aviation Safety Reporting System (ASRS), which began operations on April 15, 1976. The actual operations were handled for a number of years by a contractor, the Battelle Memorial Institute, at its Mountain View, California, office.

Input to the Aviation Safety Reporting System

As I stressed at the NSF risk and hazard colloquium, the ASRS is an interorganizational risk communication system for an entire industry, similar in that way to Wernher von Braun's system of risk sensors. Input is provided by aviation mechanics, air traffic controllers, pilots, other crew members, and occasionally by other observers. Those who send in the reports are promised both anonymity and immunity from prosecution. The analysts—former pilots and controllers—study, code, and store the reports electronically. The total input when I visited the Battelle operation in 1986 was staggering: 70,000 reports concerning 50,000 incidents. All had been received and processed without a single breach of anonymity and immunity.

The output included alert bulletins, time-critical notices about ongoing hazards such as overgrown trees blocking approaches to a runway, faulty navigational lights, and misleading runway markings. The ASRS also issued quarterly program reports about trends in the business and corrective actions taken in response to alert bulletins. The effects of these messages sent back to the aviation community cannot be quantified because it is impossible to count events that did not take place, accidents that did not happen. It is also impossible to study the system without being convinced that it has reduced risks and eliminated hazards, saving untold lives.

My NASA credentials got me in, allowing me to make the trip to the contractor's office in Mountain View. I studied its reports and had a lengthy interview with its director and research conversations with others. I interrogated the database about human factors. After I specified that the incidents had to involve a "message from one person to another," the computer found this operational definition in 61 percent of the incidents filed in the database between 1978 and 1987. The analysts helping me with the search thought this was a conservative figure. They used "information transfer" as a category as well, as their experience taught them, and found that about *70 percent of the reports* in the database included a reference to human communication as a contributing factor or serious threat to aviation safety.

We were able to break that percentage down further, finding that more than one-third of these problems of communication involved the absence of "information transfer" in situations where, in the opinion of the analysts, the information could have prevented a risky or hazardous occurrence: *the message not sent*. In another third of the cases, information transfer took place, but the message was found by the analysts to be either incomplete or inaccurate, leading in those cases to incorrect decisions regarding the flying or controlling of an aircraft: *the inaccurate message*. One-eighth of the reports involved information transfers that were correct but untimely, too late in most cases to be of assistance in avoiding a risky situation: *the message sent too late*. In one-tenth of the reports, the information was transferred or sent but was misperceived by the intended recipients: *the misunderstood message*. The remainder of the reports involved equipment problems and a variety of miscellaneous conditions: *the message not received*.

Early on the ASRS quarterly reports recognized that communication was important. For example, the message "runway two zero" was heard as "runway two," and aircraft ABC and CBA both believed they were cleared to 11,000 feet. I included another communication incident in my NSF colloquium paper. This was a report filed on an actual accident involving an airline vice president, an experienced pilot, who took over the controls of one of his company's commuter aircraft. The vice president–pilot was known to acknowledge rarely if ever the checklist items or callouts from his first officer. The aircraft was well below its assigned altitude during its final slope and the first officer made every callout to that effect. The aircraft hit the ground several miles short of the runway. This case should remind the reader of Dr. Gawande's research on concertive checklists and surgery. Certain surgeons, he found, liked to be the hero, one who does not need a checklist or people of lower status pointing out his or her responsibilities or mistakes. To broaden the principle presented in chapter 4, the ability and willingness to acknowledge the worthiness of a checklist and callouts ought to be a criterion for screening out both would-be pilots and would-be surgeons.

Discursive or Textual Work Environment

It is worth noting that epistemologically and theoretically, the ASRS analysts had no reality other than a textual one in their coding work. All they had were written reports. Today some would say that it was a totally discursive work environment. Add to that, they had to assign meaning to *written* words such as the "shape of airspace," and they were working in a purely verbal world. The airline companies and other organizations they were trying to save from disaster were merely discursive items, or as I said at the colloquium, textual: *organizations as texts*. I read a sense of insecurity in their earliest bulletins because of this textual dependence:

> During a recent visit to the Battelle office . . . , I inquired about the epistemological edginess in the early publications and was told it had disappeared. My observation that there was no way of verifying a report except by means of another report [i.e., another text] was

not contested. And perhaps the best evidence of a new symbolic or textual sophistication was produced when I pressed one of the staff members about the "reality" of the "shape" and "design" of airspace. The response was a smile and the narrative of a joke about the pilot who deviated from his flight plan. When asked why he had strayed from the assigned airspace, the pilot explained: "I couldn't see the magenta lines on the ground."[8]

National Science Foundation Colloquium on Hazards and Risks

I had what I wanted for the colloquium paper, but before presenting the data in my paper and oral report, I reported that in 1987 risk communication was a synthetic field with no academic home, described by experts on the subject as encompassing such diverse fields as cognitive psychology, consumer behavior, marketing, advertising, economics, mass communication, linguistics, anthropology, decision science, medicine, philosophy, and others. I was critical of the operational definition of risk communication because it virtually limited the field to the transmission of warnings about health or environmental risks. I could not find the word *organization* in their categories at that time. (While writing this chapter I decided to check what Ulrich Beck had to say about risk communication in *Risk Society*. The index to the English translation has one reference to risk communication: page 4. I flipped to that page and found it was part of the Introduction written by Scott Lash and Brian Wynn: "The modern sub-field of risk communication exemplifies this baneful defence against reflexivity."[9] That translates into meaning the sub-field does not question "the forms of power or social control involved," words from the sentence preceding the words quoted above. Lash and Wynn presumably speak for Beck on this matter.)

After taking that position, I introduced the ASRS and the data along with it, convinced as I was that the system and the results made the field of risk communication richer and deeper. Recall that the system begins with a message about a risk or hazard such as being assigned to the wrong runway. It is sent to a third party, a receiver who is an honest broker, a person who has no direct power over the sender. An experienced pilot, controller, or mechanic will make sense of it, enter it into the computer's database, and if the risk is still a threat or could repeat itself, the original receiver of the report becomes a sender, issuing a bulletin alerting all possible organizations who need to know.

The system thus has built into it all of the components of risk communication as I think of it: the discovery of a risk, risk analysis, a message sent to the broker, feedback to the reporter that it has been received, and another message warning and alerting the entire industry about the risks or hazards. Then I reported that I had found that up to 70 percent of the reports are *about* human communication as a risk to aviation safety. The colloquium participants gave me their total attention, showing great interest in this finding; perhaps it is not an exaggeration to say they were astonished. The organizers released the paper to the media, and I found myself on radio talk shows from coast to coast. I did a long live interview with a radio talk show host in New York City. While I was doing one in Chicago, a pilot driving to make a flight out of O'Hare called in to confirm my findings and conclusions and give the ASRS high praise based on his personal experiences. A friend showed me that my paper had even been summarized in *Popular Mechanics*. I gave a lengthy interview for a local television channel in Denver to a Mr. Shapiro, which was picked up and carried by CNN; colleagues in Australia reported that they had seen and heard it.

It is clear to me that most people *drastically underestimate* the importance of talk, conversation, orders, feedback, and other aspects of the total process of communication. The talk show hosts and their listeners were dumbfounded to know that misunderstandings, misinformation, and other forms of miscommunication are so frequent that they could produce that many risks. And they were equally heartened to learn that a communication system such as the ASRS could help prevent accidents from happening. Risk analysts factor in both the likelihood and impact, or severity, of occurrence. When one talks about aviation, even lay persons sense immediately and intuitively that the *impact* or *severity* of a risk occurring is profoundly serious.

I have tried to keep track of the ASRS over the years. During the late 1980s the media reported that efforts were being made to get the health industry to adopt something like it. Imagine a world in which nurses, doctors, and hospital administrators are able to communicate risks anonymously to an honest third party, a trusted broker. Retired doctors and nurses could process the reports or risk messages, give feedback to the sender, and then provide the alert messages to the right people. I learned from both a lawyer and a doctor that tort lawyers had organized an effective resistance to the reform. I was told that their motives were not unaffected by the lucrative business of malpractice suits.

The irony of this outcome, as we learned in chapter 4, is that Dr. Atul Gawande read the history of aviation to learn that it was the B-17, the "flying fortress," that first required a checklist for the pilot and cockpit crew to be able to fly it safely. He also made a trip to Boeing Headquarters to learn more about checklists before designing one with his team at Harvard to use in the surgical experiment discussed in chapter 4. According to carefully collected before and after statistics, the airplane checklist as adapted for surgery by Dr. Gawande reduced the likelihood that surgical incidents would take place.

But there is some good news for those wanting to promote and advance the principles of the ASRS risk communication system. In preparing to write this book I went online to check on ASRS. Indeed, interested readers can satisfy their own curiosity by going online to find entries on the history of the process and even how to file a risk report. I googled NASA's ASRS and also found an undated report by Linda J. Connell, director of the Aviation Safety Reporting System at the Ames Research Center at Moffett Field, California. The title is "Cross-Industry Applications of a Confidential Reporting Model," and at the lower right hand corner of the first page is this tag: "NASA ASRS (Pub. 62)." Connell mentions that the motivation for the creation of ASRS was an ambiguous and misunderstood communication between an air traffic controller and a flight crew—the case I introduced earlier involving the crash of TWA Flight 514. At the time Connell wrote her report, over 610,000 reports about risks from workers in the aviation business had been received by the ASRS, and the confidentiality promise had never been broken.

According to the report, seven other countries had organized an aviation safety reporting system modeled on the ASRS, including those in the

United Kingdom, Canada, and Australia. If imitation is indeed a form of flattery, then this speaks favorably of the ASRS. Connell also reported that the Department of Veteran Affairs had worked with ASRS to establish a program called Patient Safety Reporting System (PSRS). She reported that the system was bringing in reports of risks to the health of veterans, but the recent exposure of the VA for lack of accountability creates some doubt about this application. Connell also says there have been stirrings again in the general health community for some kind of risk communication system for medicine. In addition, NASA has proposed that a form of risk management be adopted for all of the life cycles in the process of developing new technologies. Risk management to NASA means "identifying and assessing risks, then establishing a comprehensive plan to prevent or minimize effects from those risks being asserted."[10] This sounds like a risk communication system.

It was not until I began writing this chapter that I saw the connection between the principles of ASRS and those of automatic responsibility as developed by Dr. von Braun at the Marshall Space Flight Center (and introduced in chapter 2 of this book). Recall that everyone at the MSFC assumed responsibility automatically for a problem or risk the moment they perceived it. The perceiver was responsible automatically for solving it if possible, and reporting it up the line in any case. This was true even if the formal responsibility for the area in which the problem occurred was assigned to another lab or division within one's own lab. But what about the honest broker in that single organizational scheme of risk communication? Von Braun had established as part of the organizational culture that one would never be punished for reporting a problem, only for hiding or failing to report a risk to the project. Karl Weick and Kathleen Sutcliffe wanted to discuss the importance of "error reporting" in their book, *Managing the Unexpected: Assuring High Performance in an Age of Complexity.* They chose to support the point with an example from von Braun's management style while in the U.S. Army: "Wernher von Braun sent a bottle of champagne to an engineer who, when a Redstone missile went out of control, reported that he may have caused a short-circuit during a prelaunch testing. Analysis revealed that this indeed had caused the accident, and his confession meant that expensive redesigns were unnecessary."[11]

Employees knew that top management under von Braun, whether in the U.S. Army or NASA, would be an honest broker about the reporting of bad news. Contrary to the old saying that good news goes up the line and bad news comes down—von Braun and his concept of automatic responsibility meant that bad news went up the line quickly and was rewarded, not punished. The ASRS achieved this for an entire industry, but with a third party, NASA, who had no authority over either individuals or their aviation organization. One can say that there is also a connection among the principles of ASRS, automatic responsibility, and open, concertive communication: the encouragement of individuals to act for the good of the whole, to serve as sensors in an earthquake prediction system. Still another similarity is that both the ASRS and automatic responsibility *empowered* those at the bottom to communicate bad news up the line.

Soon after I finished my first draft of this chapter, I met an airline pilot while both of us were getting an early evening snack in a Denver restaurant. "Oh, yes," the pilot said, "the NASA reports." The pilot said that some airlines are now using their own safety reporting systems, that there is a new sense of secrecy about problems within the airlines. Airline executives cared so much for their bonuses for "on time" departures that they locked the doors on ticket holders to leave on time. They did not want their company's problems known to the whole industry. It will be actions bordering on criminality if the airline managers have indeed weakened the ASRS, but at least we still have the principles, the practices of open communication that citizens can fight to have reinstated in the airline industry and implemented in other industries as a whole.

STOP: A WOLF IN SHEEP'S CLOTHING

Aware of the nature of this book project, Professor Larry Browning made a chapter available to me from a new book he edited with Norwegian colleagues which contains a series of 21 student ethnographies on the culture of the High North region of Norway. A woman named Nadina Ramcharitar authored a charming ethnography originally titled "A Wolf in Sheep's Clothing? A Tale of Paradox, Irony, and Coexistence in the

Norwegian Oil and Gas Industry." Before publication, however, she changed it to "Keeping Law and Order in the Norwegian Oil and Gas Industry: The Challenges of Safety Regulation."[12] Ramcharitar, the narrator, shadows Liv, a veteran of 25 years in Norway's oil and gas industry, who also can claim a fair knowledge of its culture. Part of that is influenced by the health, safety, and environmental concerns, or HSE. Liv's current role is being somewhat of a cop for HSE. Her job is to keep people safe on their job. Given the risks of the industry, this is a serious responsibility.

Liv is a rules enforcer, ensuring compliance. This would be well and fine if all the rules from above were sensible, but some seem "a bit silly even to her, which often happens when bureaucrats or lawyers write them, since they tend to view the world from behind a desk rather than out in the field."[13] The rules themselves don't recognize the nuances that Liv and her charges see every day. Another problem arises among the employees she is supposed to manage: they are either over-compliant, mindless followers or rebellious in a sneaky way—independent "smarties." She calls the first group the sheep and the others she calls wolves. When asked if, given her job, she didn't want them all to follow the rules, Liv's reply was yes, you want them to follow the rules—and here she echoed what those forest rangers requested: to follow the Fire Orders—"'You want people thinking on the job, using all their critical faculties, not blindly following a worn path,' she says."[14]

The wolves, on the other hand, are clever canines who actually value safety as much as their sheepish counterparts, and in fact are always looking for safer and more efficient ways of doing the work. Often this involves taking shortcuts and not quite complying with the rules. Ramcharitar at this point begins to suspect that Liv is ironically a bit wolfish herself, and she adds this thought not spoken by Liv: "They're even more like lemmings than sheep."[15]

The Infamous Handrail Policy and Discursive Compulsion

Liv illustrates her point of view with the rule that everyone must hold onto the handrail while walking up or down stairs. That is the policy. No exceptions. Ever. This makes sense when at offshore facilities, given the high winds and waves, but at onshore facilities also? Always? The likelihood of a serious injury is low under safe conditions. The sheep, however, never think about it. They hold onto the handrail while walking up or down stairs whatever the conditions. The wolves question the rule, and according to Liv, they have a good reason for noncompliance during the flu season: the germs they could pick up from the handrail. Yes, they could catch the flu just because they followed the safety rules. In addition, holding onto the handrail means wasted time spent sanitizing hands after every contact with the handrail. Liv, says Ramcharitar, is clearly conflicted by the responsibility for enforcing this rule.

The STOP Game

Despite this internal conflict, Liv accepts that, as HSE manager, she must enforce these rules. And she has a small army of enablers to help her: the employees themselves. Whether it's the handrail policy or another safety rule, her company has implemented a "game"—or so they call it—for monitoring offshore HSE compliance. Called the Safety Training Observation Program (STOP), it was originally created for DuPont. This Orwellian "game" involves employees monitoring and reporting any acts of noncompliance they observe in their coworkers' behavior, regardless of how minor the infraction. The program combines teamwork (an irony there?) with surveillance to control worker behavior.[16]

It works this way: If an employee sees another employee breaking one of the rules, he or she must follow the STOP rules. First, he or she has a STOP conversation with the offender. The next step is to complete a STOP card documenting the infraction and the conversation with the offender. The STOP conversations and cards are supposed to prevent risks from occurring, and their requirement at first seems well intentioned, but here is still another rule: "Employees are obliged to fill out one card per shift. Again, *no exceptions.*"[17] So how did the wolves handle what the critical theorists might call "discursive compulsion"? They craftily figured out how to combine the two rules, thus neutralizing them and keeping their hands sanitary. They purposely did not touch the handrail so members of their wolf pack could fill out a STOP card, fulfilling their daily requirement.

In a brilliant insight, the ethnographer, Ramcharitar, asks the reader to note the real teamwork happening here. The wolves cooperated with each other, aware of their real priorities while working on a platform during a 12-hour shift. Their cooperative strategy helped them cope with the onerous requirements and yet the wolves "take the STOP card practice very seriously when they see something really worthy of being reported."[18]

Ramcharitar closes the essay with some last words from her ethnographic quarry. Liv says rules are a lot of words, and no matter how well they are written, they are hard to communicate. Then she says something similar to von Braun's warning about not making "foul compromises." Liv seeks the "correct tradeoff" of the natural instincts of both the sheep and wolves to maintain robust standards that are good for all.

I decided to pursue the STOP phenomenon and found a master's thesis about STOP and two of its competitors written at the Rochester Institute of Technology by Herbert Byrd and submitted on September 17, 2007. It is a comparison of the DuPont STOP program, Safety Performance Solutions, and Behavior Science Technology. I remain unconvinced that these packages are as effective as would be the case if management and the workers were all trained in participatory decision making and the original ASRS principles and were allowed to make and enforce the rules.

SAFE2TELL: AUTOMATIC RESPONSIBILITY REVISITED

I got up in the morning on December 24, 2013, to write the first draft of this chapter. But first I had breakfast while scanning our local newspaper, the *Denver Post*. In it was a front page article by Colleen O'Connor, the headline of which read, "Early Reporting May Keep Crises from Escalating" under a generic heading, SCHOOL VIOLENCE. It begins with this sentence: "Since the beginning of this school year, reports of 16 planned attacks—that someone had a hit list or was coming to school with a gun—were made to Safe2Tell, the anonymous hotline where people can report threats against themselves or others." Following the story to page 7A, I learned that after Colorado's infamous school shooting tragedy, the Columbine Commission suggested such a hotline in 2004. Safe2Tell was created shortly after that and had received 282 reports of planned school attacks, all of which were investigated by law enforcement officials and school administrators. Of that total, 251 were classified as high-risk threats, and "31 were called very high risk—prevented just in time." Police were able to thwart a planned gun attack on the Trinidad, Colorado, high school, by a tip that two boys, ages 15 and 16, were planning the attack in response to bullying.

O'Connor explained that Safe2Tell is a private, nonprofit organization that partners with various state agencies but has to raise its funds from grants and donations, exasperating some local violence prevention experts. The state of Michigan was so impressed with Safe2Tell that it passed legislation the previous week to create a program modeled after it called OK2Say, and the bill included $4.5 million in appropriations. I dashed off a letter to the editor of the *Denver Post*. On December 27, three days later, the newspaper ran the following under the heading THE OPEN FORUM, LETTERS TO THE EDITOR:

Addressing school violence
Re: "Early reporting may keep crises from escalating," Dec. 24 news story.
Bravo to The Denver Post for publishing Colleen O'Connor's timely and useful article about Safe2Tell and the carnage it has prevented in Colorado Schools. Safe2Tell uses the same risk-communication principles as the industry-wide Aviation Safety Reporting System, which has saved an untold number of lives and has been adopted in other advanced countries. We need to encourage more people, including students, to report suspicious behaviors that may lead to a school attack. Having an anonymous hotline answered by trained people who will report risks to police and school administrators is

vitally important to the success of such a system. O'Connor reports that Safe2Tell has no direct state funding. We need to correct that. Bravo to The Post and reporter O'Connor.

Phillip K. Tompkins, Denver

Reporter O'Connor answered my e-mail message to her, thanking me and promising to do another story on state funding, which was later printed. This is an apt conclusion for this chapter because I had planned to say that even if the ASRS had changed over the years because of new technology or new motives among some airlines, it is the *risk communication principles* it embodied that are important and need to be used as a model. I plan to support state funding for Safe2Tell, and I now appeal to the reader to accept and promote the principles of automatic responsibility and the ASRS and act to have them adopted for their home state and for the nation's health and medical system.

Final Thoughts

Kenneth Burke wrote a famous definition of man many years ago. I have rewritten it in gender neutral language and offer one clause here:

Humans are separated from their natural condition by instruments of our own making:
Consider the ways in which we have ravaged our environment with instruments of our own making in order to provide each of us with the amount of electricity needed to make life "natural." We have built power plants fueled by fossil and nuclear energy and have spoiled the environment with their byproducts. Electrical grids and power lines distract us from beautiful vistas. In the process of building electrical transformers, a company dumped the chemical PCB into the Hudson River with deleterious effects on fish and, quite logically, fishermen.[19]

By separating ourselves from our natural condition, we have now made the distinction between hazards and risks disappear. But whatever the cause of risks and hazards, the ASRS has given us a model, a communication model, of how to reduce the threat of risks. The original practices, at least, were interorganizational in nature, industry wide. There was an honest, expert, and economically disinterested broker to read the reports of risks. The reporters were provided anonymity and immunity from prosecution. This provided them, ironically, the protection to participate in open communication. The receivers classified the reports and fed alerts and warnings back into the interorganizational system. They lived in a world of organizations-as-texts, and the results were greatly beneficial.

It was some time before I realized how much the ASRS and automatic responsibility have in common. The latter was limited to one organization, while the ASRS was processed for an entire industry. Both reduced the time in which risks can be observed and reported to agents who can mitigate or eliminate them. Both allowed channel redundancy, increasing the reliability of agents making sense of the messages, or better sensemaking. Sadly, the one has disappeared from NASA, and the airline companies appear to be weakening the other.

In regard to the STOP study, it is clear to me that it is close to being a case of the pseudo-participation of employees. As we shall see in the next chapter, one experienced expert says there is a world of difference between asking for consultation and asking for participation. The discursive compulsion to report a colleague as having broken a rule is the opposite of teamwork. The only true teamwork in Ramcharitar's ethnography was the informal teams of wolves who reported each other for not touching the germ-ridden handrails. It was heartening to learn from that essay that the company Liv worked for, based on the experience described, started hiring more wolves than sheep, giving us confidence that there will be more people thinking about risks and reporting them rather than sheepishly following the rules.

The principles of the ASRS are what we must promote, guaranteeing anonymity to those who report risks to an office with the ability to know when and why to alert an entire industry about imminent threats brought on by increasing complexity. Those threats can be to the very existence of the organization.

We move now to chapter 10 so that we may concentrate on the findings about the general effectiveness of participation, teamwork, in organizations as perceived and described by academics as well as by business owner-managers.

Notes

1. Deborah Lupton, *Risk,* 2nd ed. (London: Routledge, 2013), 78–79.

2. Ibid., 79.

3. Charles Perrow, *Normal Accidents: Living with High Risk Technologies* (New York: Basic Books, 1984).

4. Kenneth Burke, *Attitudes toward History,* 3rd ed. (Berkeley, CA: University of California Press, 1984), 308–9.

5. Perrow, *Normal Accidents,* 12.

6. Ibid., 168–69.

7. Phillip K. Tompkins, "Organizational Communication and Technological Risks," in *Risky Business: Communicating Issues of Science, Risk, and Public Policy,* ed. Lee Wilkins and Philip Paterson (New York: Greenwood Press, 1991), 123.

8. Phillip K. Tompkins, "On Risk Communication as Interorganizational Control: The Case of the Aviation Safety Reporting System," in *Nothing to Fear: Risks and Hazards in American Society,* ed. Andrew Kirby (Tucson: University of Arizona Press, 1990), 203–39, 214–15.

9. Scott Lash and Brian Wynn, Introduction to *Risk Society: Towards a New Modernity* by Ulrich Beck (London: Sage Publications, 1992), 4.

10. Quoted by Linda J. Connell in "Cross-Industry Applications of a Confidential Reporting Model," *ASRS Research Papers* 62 (2004): 7.

11. Karl Weick and Kathleen Sutcliffe, *Managing the Unexpected: Assuring High Performance in an Age of Complexity* (San Francisco: Jossey-Bass, 2001), 58.

12. Nadina Ramcharitar, "Keeping Law and Order in the Norwegian Oil and

Gas Industry: The Challenges of Safety Regulation," in *Culture, Development and Petroleum: An Ethnography of the High North*, ed. J. O. Sormes, L. Browning, and J. T. Henricksen (London: Routledge, 2014).

13. Ibid., 85.

14. Ibid., 86.

15. Ibid.

16. Ibid., 87.

17. Ibid. Emphasis in original.

18. Ibid., 88.

19. Phillip K. Tompkins, *Communication as Action* (Belmont, CA: Wadsworth, 1982), 11–12. My "translation" was taken from Burke's Definition of Man in Kenneth Burke, *Language as Symbolic Action* (Berkeley: University of California Press, 1968), 16.

10

The Age of Participation

"The pyramid, the chief organizational principle of the modern corporation, turns a business into a traffic jam. A company starts out like an eight-lane superhighway—the bottom of the pyramid—drops to six lanes, then four, then two, then becomes a country road and eventually a dirt path, before abruptly coming to a stop. Thousands of drivers start off on the highway, but as it narrows more and more are forced to slow and stop. There are smashups, and cars are pushed off onto the shoulder. Some drivers give up and take side roads to other destinations. A few—the most aggressive—keep charging ahead, swerving and accelerating and bending fenders all about them. Remember, objects in the mirror are closer than they appear."

—Ricardo Semler, *Maverick: The Success Story Behind the World's Most Unusual Workplace*

This chapter begins with a very short history of the academic discipline of communication to make explicit the philosophic assumptions of it over the years, and how important historically to it has been the *practice of participation*. After looking at the analysis of academic research and commentary on the subject, the chapter examines participation as seen and experienced by members of, and commentators on, practices of the business world. The final section will look at the claim of a prophecy fulfilled.

Rhetoric as the First Communication Theory

The field of communication was the first academic discipline in ancient Greece. They called it "rhetoric," defined as the art or faculty of discovering in any situation all the available means of persuasion. Discovering all the techniques of persuasion was a way also of analyzing a society, its value premises, and its norms, or rules for correct behavior. It was a combination of what today we would call the humanities and the social sciences. Aristotle, for example, refers the reader of the *Poetics* to his earlier work, *Rhetoric*, for his prior discussion of style or the use of language for effect. The *Rhetoric* also explains how the enthymeme, the rhetorical syllogism, works: it draws from the value and factual premises of the audience, those they already hold whether spoken or not, to reach the persuader's conclusion. Knowing what value and factual premises an audience holds dear requires more social analysis. It was not difficult to praise Athenians while in Athens, but to do so in Troy would have been a different matter.

Why was rhetoric the earliest of disciplines? For a couple of pragmatic reasons, one of which was that the citizens of Athens could not hire lawyers to represent them in court when they needed to defend themselves or to sue or accuse someone else. They needed to know how to use Logos, or logical proof, in order to construct a deductive oral argument, the enthymeme, based on the beliefs or value premises of their audience, and how to use inductive proof by means of a careful choice of one or more examples to arrive at a more general conclusion. Aristotle taught that Logos was the most important of the three types of proof or modes of persuasion. Pathos was emotional proof to be used by the citizen in the lawsuit to move the audience by, say, eliciting pity for one example. Ethos, taught Aristotle, was the most powerful of the three forms of proof. Today we might call it source credibility or ethical proof; the rhetor or persuader was taught to speak so as to appear to the jury, judge, or audience as a credible man (no women or slaves were citizens then)—a man of good character, good sense, and good will. To provide such a theory, Aristotle had to be something of a social scientist to know the opinions and beliefs of the community.

There was another reason that rhetoric was the first subject to be taught and learned in Athens. Aristotle taught that there were three broad categories of rhetoric, one of which, forensic or courtroom rhetoric, the one we have already briefly considered. Citizens also needed to know how to speak and listen to ceremonial speaking—the epideictic—the speech of blame or praise. Most importantly, when the citizens of Athens began to experiment with democracy, they needed to know how to practice deliberative, or political, oratory. They had to know how to promote a piece of legislation and to recognize a specious argument in order to refute it. The Greeks became so good at it that the teaching of argumentation in grammar, logic, and rhetoric, as we shall see in the Epilogue, helped them develop mathematics.

From the beginning, rhetoric thus had practical, pragmatic purposes, particularly functional to an open democratic society. As it was imported into other societies, for example Rome, it became less fundamentally practical after the republic became an empire. Cicero was executed for deliberative remarks he made in the Senate, and thereafter the rhetoricians such as Quintilian paid more attention to the ceremonial output of speakers. Communication professors with a historical perspective teach today that throughout history, rhetoric flourished in democratic countries with a parliament (e.g., Great Britain), and by contrast that there were no popular rhetorical textbooks in German history, making its people susceptible to, and easily duped by, the incendiary and disastrous rhetoric and propaganda of Adolph Hitler and his Nazi Party.

Despite being the most practical, pragmatic discipline in democracies, and a dangerous set of ideas and assumptions within dictatorships and totalitarian societies, rhetoric was attacked by other disciplines in the academy. From the beginning, philosophers such as Socrates belittled rhetoric as sophistry and rhetoricians as sophists, speakers who sought victory rather than the ultimate Truth, as he believed philosophy could. Within the humanities, the more aesthetically inclined fields such as literature and art belittled rhetoric for being practical and mundane as opposed to lofty and beautiful. Kenneth Burke, in his book *A Rhetoric of Motives*, wrote:

Precisely at a time when the term "rhetoric" had fallen into greatest neglect and disrepute, writers in the "social sciences" were, under many guises, making good contributions to the New Rhetoric. As usual with modern thought, the insights gained by *comparative culture* could throw light upon the classic approach to the subject; and again, as usual with modern thought, this light was interpreted in terms that concealed its true relation to earlier work.[1]

What Burke is saying is that the anthropologists and other social scientists established new disciplines by doing what the rhetorical theorists had done, going into the culture of their own or other countries and describing them, concentrating on such items as norms or rules for correct behavior and the highest values, just as Aristotle and other rhetoricians had described their *topoi* as possible premises or lines of argument acceptable to the audiences of ancient Greece. The social scientists may have been ignorant of the rhetorical tradition as taken over by anthropology, or some may have eagerly wanted to integrate it into their new social science. It was inevitable that the rhetoricians would move back into what had become the social scientific turf with modern names: interpersonal, organizational, and mass communication studies.

The United States of America was founded as a democracy, one calling for participation by all citizens, except those who, as in Greece, were slaves or women. The United States also produced the school of philosophy known as pragmatism. As we all know, it took some powerful rhetorical movements to get women and blacks the right to vote and other rights. Citizens were expected to participate by running for office, by giving campaign speeches; others were expected to speak out on behalf of local and national candidates they favored. They were also expected to partic-ipate in local problem-solving deliberative discussions in their states and towns. Back on the campuses, rhetoric as known to the Greeks came to be little more than a quaint and ancient subject taught in the classics depart-ment, not as something to help prepare student citizens to speak out and participate in politics. The social sciences continued to analyze the norms and class structure of the American society. The need for practical courses in public speaking, debate, and discussion, however, continued and was met by the creation of speech departments, particularly in the land-grant universities that were founded by Abraham Lincoln to teach *practical* arts and sciences, and other public institutions of higher learning.

Other departments often required their students to take a public speaking class in the speech department. Courses in group discussion, in which students learned collectively to move through the steps of reflective thinking or steps of problem solving identified by the pragmatist, John Dewey, were developed. The students would practice as a group trying to analyze a social problem, developing criteria for evaluating solutions, list-ing all possible solutions, and then applying the criteria as a method of choosing a solution or combination of them. They were also taught lead-ership functions that must be performed in a group, by any and all of its members, if the group was to succeed. The students were graded in part on how well balanced the participation was in their group, how equally all participants joined into the discussion and performed the leadership functions such as summarizing, verbalizing group agreements, or calling on the more reticent members. Perhaps most important was the quantity and quality of data or information embedded in students' arguments after thorough research.

Courses in argumentation and debate also gave students practice in making a case, refuting the opposing side, defending their own proposals, and then switching sides—a good way, incidentally, of reaching one's own personal position on issues. Research by faculty and graduate students was often conducted on what was called "public address"—speeches as docu-ments or texts given by prominent orators, historical and modern, trying to isolate the causal factors of eloquence, persuasiveness, and rhetorical failure. The connections I have been trying to make in the reader's mind were condensed and expressed as the title of a book published in 2009 by Omar Swartz, Katia Campbell, and Christina Pestana: *Neo-Pragmatism, Communication, and the Culture of Creative Democracy;* I was honored to write its Foreword.[2]

In the 1950s and 1960s, many members of the speech field were themselves persuaded to accept the doctrines of logical positivism, a school of philosophy defined by *The Cambridge Dictionary of Philosophy* as a "movement inspired by empiricism and verificationism."[3] In practice it called for empirical observations to be translated into quantitative data, then analyzed according to theories of inferential statistics, often with a large institutional computer. The field of speech began to conduct empirical, quantitative studies of interpersonal, group, and mass communication. Many speech departments changed their name, and the Speech Association of America ultimately became the National Communication Association.

Some courses that had been given under the title of Business and Professional Speaking over time became Business and Professional Communication, and ultimately Organizational Communication. Some with new PhD degrees in the field became consultants to various organizations, and some came to identify with those who hired and paid them—management. The main journal for organizational communication today is *Management Communication Quarterly,* not the *Worker's Communication Journal.* (To the reader not familiar with communication journals, the *WCJ* is a fiction, the name of a journal I made up to make my point.) The empirical studies of communication in organizations continued, but over the years more and more of them became qualitative, using verbal interview data rather than the quantitative sort from, say, forced-choice questionnaires. Although most members in the field still had faith in the importance and effectiveness of participatory decision making, they now felt they had to take into account the private interests of corporations and smaller business organizations, as well as the desires of individual employees. The belief in participatory processes as important to democracy was still there, but it was now qualified by new paradoxes discovered by researchers and commentators.

A Synthesis of Paradoxes in Participatory Processes

In 2001 a 50-page article, "Participatory Processes/Paradoxical Practices: Communication and the Dilemmas of Organizational Democracy," by Cynthia Stohl and George Cheney with 125 references to studies and commentaries, appeared in *Management Communication Quarterly.*[4] In a table, the authors present the "paradoxes of employee participation and workplace democracy," listing 14 paradoxes under the four main headings I reproduce here:

A. *Paradoxes of Structure:* Concerning the architecture of participation and democracy—for example, "Be spontaneous, creative, vocal, and assertive in the way we have planned!"

B. *Paradoxes of Agency:* Concerning the individual's sense of efficacy within the system—for example, "Do things our way but in a way that is still distinctively your own!"

C. *Paradoxes of Identity:* Concerning issues of membership, inclusion, and boundaries—for example, "Be *self*-managing to meet *organizational* goals!"

D. *Paradoxes of Power:* Concerning the locus, nature, and specific exercise of power in the organization—for example, "Be independent, just as I have commanded you!"[5]

These excellent examples make the categories of paradoxes clear. And some of them may be examples of what I called "pseudo-participatory schemes" in chapter 9, in which consulting companies' employee participation programs were discussed. Many could be paraphrased by Peter Block's apt statement: "When we command people to participate, we get participation in name only."[6] The paradoxes seem to fit Block's general observation, except for those that refer to the employee giving up more of her or his rights and time to the group than is desirable. Stohl and Cheney mention the study of the Grameen Bank discussed in chapter 3 of this book, repeating that some of the bank employees worked themselves too hard for the good of the cause. They also mention the concept of "cooptation," assimilating people into a group in order to neutralize their desire for change.

Paradoxical Paradox

The theory of concertive control developed by Cheney and me is discussed by Stohl and Cheney, and in that context they shift from paradox to another type of incongruity to say this about a study by Alder and me: "The increased vertical (electronic) and horizontal (peer-based) monitoring of work is one of the greatest *ironies* in an age of so-called employee empowerment."[7] Once again, management actually increases the total amount of control in the system—the organization—while seeming to be giving up decision-making authority to employees. All of these various paradoxes might seem to be daunting to those who believe in participatory decision making—teamwork. Stohl and Cheney add that they do not wish "to leave the reader with the impression that classification of paradoxes is our only concern here."[8] They need not have worried. What they have given readers is an exhaustive analysis of the available academic research on participatory processes. The bonus is that the paradoxes and ironies provide an additional insight, a trend toward greater *complexity* in the organizational use of employee participation.

Stohl and Cheney are concerned, for example, that employees are becoming involved with global colleagues or peers in participatory decision making, thus greatly increasing complexity. Electronic monitoring of work was mentioned in the previous paragraph, adding new variables. We can now say that an even greater paradox emerges from Stohl and Cheney's analysis of participatory practices. Part of this new or paradoxical paradox was established in chapter 3 of this book—that is, that increasing levels of complexity are best handled by teams, not individuals. The rest of the new paradox is supplied by Stohl and Cheney: as teams tackle modern problems, the team processes *themselves* are also increasing in complexity. This does not in any way, however, weaken the need for participatory decision making. No, it makes it all the more important that we continue to study and promote it in the hope of gaining a better understanding of how to cope with even greater complexity so that we may *reduce risks*, a theme of this book.

In addition, I do not want to give the impression that Stohl and Cheney concluded with a different or more negative attitude toward participation. To the contrary, they wrote this in their conclusion: "We believe that the strong, diverse, and dynamic linkages comprising participation networks potentially enrich and empower individuals, organizations and society.... *We hope our efforts will help to contribute to the fulfillment of the promises of participation.*"[9] While considering this comprehensive survey by stellar academics, I wondered what Ulrich Beck had to say about participation in *Risk Society: Towards a New Modernity.* The several references I found referred to participation in politics, an example being: "Sub-political innovation institutionalized as 'progress' remains under the jurisdiction of business, science, and technology, for whom democratic procedures are invalid."[10]

The Views of Practitioner-Advocates

There had appeared in 1993, eight years before the Stohl-Cheney synthesis, an unusual book, a first-person narrative that presents the autobiography of an organization and its owner in Brazil that had gone to the apparently maximal heights of participatory management. The author, Ricardo Semler, son of two Austrian immigrants to Brazil, was in his 20s when he took over Semco, his father's traditional, rule-bound company with a pyramidal structure. In the first chapter of his book, *Maverick: The Success Story Behind the World's Most Unusual Workplace,* Semler provides a snapshot of the changes he had made in the preceding years:

When I took over Semco from my father twelve years ago, it was a traditional company in every respect, with a pyramidal structure and a rule for every contingency. But today, our factory workers sometimes set their own production quotas and even come in on their own time to meet them. They help redesign the products they make and formulate the marketing plans. Their bosses, for their part, can run our business units with extraordinary freedom, determining business strategy without interference from the brass. They even set their own salaries, with no strings. Then again, everyone will know what they are, since all financial information at Semco is openly discussed. Indeed, our workers have unlimited access to our books (and we only keep one set).[11]

The rest of the book is as exciting as a novel or film, except in revealing the real names of real people and real companies that succeeded and failed during the period of narration. The story tells how Semler introduced participation into a traditional shipbuilding organization in São Paulo and the results produced: higher profits, lower costs, and the acquisition of other companies that were also transformed into participatory units within Semco. The brilliant opening analogy of the pyramid and the superhighway presented as the epigraph of this chapter is from Semler's book and illustrates that communication and its channels were always foremost in Semler's mind and agenda. Indeed, he incessantly seeks open communication and teamwork. The assembly line is broken into shapes that fit the teams of workers in Semco's manufacturing plants, which make a variety of products, from pumps for ships to kitchen equipment. More and more, however, Semco has moved toward providing services to other organizations and consumers.

Much of Semler's narrative is devoted to shattering paradoxes in the real world similar to those introduced by Stohl and Cheney earlier in this chapter. For example, Brazil is a highly unionized country, and the local chapter gave Semco trouble for offering its workers improvements in hours or wages because they did not emerge from collective bargaining. The paradoxes were resolved, and Semco later received a national award for its excellent labor relations. Indeed, Semler recognizes the paradox of paradoxes by writing that the era of using people as tools is coming to an end, but he warns that "participation is infinitely more complex in practice than conventional corporate unilateralism, just as democracy is much more cumbersome than dictatorship."[12] Semco has gone so far in the direction of democracy that *everyone* in the corporation has a vote on major decisions, such as whether or not to acquire a new company.

Semler not only tossed out the pyramid, he substituted a new geometric symbol for Semco: three concentric circles with tiny triangles within them, emphasizing the circularity of open communication and teams over the vertical hierarchy of a pyramid. In addition to the many cognitive solutions, Semler also acknowledges the affective changes. In speaking of a company Semco had acquired and then reformed into an organizational democracy, Semler writes that the old firm had become unrecognizable, "not so much physically, of course, but organizationally and, if I may say so, spiritutally."[13] He is referring here to that quasi-religious feeling of oneness with others who have achieved success, accompanied by a feeling of pride in both one's own role and the outcome of the group's achievements. I felt its power when the first men walked on the Moon, and during the processes leading up to it as well. Kenneth Burke refers to identification as a significant part of the new rhetoric, not a one-way presentation of all the available means of persuasion, but a combination of self-persuasion and pride in one's group or sect. Watch it when a team of professional athletes wins the big game.

Kenneth Burke also points out how we could see the way toward regarding a team's success as a spiritual or religious phenomenon by teaching his readers that the original meaning of the very word *hierarchy* is *priestrule* and has connotations of celestial mystery. Even the lowly flock feels what Burke calls a "mystic *participation*,"[14] using the magic word itself. Even though Semler had flattened the pyramid, had reduced the bureaucratic levels of Semco from 12 to 3,[15] there was still a short hierarchy with a lay priest at the top with his flock assembled in circles. Burke's new rhetoric helps explain the extraordinary effort of brains and skill made by Semco's flocks of believers.

A favorable reference to Semler's book is made in a comprehensive book published two years later, in 1995, with this extraordinary title: *The Age of Participation: New Governance for the Workplace and the World,* by Patricia McLagan and Christo Nel, with a foreword by Peter Block.[16] Despite the title, the book did not literally announce the arrival of the New Age, merely the beginning of its arrival. McLagan had founded a consulting company and at the time of the book's publication was teaching in South Africa at what was then Rand Afrikaans University at Johannesburg. Her coauthor is a South African who had been assisting change in the public and private sectors of his country, including work that "helped to bring about the end of apartheid in South Africa," according to the dust cover of the book.

The book is a curious mixture of argument, scientific evidence, prediction, and how-to-do-it. In it the authors said that the Participation Age may not be here yet—in 1995 when they wrote—but it was definitely coming, in all walks of life and human governance. They cite academic research studies that show that participation works well for successful businesses. They also cite cases from their worldwide consulting, providing evidence of what works and what does not. Their final chapter, "Taking the Transformation beyond the Workplace," contains headings such as GLOBAL AND NATIONAL GOVERNANCE and targets a need for more participation and democracy in such institutions and organizations as schools, universities, churches, local government, families, and business.

McLagan and Nel write that the Participation Age, characterized by a shift from authoritarianism to participation, was inevitable and necessary because of the complexity of the times. Contributing to that complexity were globalization and technology, and that the "new science of complexity is the emerging science of participation."[17] These predictions are identical with the thesis of the book in the reader's hand at this moment. So are the statements by McLagan and Nel that participation makes sense both in theory and in *moral* terms.

Here is a statement that could have been made by Marshall Space Flight Center director Wernher von Braun to justify the appointment of his working groups in NASA: "First, much work is complex and requires several people with diverse skills and experience to contribute parts of the solution."[18] They also anticipate the Paul-Tompkins law of risk communication, demonstrating that early detection of risky problems is vital: "Executives play a key role in the detoxifying of information. Leaders must be models of *openness*, talking about their own learning, and supporting *early* identification of problems."[19] McLagan and Nel even think the New Age provides us with existential issues. I agree: Human *being* is better characterized by participation than by mere obedience.

Thinking it would be interesting to compare and contrast the academic views presented earlier with those of persons in business, I have summarized Ricardo Semler's work as well as that of McLagan and Nel; I now turn to a book with an unusual title written by a businessman in Denver, Colorado: Chuck Blakeman. It comes third for a chronological reason. The striking title of his book is *Why Employees are Always a Bad Idea (and Other Business Diseases of the Industrial Age)*.[20] Before the reader is tempted to consider this an incomprehensible title worthy only of quick dismissal, she or he must be advised that it is the word *employees* that the author is demeaning, not the human beings it applies to. Readers should also know that he treats the word *manager* with the same disdain. I hasten to explicate those and other terms used by Blakeman in this unusual book.

In the preface of his book, Blakeman says he's going to call the period of human history from 1700 to 1970 the Industrial Age and the period of 1850 to 1970 the Factory System Period. From 1970 on we have been in what Blakeman calls the Age of Participation. In case you missed it, the Age has already arrived. He forecasts that he will talk about his own company, the Crankset Group, saying that one "intention" of the organization is to solve the problem of poverty in Africa. He also discusses companies he worked with as a consultant and others he discovered in doing research for his book. He promises that many of the examples he will use are in the manufacturing industry because of the rhetorical necessity of having to refute claims that the Participation Age is taking place only in the service and technology industries.

Part I of Blakeman's book is given to what he calls the seven core diseases of the Industrial Age. The first is "the problem with big." Blakeman ushers in some historical facts, pointing out that both the number and size of organizations that survive over hundreds of years are relatively small, implying that bigness decreases the likelihood of long-term survival. The desire to be big is the wrong motive, he argues, pointing out that half of this country rails against Big Government and the other half lambastes Big Business. Blakeman advances these two claims relevant to our interest in complexity and risk:

1. The bigger they are, the more problems their complexity creates for themselves and the world around them.
2. The bigger they are, the greater impact their mistakes and problems have on the world around them.[21]

Blakeman's second disease of the Industrial Age is borne by the 21st-century industrialist. This disease has many symptoms, among them the resistance to change, a time-based orientation, and closed markets. And according to Blakeman, the companies ailing with the Big Disease produce a decrease in jobs. The third and fourth diseases are similar: Blakeman states that the terms *employee* and *manager* are always a bad idea and should be replaced by the word *stakeholder*. His book contains a table with contrasting descriptions for *manager* and *leader*.[22] The latter, highly preferred in the Participatory Age, is characterized with such phrases as "focuses on results," "frees people to be smart and motivated, because they are," and "encourages creativity, innovation, asking why, open communication." Number five is the "9 to 5 disease." Blakeman cites research indicating that we work best in spurts. Work should be interrupted with breaks in which stakeholders do something different that they enjoy. In the Participation Age, many stakeholders do not have offices. The author reports that 70 percent of the stakeholders at PricewaterhouseCooper telecommute, as do 90 percent of the staff at Intel. The sixth disease is trying to separate work and play, a management principle advocated by Frederick Winslow Taylor and his theory of scientific management that Blakeman wants to refute. In the Age of Participation, work is designed to be as close as possible to play, something enjoyable. The seventh and final disease is retirement—a bankrupt Industrial Age idea—and captured by Blakeman in a typically bold phrase: "Carpe freaking diem already."[23]

Part II of Blakeman's book is "Embracing the Participation Age." Blakeman recommends his own company before moving on to a listing of all-star organizations, such as Crankset Group, a small outfit formed in 2006. Crankset is still quite small, with 8 full-time and 12 part-time stakeholders "mucking around in seven countries on four continents."[24] Crankset is in the consulting business, helping other companies make the transition to participation. (I heard an unusual plug for Blakeman and his book on Colorado Public Radio when I tuned in to hear classical music; it sounded interesting and relevant to my work so I ordered it from the Crankset Group. When I opened the package I found a sticker on the dust jacket: "Top 10 Business Book of the Year!")

Blakeman's description of the Crankset Group is of its practices, principles, and beliefs as they add up to his view of participation: "1. We are all owners. 2. We are all adults. 3. We are results based."[25]

Other practices scattered throughout chapter 11 are headings such as NO MANAGERS—ONLY LEADERS; NO VACATION OR SICK DAYS; NO BENEFITS; NO DEPARTMENTS; PROFIT-SHARING AND STOCK. At least two of those headings need some unpacking: "No benefits" means that Crankset pays a salary to the stakeholders and then adds a sum of money by which they can buy their own health insurance plus retirement plan and thereby can take these with them if they move on. "No vacation or sick days" translates into a policy in which each person takes time off whenever it is needed or desired.

Blakeman then moves on to other companies that illustrate the Participation Age. These are not scientific studies that academics might conduct, but then Blakeman identifies by name nearly every company he brings up, thus allowing an independent check that most academic studies of organizations don't allow because the identities are disguised. This does add some commonsense credibility to his claims.

Let's take a look at chapter 12, "Companies Thriving in the Participation Age." The reader runs into another heading: A BIG THAT FIGURED IT OUT DECADES AGO.[26] That would be perhaps his prime or all-star model:

W. L. Gore & Associates. Blakeman begins his analysis of Gore, the makers of Gore-Tex, with four descriptive phrases appearing in Fortune magazine with the year they appeared: ownership of their work, 2010; no hierarchy, 2011; company ownership and self-evaluation, 2012; leaders as servants, not mangers, 2013. The word team appears twice in the descriptions of Gore.[27] When I read those phrases taken from Fortune's annual reviews of Gore, I mentally italicized the word team both times it appears because it fits the thesis of this book so neatly. The next two pages of Blakeman's analytic description of Gore fit another theme of this book: open communication.

Blakeman provides another box with the heading THE LATTICE PR-GANIZATION.[28] Lattice is the metaphor that founder Bill Gore used to explain his organization. My 1965 *Shorter Oxford English Dictionary* defines the lattice as a "structure made of laths, or of wood or metal crossed and fastened together, with *open* spaces left between" (emphasis added). Note that the traditional metaphor for an organization is a pyramid, a structure with no lattice-like open spaces through which one can peer. Gore pointed out that every successful organization has a lattice underlying the façade of authoritarian hierarchies. That would seem to be the informal organization, the networks people create in communication with others in almost all organizations in order to get things done.

Blakeman has a claim about the lattice organization that supports the basic thesis of this book as well as his: "Any decision" in Gore and other lattice organizations "that creates risk for the company, has to be made in the context of the team, not by yourself."[29] I sent this quotation to a friend who is a long-term associate at Gore and asked for his opinion about it. This is his response:

> I do not know the reference for the statement about Gore on risk. But, from what you've said, it sounds to me like one of the many claims about Gore written by someone who doesn't have any sophisticated understanding of the company or the culture. Things are rarely black and white at Gore. So, I can imagine times when an individual takes sole and full responsibility for a risk, times when an individual consults with fairly wide-ranging groups of Associates

(who aren't a team) before deciding whether to take a particular risk or not, and situations where a team owns the risk decision.

Other Particpation Age Companies

In his book, Blakeman includes a list of Participation Age Companies in Every Industry, some of which will be well known to readers of this book, including TDIndustries, a construction company that does not hire and fire according to the nature of their contracts. It is completely owned by its 1,600 stakeholders, who also elect the members of the board of directors. Whole Foods also receives coverage, one of the 13 companies to make the list of 100 best companies to work for and be identified as an all-star company. All Whole Foods team members are eligible for stock options and share the wealth. Another grocery store chain discussed, Wegmans, which is on the East Coast, has never laid off a stakeholder in its 94-year history. It is "fanatic" about the health of its stakeholders, offering them a smoking cessation program and a 24/7 health hotline. The people who work there are so pleased with their work that they recruit family members, with the result that 20 percent of the stakeholders are related to at least one other stakeholder.[30]

Blakeman discusses and lists other companies included in the Participation Age and presents the WorldBlu List of Most Democratic Workplaces, as well as Firms of Endearment, a list of companies that have a purpose broader than making money: "Container Store, Costco, Harley-Davidson, Honda, JetBlue, Johnson & Johnson, New Balance, Patagonia, Southwest Airlines, Starbucks, Timberland, Trader Joe's, UPS, Wegmans, Whole Foods, and others."[31] I did find one company in the list that has a store in Denver—Trader Joe's. In doing so I recalled a statement from Semler's book that I now quote: "What people call participative management is usually just consultative management."[32] I visited a Trader Joe's store twice, conducting "research conversations" with six employees representing three hierarchical levels: crew members, mates, and captain. The employees obviously enjoyed working there, and a mate told me some of their best ideas come from the workers. But it was made clear by all that this was made in consultation, not participation. The captain heard about me and approached me with her card and the telephone number of "National," advising me to contact the national office if I wanted more information. Despite high morale on the part of the crew members, it was clear that this is a consultative system. We also had a laugh when I asked one crew member if the titles imply a naval military organization. "Oh no," said the young woman, "I think Joe must be a pirate."

This and the quotation in the previous section from my friend at Gore, among other things, make me somewhat skeptical of Blakeman's blanket claims about all of the companies he lists as participatory but for which he does not provide statements about how he reached this conclusion. Nonetheless, consultative management can be at least somewhat better at discovering risk than strict hierarchical management with little interest in employee opinions and ideas, even though it can't solve problems as well as full participation—teamwork.

Final Thoughts

In this chapter, Stohl and Cheney provide us with an encyclopedic discussion of research on participation, open communication, and teamwork. Their analyses of paradoxes provide lessons on what to be careful about while introducing participation in an organization. Their paradox of paradoxes is that group problem solving has itself become more complicated in a Global–High Tech Era, making it more difficult to introduce open communication and teamwork. Semler gives us a firsthand account of introducing participation—and details about how well it works. McLagan and Nel announced that the Age of Participation was on the way, had even begun, providing research about and experience with the firms practicing it. Blakeman announces that the Age of Participation has arrived, giving the reader examples of well-known corporations, thus fulfilling the prophecy of McLagan and Nel, even though he may have included companies practicing consultation, not participation.

Blakeman also talks about a potential problem for organizations and democracy in working with a company of 50 employees that wanted to become representative and make the transition from pyramid to participation: "about fifteen of the fifty people, or about 30 percent, realized they did not want to become Stakeholders, and left."[33] There may be a minority percentage of people who do not want to participate in making decisions at work or even at the ballot box, but one cannot use the 30 percent figure as more than experience in one unnamed company.

Stohl and Cheney also show us the paradoxes of teamwork and participation, and how the process has increased in complexity during the recent history of organizations. That does not dampen their enthusiasm for teamwork and participation to be used by modern organizations. The other commentators on participation, open communication, and teamwork summarized in this chapter are even more enthusiastic, and some can talk from direct experience—implementing participation in their own organizations—and by the indirect experience of helping other organizations adopt participatory decision making. They also introduce different kinds of criteria and data—organizations known by their name to be successful financially—to support their claims about the effectiveness of participatory decision making. They call out for more research in the organizations described.

Notes

1. Kenneth Burke, *A Rhetoric of Motives* (Berkeley: University of California Press, 1969), 40.

2. Omar Swartz, Katia Campbell, Christina Pestana, *Neo-Pragmatism, Communication, and the Culture of Creative Democracy* (New York: Peter Lang, 2009).

3. Robert Audi, ed., *The Cambridge Dictionary of Philosophy*, 2nd ed. (Cambridge: Cambridge University Press, 1995), 514.

4. Cynthia Stohl and George Cheney, "Participatory Processes/Paradoxical Practices: Communication Studies and the Dilemmas of Organizational Democracy, *Management Communication Quarterly* 14 (February 2001): 349–407.

5. Ibid., 360. The information is presented in Table 1.

6. Peter Block, foreword to *The Age of Participation: New Governance for the Workplace and the World* by Patricia McLagan and Christo Nel (San Francisco: Berrett-Koehler Publishers, 1995), xiii.

7. Stohl and Cheney, "Participatory Processes/Paradoxical Practices," 386.

8. Ibid., 390.

9. Ibid., 398–99. See also George Cheney and Dana Cloud, "Doing Democracy, Engaging the Material: Employee Participation and Labor Activity in an Age of Market Globalization," *Management Communication Quarterly* 19 (2006): 501–40; Tom Webb and George Cheney, "Worker-Owned-and-Governed Cooperatives and the Wider Cooperative Movement: Challenges," in *The Routledge Companion to Alternative Organization*, ed. M. Parker, G. Cheney, V. Fournier, and C. Land (London: Routledge, 2014), 64–88.

10. Ulrich Beck, *Risk Society: Towards a New Modernity* (London: Sage, 1992), 14.

11. Ricardo Semler, *Maverick: The Success Story Behind the World's Most Unusual Workplace* (New York: Hachette Book Group, 1993), 1–2.

12. Ibid., 107.

13. Ibid., 84.

14. Burke, *A Rhetoric of Motives*, 306–7.

15. Semler, *Maverick*, 6.

16. Patricia McLagan and Christo Nel, *The Age of Participation: New Governance for the Workplace and the World* (San Francisco: Berrett-Koehler, 1995).

17. Ibid., 17.

18. Ibid., 84.

19. Ibid., 126. Emphasis added.

20. Chuck Blakeman, *Why Employees are Always a Bad Idea (and Other Business Diseases of the Industrial Age)* (Highlands Ranch, CO: Crankset Publishing, 2014).

21. Ibid., 20.

22. Ibid., 81.

23. Ibid., 116.

24. Ibid., 145.

25. Ibid., 151–52.

26. Ibid., 162.

27. Ibid., 163.

28. Ibid.

29. Ibid.

30. Ibid., 170.

31. Ibid., 172.

32. Semler, *Maverick,* 83.

33. Blakeman, *Why Employees are Always a Bad Idea,* 160.

Epilogue

"Self-affirmation is the essential nature of every being and as such its highest good. Perfect self-affirmation is not an isolated act which originates in the individual being but is participation in the universal or divine act of self-affirmation."

"The self affirms itself as participant in the power of a group, of a movement, of essences, of the power of being as such."

—Paul Tillich, *The Courage to Be*

F inding the balance between temerity, or rashness, and cowardice is an important purpose of this book. The epigraph from Tillich in chapter 5 helped us find the way to a definition of *smart risk,* an informed belief that gives one reasoned courage to resist nonbeing. The two quotations in the epigraph of this Epilogue by the same existential philosopher-theologian affirm that participation—in the group, team, family, and society as I choose to interpret it—is the way to self-affirmation as well as courage. The individual affirms itself in the increased power or control of the team or movement. We can say that genuine participation in a team, organization, or political system is affirming and *self-fulfilling.* Ulrich Beck's concept of the risk society, as we saw in chapter 9, stresses the contemporary creation of fear, but allowing that emotion to dictate our decisions is to be transformed into the existential state of "nonbeing," as Tillich put it in the earlier quote. Finding that balance between cowardice and rashness happens when the group or team has the training and flexibility to provide self-affirmation for *each* of the participants.

This Epilogue picks up where the previous chapters left off and then brings it all together in a manner that at least points to that new balance. I was unable to present the paper prepared for the International Conference on Systems Engineering in Las Vegas on August 18, 2005. Dr. Stein Cass of Ball Aerospace presented it in my absence. Therefore, I begin this chapter with a discussion of that paper, not published, but bearing on issues of risk and risk management.

Communication as the Geometry of Human Organization

Being asked to speak to a mathematically oriented audience of systems engineers because it was thought that my "soft" or qualitative approach to risk might provide some insights produced both pride and defensiveness on my part, which made me hasten to show the audience that I was not totally ignorant of the quantitative. I proved that with the anecdote presented earlier, the five nines (.99999) or five *neins.* It invariably gets a laugh and helps to prove that communication by words is prior to that of numbers. It is almost a perfect pun for understanding that the *Saturn V* and Apollo Program worked so well because it was based on perceived credibility of sources, told in words, and implying a mathematical calculation. It also explains why Wernher von Braun brought along Walter Wiesman, the youngest of the Peenemünde Germans and perhaps the only non-technical one, to study potential problems in the organizational communication system at NASA's Marshall Space Flight Center (MSFC) and to call them out—in words—for all to hear.

This section will proceed by first comparing organizational communication to risk analysis and how the one can inform the other. Second, in the interest of *consilience,* a scientific word for "jumping together" (again according to my 1965 *Shorter Oxford English Dictionary*), it will show how geometry, the foundation of mathematics and physics, is a descendant of the earliest communication theory, Aristotle's *Rhetoric.* Next I shall show that communication is also the geometry of organizations. Having completed those partitioned points, this Epilogue will close with a synthesis of all 10 previous chapters and set forth some principles and recommendations for managing risk and complexity by means of open communication, including argumentation, and teamwork.

First, I must recognize a resource that was provided to me by Dr. Stein Cass. It is actually a long academic paper presented to the Colorado Chapter of the International Council on Systems Engineering on December 2, 2004. The title is "Risk Management in the Aerospace Industry: Past and Present." I shall repeat those definitions from it that were documented in chapter 1:

> *Risk:* "the likelihood and impact of potential problems or undesirable events which might occur and prevent meeting an objective."
>
> *Risk analysis:* "attempts to identify what could go wrong and what to do about it."
>
> *Risk management:* "an *iterative process* which starts at program inception and ends with program close-out."

When I was a consultant in organizational communication at the MSFC, Dr. von Braun directed me to look for potential communication problems that could cause risks. I did this by conducting deep interviews with key people. In consultation with these same people and others, I came up with recommendations about what to do about the problems or risks. Walter Wiesman, the coordinator of internal communication at the MSFC, who brought me in as a consultant, saw his position as having the full-time and iterative responsibility for keeping all of the personnel at the MSFC sensitized and disciplined to communication problems and potentials during his visits to offices and labs. So did Dr. von Braun, for that matter.

In his paper, Dr. Cass identifies the most common risks for aerospace engineers as cost overruns, schedule slips, performance shortfalls, and incorrect system implementation. The first three risks are synonymous with terms I used in understanding and explaining *topoi* and decision making at the MSFC: *cost, time,* and *reliability,* albeit in a different order. While immersed in that engineering and scientific culture, I was surprised that only the easy technical decisions were made by means of demonstration and scientific evidence. As I wrote in my first publication about NASA, "The easy decisions were made by means of demonstration and scientific evidence. *The difficult decisions were made by rhetorical or persuasive processes.* The three master *topoi* in such situations are *reliability, time* and *cost.* Most, if not all, of the arguments given in support of a particular solution had premises anchored in those *topoi.*"[1] A low level of reliability was the equivalent of a "performance shortfall," *time* was the neutral term for "schedule slips," as was *cost* for "cost overruns." It is relevant to note again that at the MSFC during Apollo, *reliability* was always listed first, and the others came after.

"But," the engineers might have asked, "What are *topoi?*" *Topoi* is a concept developed by the classical Greek rhetoricians, as reviewed in chapter 10. Aristotle, for example, defined rhetoric—the first academic subject in ancient Greece—as the faculty of discovering all the available means of persuasion in any situation. The ancient Greeks systematically classified lines of argument that could be used, say, while defending oneself in court against a charge of murder. We can also think of *topoi*, or topics of arguments, as potential premises for deductive arguments. At the MSFC it was clear that reliability, time, and cost were competitive premises for arguments. An engineer could rarely propose a solution that met or satisfied all three criteria best or equally well; hence, there was a need for tradeoffs, or compromises, among the three *topoi*. Making the necessary compromises to reach a decision required rhetorical as well as engineering skills. We sought religiously to avoid unacceptable or "foul" compromises. I am compelled to repeat that at the MSFC in the Apollo era, reliability was the first among equals; Faster, Better, Cheaper would have been incomprehensible, unthinkable, anathema to the MSFC culture of that age because we intended to keep our promise to President Kennedy to bring the astronauts back safely from the Moon. Dr. Cass persuaded me over lunch, however, that time and cost are correctly considered as serious risks from the perspective of a private contractor because failure to meet those premises invites a new risk: organizational failure, albeit financial in nature.

Cass defines Risk Factor as $RF = L \times I$, or Risk Factor equals Likelihood times Impact. He also advises his colleagues in aerospace corporations to define the likelihood and impact tables in cooperation with the customer because the customer may view risk differently. That is a sound principle of organizational communication, whether in numbers or words. This is the opposite of the position we took at MSFC—that is, we were the customer and we penetrated the contractors so that we would know when they fell short of our standards and created risks for our program. Dr. Cass forced me to see this process from another, dialectical perspective and gave me confidence in his determination to have his company practice von Braun's principle of penetration in two directions: their customer (e.g., NASA) as well as their company's suppliers or subcontractors. I am sure it would have pleased von Braun as well.

There are many other similarities between the mathematical and communicative approaches to risk analysis, but I must turn to the second point forecast or promised earlier: to show in the interest of consilience how geometry, the foundation of math and physics, is a relative or descendant of the earliest communication theory—Aristotle's work titled *Rhetoric*.

After reading how important Euclid's *Elements* was to the foundation of mathematics and physics, I pulled a copy from the row of The Great Books on our bookshelf. While reading it I was amazed because it contains no numbers and no equations, only some diagrams. It is a series of verbal arguments about figures. How can these be the foundation of mathematics? Because the verbal reasoning about the figures is so tight, readers could see how shorthand arguments or equations would work.

We know little of Euclid other than he was Greek, studied with Plato's students (which included Aristotle), and flourished at about 300 BCE in Alexandria. We know that he was aware of the work done by Antiphon, an earlier Greek of the fifth century BCE, and was described as a "Sophist philosopher" who "enunciated the 'principle of exhaustion,' which was to have a profound influence on mathematicians."[2] Sophists were a subdivision of rhetoricians. Aristotle (384–322 BCE) was one of Plato's students and made unique contributions to the arts of argumentation. Euclid may have studied under him; in any case we can be sure he knew Aristotelian thought. The 20th-century expert on Aristotle, Richard McKeon, wrote that

there are "three universal arts of argumentation—dialectic, rhetoric, and analytic." Aristotle applies the word "logic" or "logical" loosely to any of these universal arts, and what is called logic today is a historical outgrowth of Aristotle's universal art developed and systematized as analytic, dialectic, rhetoric, sophistic, mathematic, or syntactic.[3]

Leonard Mlodinow, who argues that Einstein's relativity theory and Witten's string theory are best seen as subsequent revolutions in Euclid's geometry, thinks the most important contribution of *Elements* is "its innovative logical method: first, make terms explicit. . . . Next make concepts explicit . . . so that no unstated . . . assumptions may be used. Finally, derive the logical consequences of the system employing only accepted rules of logic."[4] As mentioned, there are no algebraic equations, no numbers in *Elements*, only words and the figures made by ruler and compass, called "constructions." It is clear that Aristotelian argumentation, including rhetoric, was necessary to the development of mathematics. We should not therefore be surprised that my academic tradition—rhetoric, including logical proof, and communication—can today complement mathematical approaches to risk analysis.

To come at it from another (geometric) angle, a close colleague of mine, Dr. Elaine V. B. Tompkins, prepared an unpublished text, "Progressive Argumentation," a detailed outline with definitions, principles, and examples, for university students in her argumentation and debate classes. The affirmative debaters, who had the burden of proof, had to prove the existence of a problem in the status quo and then propose a solution that would solve or minimize it, and not cause new and greater problems, called respectively, "the need," "the plan," and "benefits." The affirmative side had to win all the issues or the old policy, the status quo, would continue. In general people resist change, so the status quo always has presumption. Similarly, a person's personal beliefs have presumption (we hold them because we think they are true), and everyone who truly wants to change our beliefs must assume the burden of proof.

The negative team, with the presumption, could attack the other team's need or plan or both, but only has to win one of them to show that the current policy should be continued. The issue of the problem is usually a social or political one. The text looks at the problem or need in a way similar to Cass's mathematical approach: $RF = L \times I$. The argumentation text uses the term *probability* for likelihood and subdivides impact into two terms: *extent* and *severity*. The debaters were mathematical to the degree that they used statistics to prove the extent and pervasiveness but needed also to prove the severity of the harmfulness of the problem or need. This set of terms is not only similar to the mathematical approach, but the subdivision of *impact* into *extent* and *severity* might be a helpful move for mathematical risk analysts to make in some situations if not in all.

The argument that communication is the geometry of human organization is related to the previous argument in that Euclid used the communication theory of argumentation to create geometry, the bed or foundation of mathematics and science. Euclid's triangle is also the shape of most

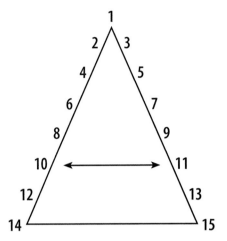

Figure 4 Fayol's gangplank

organizations. The lines of his triangles are the lines of communication among organized humans. The communication between and among the people at different levels of the hierarchy are constitutive of the triangle, or any shape of the organization, even for flatter ones or concentric circles. Organizational theorists, however, have found the triangle or pyramid to be an irresistible metaphor in describing human organizations.

Figure 4 is an example of geometric creation, a depiction of a concept introduced by Henri Fayol (1841–1925), a French engineer who made an important contribution to management and organization theory. I shall argue that the main benefit of it has been to the practice of organizational communication. The apex of the triangle represents the central authority. The sloping lines or sides of the figure represent the formal lines of communication that Fayol said were used for the managerial functions of commanding, coordinating, and controlling; again, these lines of communication constitute the geometric form and the organization. The scalar chain of communication is that line of superiors and subordinates—many playing both roles—stretching from the apex, or centralized command point, to those points at the base of the triangle where we picture the workers who execute the commands.

Aerospace engineers should find it particularly interesting that Fayol preached a principle called the "unity of command," the notion that employees should receive orders from only one supervisor. NASA Headquarters imposed on MSFC a new geometric figure, the matrix organization, in which program and project offices were created downward on a line parallel to the traditional line organization. The program and project officers, in their boxes, could then enter the other boxes representing the laboratories from a lateral position with carefully worded orders or requests. The traditional laboratory directors had at first a difficult problem with this new geometric arrangement that is now rather widespread. The principle of unity of command was tested and finally watered down, and the lab workers continued to identify most with the lab and not the project or program office.

The final aspect of Fayol's triangle I explained to the aerospace systems engineers was the gangplank, or bridge, formed by the two-way lateral channel connecting, for example, supervisors 10 and 11 in Figure 4. Historically, from the beginning of organizations to the time when Fayol published his work, 1916, such lateral or horizontal communication was forbidden. The expectation was that an upward-directed message had to move all the way to the ultimate authority and back down to the intended receiver. If 10 and 11 had a common problem, they could not take action about it. Each had to go up the scalar chain to get approval for joint action. Fayol's bridge allowed them to communicate with each other (a) if 8 and 9 authorized such interaction; and (b) if 10 and 11 are in agreement about the course of action; and (c) if 8 and 9 are informed of the action to be taken. Problems at times could be solved in one sitting as opposed to necessitating seemingly endless serial reproductions of written messages up and down the line, thus shortening the vertical semantic-information distance so crucial to risk management communication. Fayol thought that top management's encouragement of the gangplank's use would lead to the habit of seeking responsibility.[5]

That habit of seeking responsibility reached its apex so far as I know in automatic responsibility, the charge to all people at the bottom of the MSFC's triangle that the moment they perceived a risk they assumed responsibility for it, not just by going laterally to the lab assigned to the problem, but by going directly to the top, the point of ultimate power and control. The Monday Notes could be used in the same way, shortening the triangle. And as we saw in Figure 2 (chapter 1), the Paul-Tompkins law of risk communication, shortening the height of the triangle when dealing with problems of high likelihood and severe impact is of great benefit. Semantic-status-information distance is also reduced, making for better understanding.

I developed for the engineers the analogy of geometry and organizational communication by mentioning that the coordinates in geometry are suggestive of the coordination needed in a human organization, and that organizational and communication theorists used to speak of tall and flat organizations, the variable being the number of supervisory layers between the base and the apex of the triangle. Euclid's *Elements*, Book IV, Proposition 13, allows us to see a circle within a pentagon, suggestive of a meeting the secretary of defense might conduct at a roundtable where all can see, hear, and talk with everyone else. And because of the title of this book—at least the *Open Communication and Teamwork* part—it follows that circles in organizations are recommended. The proliferation of circular working groups I observed at the MSFC led to the development of the theory of concertive control, the effectiveness of which was later demonstrated in chapter 3 by the Barker study of an electronic manufacturing company and the Larson study of an aerospace company. Subtract the "e" from *equality*, add the word *circle*, and one has *quality circle*, an important geometric form in human communication.

There is now a related "academic" issue in higher education manifested in an acronym—STEM—which stands for science, technology, engineering, and mathematics. The National Science Foundation has been promoting these four fields for support and higher funding, which means a decrease in that provided to the humanities and social sciences. The issue is well illustrated by a newspaper article written by Nick Anderson of the *Washington Post:* "Can the English Major Be Saved?" Enrollments have been decreasing in English and other departments in the humanities since the Great Recession and the emergence of STEM. A professor of English at the University of Maryland, Kent Cartwright, is quoted as saying "We are so completely STEM-driven," and that the humanities are not considered part of the well-being of the university. The president of Maryland,

Wallace D. Lob, disagrees. He thinks of the university as a flower: "That flower has a long and very sturdy 'STEM,'... But at the top of that STEM, there's a flower, a blossom. And that flower is the humanities."[6]

This incomplete metaphor was troubling to me until I realized that a sturdy stem and beautiful blossoms need nourishment, support, and stability. *Roots*, that's what they need. I submit that the main or tap roots for this stem and blossom are what Richard McKeon, quoted earlier, called the "universal arts of argumentation": grammar, logic, rhetoric. As we saw, these disciplines were needed prior to the development of math and science. Five *neins* are prior to .99999. Rhetoric and communication, or speaking and writing grammatical, rational, and persuasive discourse, are still necessary to success in, yes, even the STEM fields. Grammar, logic, and rhetoric constituted the trivium, or first three of the ancient liberal arts. As such they were considered by the ancients to be the basic, necessary parts of an education *worthy of a free person*—that is, one who can participate effectively in the discourse and decision making within a democracy. They still are.

At the micro-level of the sciences and humanities, we read in chapter 3 about a study in which more and more scholarly research, including research in the STEM fields, is being conducted and published by *teams*. That goes for quality as well as quantity, as measured by the higher citation rate for team-produced research than research produced by an individual. We know that communication, discourse, and argumentation are constitutive of organization at the macro-level as well, having seen that a man of technology and science, Dr. von Braun, gave communication the highest priority in managing risk and complexity.

Synthesis

Chapter 1 laid out the concertive control theory; the three visual figures—Paul's law (Figure 1), the Paul-Tompkins law of risk communication (Figure 2), and semantic-information distance (Figure 3)—showed that the virtues of early testing and energy expenditure during the life of a project could be a great advantage to an organization, particularly if the likelihood and impact of a risk were quantitatively and qualitatively high. Figure 3 demonstrated how the semantic-information distance units affected speed and energy in communicating and fixing a risk. Chapter 2 showed how Dr. Wernher von Braun seemed to grasp all of this by his emphasis on early and frequent testing. Complementing this was the regular redundancy of channels and messages: briefings, Monday Notes, penetration, and perhaps most of all automatic responsibility, which eliminated layers of organization and bureaucratic delays in getting word about a risk to the top of the triangle. Automatic responsibility also shortened the *lateral* semantic-information distance between and among other labs concerned with the same problem or risk. Von Braun's use of working groups to attack risks that individual disciplines (labs) could not handle suggests the principle that the collective expertise of the individual members of a group or team should be *equal to or greater than the degree of complexity of the problem*. No individual is complex enough, but separate experts can pool their knowledge to match the complexity of the risk.

Chapter 3 began with a discussion of a stunning and massive study of scholarly publications. Most surprising in the results of this survey is the fact that the humanities, the social sciences, and the arts have joined the scientific and engineering disciplines in the team approach to research and scholarship. Approximately 20 million publications and 2 million patents proved that knowledge has become so complex over the years that it now requires a team approach, concertive or participatory research, to make new advances. It may have surprised some academics to learn that today teamwork also produces higher *quality* results than the great genius working alone. The citation rates or quotation rates for the products of teams are higher than the publications and patents produced by single authors.

Also in chapter 3 we looked at Barker's celebrated study of concertive control in ISE, the electronic manufacturing company. The results demonstrate emphatically that these ordinary workers who had been trained for participatory decision making readily accepted the responsibility of making decisions about their work rules, enforcing them, and changing them when needed. The company made a profit after the change, but because

ISE was bought out by a larger company seeking its patents, we cannot go back to see how it is operating today.

As a resident of the state of Colorado, I can report to the reader that JAR, the aerospace contractor studied by Larson, has flourished since the study. Yes, management at JAR was tempted by NASA's attempt to switch decision premises from reliability, time, and cost, to Faster, Better, Cheaper. But JAR's engineers stood in concert against lowering their technical standards, and even management became ambivalent in the face of resistance in their own ranks. The engineers won that battle, I am happy to report, and without revealing the identity of the real company I say here that it has distinguished itself with the success of its missions into space.

The Grameen Bank study is an inspiration to all. It has had an effect similar to that of the Manned Flight Awareness program—a Womanned Flight Awareness program in this case—creating determination in the women to repay their loans so that other women could then borrow money to elevate their status. The women of Bangladesh who have been able to participate in the concertive loan company have become emancipated. The world is a better place for that teamwork, and it is reassuring to be able to provide an update that is still inspiring.

Chapter 4 featured Atul Gawande, the son of immigrants and a surgeon and Harvard Medical School professor who does his own research about how to organize the field of medicine in ways that reduce risks to patients and bring down the costs at the same time. Although Dr. Gawande gives most of the credit to the use of checklists, I think the fact that the most effective checklists are put together and enforced by a competent team with hands-on experience with the process gives considerable credit to concertive decision making or teamwork. (And lists not created by a team can be hazardous or even deadly, as we have seen with the U.S. Forest Service's Standard Firefighting Orders.) Dr. Gawande also discovered that the complexity and riskiness of the construction of high-rise buildings and flying airplanes also require checklists and teamwork.

In chapter 4 we also learned from the medical community in Grand Junction, Colorado, that both risks and costs are reduced when doctors team up, sharing electronic health data and agreeing on fees. If the medical establishment heeds these reforms, this rich country should move up the ranks from its shameful position today into those of the other advanced countries of the world. The Grand Junction experience teaches us that the *Carte Vitale* could work in the United States as well as in France and Germany at a great cut in medical costs to the patients.

Chapter 5 showed us again the value of repeated data points while studying organizations. The U.S. Forest Service has been a much admired organization since the publication of Herbert Kaufman's book *The Forest Ranger: A Study in Administrative Behavior* in 1960. In it Kaufman provides an overall description of the agency as well as such important variables as identification with the organization and its effect on decision making. Connie Bullis followed up 25 years later with a study of the same organization and variables and found that the level of identification had decreased, no doubt because of increased bureaucratization which was in turn a reaction to external pressures. The Rules, the Standard Firefighting Orders, had become a contentious list, unhelpful in emergency situations, and the cause of discursive closure, according to the work of Jennifer Ziegler.

Ziegler argues that some progress has been made in the USFS and some degree of discursive opening has occurred. However, we see that as early as 1969, student of public administration Orion F. White Jr. had looked at government agencies and saw a trend in which they were becoming more and more bureaucratically mechanical, and less responsive and flexible. He gave us a descriptive neologism to apply to what the USFS bureaucrats had done to the memory of their firefighters who had been killed in the line of duty fighting wildland fires: They used the 10 Standard Firefighting Orders, the Rules, as *a tool for creating* "blamability," blaming the dead for not following sheepishly a set of rules which, if followed literally, would have produced paralysis, or what Tillich called the fearful state of "nonbeing." We also considered the hypothesis that the process of aging may have had a deleterious effect on the USFS and may be a general condition among governmental and nongovernmental organizations.

We closed the chapter with a recent study of employee commitment in U.S. government agencies showing the USFS in a dismal ranking, near the bottom. Commitment is the behavioral manifestation of identification, once a proud characteristic of the rangers. All of this shows the value of repeated data gathering in organizations. Then there was Craig Melville, the fire seminar graduate who joined the Helena Hotshots to fight fires so that he could understand the Fire Orders and the teams using them. He gave us a more balanced view of risk and foreshadowed McCurdy's discussion of the normalization of risk. Melville gave us a modifier, *smart*, in advising when to take a risk that may help us find a balance between cowardice and brashness. Inspired by his exploration I offered a definition of smart risk as "the willing and courageous acceptance of the probability of threat because it is balanced by the ability and resources to resist nonbeing." Another phrase for it might be *reasoned courage*. After writing that definition I realized that it might also cover a corporate cabal; a small group of executives could secretly plan shortcuts in their products that could *create* risks to employees, customers, and society at large.

I recalled a paper written with a former undergraduate student in the early '70s who had gone on to Harvard Law School and kept in touch. He taught me the law about conspiracy so that we could put it in our paper delivered at a national communication convention. The title is "Conspiracies, Corporations, Communication."[7] It begins with a quote from Kenneth Burke's *A Rhetoric of Motives* paired with a definition from my 1965 *Shorter Oxford English Dictionary:* "Conspiracy is as natural as breathing" and "Conspire ... *conspirare* lit ... 'to breathe together.'"[8] To give a brief summary, the conspiracy law did not apply to members of the same corporation! Why not? Because a corporation is an artificial person, and everyone knows a person cannot conspire with him- or herself. We called for a change in the law. I still believe the law should be changed.

In chapter 6 we returned to NASA for several more data points—namely, the tragic failures of the space shuttles *Challenger* and *Columbia*. Research shows that the exemplary open communication practices and teamwork that von Braun fostered during the early period of NASA's existence, the original technical culture, were no longer in use. The *Challenger* accident would not have happened if NASA had continued the hallowed tradition that the contractor had the burden of proof. The OTC had given way to the new culture captured by the slogan, "Faster, Better, Cheaper," hence there was the time pressure to launch *now*. Budget cuts and a diminished financial and popular commitment to the space program after the successful trips by astronauts to the Moon and back created a new culture, one that abandoned the smart risk approach of the Apollo Program and the OTC and instead emphasized the meeting of schedules, the cutting of costs, and an unwarranted temerity or boldness—the unwarranted courage of Tillich. *Columbia* brought us more of the same. The mission management team valued keeping on schedule over aborting the flight or even taking more imagery, as requested by the engineers, to determine the extent of damage the "foam" bricks had caused.

While still teaching on the campus of the University of Colorado Boulder, I was asked to have dinner with a guest speaker sponsored by the engineering schools. We were joined by one other faculty member, Patricia Nelson Limerick, who would later introduce the speaker, Roger Boisjoly, the Morton Thiokol engineer who recommended against the launch of *Challenger* during the conference call the night before because he did not have data appropriate to the cold weather at the time of the launch. Earlier at dinner Boisjoly answered our questions about the effects of his stance for technical standards. The corporation and the community had decided he was the blamable one. People put dead animals and other foul objects in his mailbox. He was shunned by members of his church at home in Utah. But when Professor Limerick introduced him to the audience, the engineering students gave him a standing ovation. A hero's welcome it was indeed. This gave me some faith in what the engineering students were learning. I later wondered, when they take jobs will they also resist managers who order them to make things Faster, Better, Cheaper?

Howard McCurdy, as we saw, had cited Orion White's 1969 article on the increasing bureaucratization of governmental agencies over time, with aging. Bringing the topic up to date, McCurdy concluded that as NASA matured and left that period when it could do no wrong, it did lose administrative flexibility and high standards because of increasing bureaucratization.

Chapter 7 was a narration of reactions to my book on *Apollo, Challenger,* and *Columbia,* demonstrating the wide interest in hearing how open communication and teamwork can serve as risk discovery, analysis, and management. Even NASA took notice of the subtitle, *The Decline of the Space*

Program, and invited me in 2005 and 2006 to talk about the communication practices of Apollo so that its young managers and engineers could learn how we did it, how we went to the Moon.

"At risk" and "risky" are our homeless neighbors in chapter 8. I had reported that the homeless shelter we toured—the St. Francis Center—had an employment office that had found more than 200 full-time jobs for homeless guests in 2012. This morning, a day in the fall of 2014, I received an e-mail message from the director of the SFC, Tom Luehrs, who had read the first draft of chapter 8. This is an addition I gladly make: "Our employment office got jobs for 465 people in 2013." Now I am curious: Did the employment office get better? Do employers have more trust in the SFC employment office? Is the economy improving that much? Or is it all of these and more?

In the larger society we found encouraging the experiments the cities of Denver, Phoenix, and Nashville, among others, have conducted with the Housing First program and how they have more than paid off. These cities have saved money and reduced the risks for the most vulnerable persons in our society: the chronically homeless. It also supports the thesis of this book that this risk reduction has been accomplished because of the cooperation, argumentation, and conciliation by disparate elements of these cities: homeless people, care providers, and politicians, plus representatives of businesses and churches who served on commissions to help mediate the risks. Their open, concertive communication and teamwork have shown the way. New increases in the population of homelessness was hypothesized as being caused by an increasing, unprecedented *income inequality* in the United States, the privatization of risk in a risk society, and rising housing costs. The logical connection between income inequality plus rising costs of housing and homelessness *must* be thoroughly researched. Recommendations must come that will reduce inequality.

Chapter 9 showed again how ideas first introduced in the Introduction and chapter 1 have interacted with case studies to provide new insights about managing complexity and risk by means of open communication and teamwork. The Aviation Safety Reporting System is the epitome of this integration. With the *original principles* of the system, the written report is an open communication channel in which to report potential risks in a complex, dangerous business. The reporters remain anonymous. The reports are coded by a neutral third party, and the entire industry is alerted about the hazards and dangers. Two communication practices, automatic responsibility and the ASRS, promoted by different organizations (the former by NASA, the latter by the Federal Aviation Administration), have given people the chance to take responsibility for risks and dangers, and they prove that people will do it when they know that no harm will come to them for reporting the truth. These practices should be models for the future.

I shall continue to watch Safe2Tell. Since the shootings at Columbine High School, in Colorado we have desperately needed an organization like this to help us prevent people from taking guns and bombs into our schools. I am happy to report that in the time since I wrote chapter 9, members of both the Republican and Democratic parties in the Colorado State Legislature have promised to give Safe2Tell state backing. It bears repeating that this organization came about because of the cooperation of people in different government agencies and citizens. It is interorganizational concertive communication and teamwork that have brought us this far.

In chapter 10 we looked at academic and business studies of participation. The Age of Participation had been proclaimed, but none of the authors in either camp also invoked the other Age, the Age of Risk. I have consciously brought these two Ages, Risk and Participation, to a confluence in our collective awareness and to claim that participation is an answer to risk, particularly if we use reasoned courage and smart risk. The business writers used the word *risk* more often than the academics, but their usage was to denote financial loss, and they tend to use *risk aversive* as a negative term for companies that are afraid to test new ideas. We should all have some of that, but let's call it *dumb-risk aversive*. We should think of one Age as the antidote to the bane of the other. The Age of Participation can modify if not replace the Age of Risk.

One of the most educational experiences I had while composing these chapters was to see how different sections of our society are linked with regard to complexity, risk, and effectiveness. Kenneth Burke wrote that the "most practical form of thought that one can think of . . . has been described as analogical extension . . . ,"[9] his word *practical* bringing us back to pragmatism. There is a kind of pragmatic beauty also in the *analogical* genius some of the characters in our drama have shown. Atul Gawande, for example, saw the relevance of taking a trip from Harvard to the Boeing Company in Seattle because he saw an analog in checklists for flight crews that he thought might help surgical teams. The same genius made him take the trip up the high-rise building being built near his hospital in Boston. He must have seen some parallel resemblances to think he would learn again how to improve surgery, this time the need for communication points in a checklist for a complex operation. These were all positive advances, as opposed to the list of Fire Orders, which were developed by administrators to place blame and did not work because the steps were not in order and did not have that "all-or-none" quality that Dr. Gawande mentioned. Oh, and Gawande also pointed out the redundancy in the human body, what with its multiple pairs of organs and parts.

Another way we saw the analogical power at work was when Karl Weick discovered in a single fire—the Mann Gulch disaster—some parallel factors that he could see led to the collapse of sensemaking in organizations in general. Dr. Berwick read Weick's essay and discovered analogical lessons he began to preach to his medical colleagues, lessons from firefighting that improve the practice of medicine—for example, using an escape fire and dropping useless tools. We must remember that Berwick also saw teamwork in quality circles and other forms of industrial teamwork that would prove to be useful to the medical community. I think we can also count the solvability link between Apollo and Housing First made by Rachel Maddow. And the genius of von Braun in seeing analogies, what with earthquake prediction sensors in strategic networks. And who can forget the five *neins*?

I would submit that as we learn more about complexity, risk, and their resolution, people with this analogical ability who also *seek* analogs will become highly valued problem solvers.

We also saw the possibility of the disastrous effects of aging on organizations in the case of three government agencies: the USFS, NASA, and the Veteran's Administration. This suggests that external reviews and analysis by independent researchers should be tied to the chronological age of organizations. MSNBC's Rachel Maddow linked the Apollo Program's record of solvability to that of Phoenix's record of eliminating homelessness among the veterans of that city: the impossible became solvable. We also saw how the principles of the ASRS could be successfully adapted analogically to other risk-reduction efforts such as Safe2Tell.

These and other connections suggest an overall strategy of dealing with complexity and risk in the future, one broader than the specific conclusions that follow. The plan begins with cataloguing the riskiest organizations in the country and demanding that they adopt, on an industry-wide basis, the basic principles of the ASRS as described earlier. In addition, the riskiest industries and other organizations should be required to develop a risk communication system, or RCS. The RCS should satisfy several criteria, one being that it instills something similar to automatic responsibility in all employees or stakeholders, from bottom to top. Other criteria would be that it reduces vertical semantic-information distance and time with regard to perceived risks. In addition, the RCS should allow for redundant channels of communication, particularly for an upward-directed alarm clock to awaken everyone. Finally, all organizations should consider how to increase the participation of all stakeholders. We should spread the value to the individual and society by preaching automatic responsibility in regard to risks in political, business, educational, and nonprofit organizations.

Conclusions and Afterthoughts

There are some specifics that can be enumerated. They are based on observations, conclusions from research findings and first-hand experiences, and as we just saw, some analogical perceptions that should help improve the management of risk and complexity.

1. *Open communication* means that anyone in an organization with competence to perceive a problem, if not solve it, should feel free to bring problems and risks to the attention of all members of the organization, particularly colleagues and, simultaneously, those at the top, and without

any fear of reprisal. It is illustrated by the MSFC's automatic responsibility and the original principles of the ASRS. A person who discovers a risk or problem should be able to trust that he or she can bring it into the open without being punished. (Remember the engineer who made a mistake, admitted it, and received a bottle of champagne from von Braun.) This practice of open communication by members will benefit the organization and society as a whole, and the individual will grow with the exercise of reasoned courage and integrity that goes with truth telling. I have come to believe there should be a whistleblowing civil right for all Americans, to the degree of calling out risks to workers, consumers, and society.

2. The normal scalar chain of command in organizational hierarchies should have provisions that allow for either eliminating or shortening or bypassing it whenever a serious risk and the creation of problem-solving teams to eliminate it is discovered at lower levels and requires additional resources to manage it. *Shortening* in this context applies to both the length of the chain of command and the time taken to communicate the problem or risk upward. The Paul-Tompkins law of risk communication reminds us that early awareness of a risk and creation of problem-solving teams to eliminate it are essential for safety, lowered costs, increased profits, and the success of the organization's projects.

3. Teamwork or participation, as opposed to consultation, characterized by open and participatory communication within a group, has been shown to work, increasing profits, increasing control, and reducing risks. It has worked in making circuit boards, going to the Moon, improving surgical outcomes in an international experiment, using escape fires, and emancipating women in Bangladesh, and in recent years it has turned out more and better scholarly research papers than have solo researchers. Several of these successes have occurred in enterprises with the highest known rates of complexity and risk. We must note, however, that participatory groups I watched at work at NASA ran into complicated risks that they had to send up the hierarchy. Von Braun seemed to know that a new working group had to be appointed in such a case, loading the group with people of different disciplines, making the complexity in the group equal to that of the risk problem.

4. There is some evidence, however, that team members need to learn the skills of argument and group problem solving—for example, how to disagree in an agreeable manner. As experienced team members need to be replaced, newcomers should be trained. Oh, yes, and managers should definitely receive training also. Personnel considerations should include the consequences for someone who insists on playing the role of heroic star, unwilling to listen to others.

5. Organizations should *formally and explicitly* establish the presumption and burden of proof in significant transactions with suppliers and customers. Otherwise the presumption should be with the buyer and the burden of proof with the seller because of the asymmetry of relevant information. Let the buyer beware enough to demand that the seller assumes and exercises the burden of proof to the buyer's satisfaction. Appropriate assignment of presumption and burden of proof should be established for all major contracts, especially when dangerous risks are likely to emerge.

6. Risks to organizations, workers, consumers, and society can be managed best by a combination of verbal and mathematical risk analysis. The mathematical approach needs to be used *with* verbal arguments, including oral, face-to-face discussions: they complement each other and provide redundancy. Risks to organizations, workers, consumers, and society can be managed best by a somewhat redundant combination of verbal and mathematical risk analysis.

7. Lists have been used in both positive and negative ways. No list can anticipate *all* of the surprising events that can occur in the enterprise it is supposed to control. Lists obviously should *not* be made to create "blamability" in risky occupations. Lists seem to work best in complex enterprises when they specify steps that must be executed in a precise order. Checklists work in complex activities if they are created by teams who collectively have a degree of complexity equal to the problem, have breaks or steps in order to call all specialized members together for communication and decision making by the team; it is also most effective if the checklist is created, enforced, and modified as needed by competent team members, participatory colleagues. The notion of smart risk should be taught in all risky occupations, stressing the flexibility of teams to respond to changes in reality.

8. The practice of internal penetration—two layers up and two down—should be attempted by managers and supervisors in complex, vertical institutions. External penetration of suppliers and customers is strongly recommended on any new projects if there is a possible risk and the organization has the technical capacity (experts) to commit to it.

9. In an organization in which either the likelihood or impact of a risk is judged (quantitatively or qualitatively) to be high, redundant channels of communication *must be created* and made known to all members in a position to affect those risks in any way.

10. The *social* problems of cities and states should be addressed by teams of disparate stakeholders in the community. The teams should be led by a chair who realizes that on complex problems and risks, the members should be willing to let others have what they want or need for its own sake in order to gain what they want or need for its own sake: *coordinated action* with smart compromises. Organizers should seek members on a bipartisan interest basis, including but not limited to people from business, education, labor, and those who suffer from the social problems.

11. We live in what is called a "risk society" in part because we cannot avoid all of the old hazards and new risks. To be totally risk aversive would produce *nonbeing*, to use Paul Tillich's existential term. Nor should we be so bold as to be fearless, or we will again succumb to nonbeing. We must seek the balance between temerity and cowardice, but as life becomes more complex and riskier, we should think of living with smart risks and reasoned courage. We should work toward merging the Age of Participation to the point of dominance over the Age of Risk. For persons who cannot accept the responsibility of participation and open communication, there will remain for some time to come jobs that have no such requirement.

12. Organizations should invite outside researchers to conduct holistic, idiographic or diagnostic studies of them periodically for at least two reasons: (1) to find communication problems that may be producing or failing to reduce risks, and (2) to check for the unsuspected effects of organizational aging. If they cannot afford one of the professional consulting companies, which in general have received withering criticism from

within, by an insider,[10] they should get in touch with local universities to find graduate students and faculty eager to do such research.

* * *

I started writing this book by stating premises that could lead to conclusions, but when dealing with complex realities, a chain of minor premises could go in different directions and dictate unexpected conclusions. The epigraph at the beginning of chapter 1 is by Richard Rorty, who composed it for an assignment to describe the future of religion. He wrote that anticlericalism and atheism were among his basic beliefs, that he had been a Socialist but was rethinking his faith in that system. He could not imagine *any* past event as holy, only the ideal future that he described in the following major premises: "Communication would be domination-free, caste would be unknown, hierarchy would be a matter of temporary pragmatic convenience, and power would be entirely at the disposal of the free agreement of a literate and well-educated electorate."[11] Paul Tillich was fired from his university job and had to leave Germany because he publicly opposed Hitler and Nazism. Good recommendation say I. Participation for him seems to be a courageous way of being by transcending egoism.[12] Again, there is religious and moral support for open communication and participation, even for atheists.

What if the best way to face increasing complexity and risk in the future is not by seeking a new and grand theory? Cynthia Stohl admits she was "naïve" to search for a unitary and comprehensive theory in her studies of globalization.[13] I came to the same conclusion after working on the theory of concertive control. Theories also change with new technologies and new ideas about ways to work. The frequent changes in our theories are well described in the Epilogue of the book by George Cheney and colleagues, *Organizational Communication in an Age of Globalization: Issues, Reflections, Practices*. Could it be that the way to achieve Rorty's vision is not by a grand theory of organizational communication, but instead by pragmatism, or combined with critical realism, a set of practices and principles that have worked to liberate as well as produce? In discovering another Fayol's bridge? We could save and gain so much if we simply adopted the *Carte Vitale,* France's national health insurance card discussed in chapter 4. Globalization provides other practices we should adopt. The most exciting organizational experience of my life, however, was when we escaped globalization by leaving this planet. It was ever so risky and complicated, but we did it. One of the big surprises to me was the importance of welders to the project—the need for them to reduce risk by finding the proper method of welding exotic metals together for the first time. We did it, in short, not so much with a grand theory as with able, pragmatic people taking smart risks with reasoned courage by means of lessons learned through and about open communication and teamwork. Okay, we did have some geniuses, but they could not do it alone.

In our ever changing world, organizations need to fight the tendency to succumb to arthritic bureaucracies, be blinded by profit, and demean those who work for them. Organizations should be encouraged to use those practices of communication that have proved to work for people all over the world, and look for new ones as well to reduce risks for everyone and move us all ever closer to first, the Age of Participation, and second, Richard Rorty's ideal communication situation.

Notes

1. Phillip K. Tompkins, "Management Qua Communication in Rocket Research and Development," *Communication Monographs* 44, no. 1 (1977): 24. doi:10.1080/03637757709390111.

2. Petr Beckmann, *A History of Pi,* 3rd ed. (New York: The Golem Press of St. Martin's Press, 1976), 37.

3. Richard McKeon, *Introduction to Aristotle,* 2nd ed. (Chicago: The University of Chicago Press, 1973), xviii.

4. Leonard Mlodinow, *Euclid's Window: The Story of Geometry from Parallel Lines to Hyperspace* (New York: Simon and Schuster, 2001), 30.

5. Phillip K. Tompkins, "The Functions of Human Communication in Organization," in *The Handbook of Rhetorical and Communication Theory,* ed. Carroll C. Arnold and John Waite Bowers (Boston: Allyn & Bacon, 1984), 659–719.

6. Nick Anderson, "Can the English Major Be Saved?" Reprinted from the *Washington Post* in the *Denver Post,* April 13, 2015, 3C.

7. Phillip K. Tompkins and Michael A. Lampert, "Conspiracies, Corporations, Communication" (paper presented at the annual meeting of the Speech Communication Association, New York City, November 14, 1980).

8. Kenneth Burke, *A Rhetoric of Motives* (New York: Prentice-Hall, 1950), 166.

9. Kenneth Burke, *Permanence and Change,* 2nd ed. (Indianapolis: Bobbs-Merrill, 1965), 96.

10. Matthew Stewart, *The Management Myth: Why the Experts Keep Getting it Wrong* (New York: W. W. Norton, 2009).

11. Richard Rorty, "Anticlericalism and Atheism," in *The Future of Religion,* ed. Santiago Zabala (New York: Columbia University Press, 2005), 40.

12. Paul Tillich, *The Courage to Be* (New Haven: Yale University Press, 1952/1980), 156–57, 165, 181, 187.

13. Cynthia Stohl, "Globalization Theory," in *Engaging Organizational Communication: Theory and Research,* ed. Steve May and Dennis K. Mumby (Thousand Oaks, CA: Sage, 2005), 247.

Acknowledgments

First, I would like to express my thanks to Marifran Mattson, head of the Brian Lamb School of Communication at Purdue University. We met because of her wonderful outreach work with alumni of the Department and now School of Communication. She first suggested back in late 2013 that a book that was still completely inside my skin might be published by the Purdue University Press. She encouraged me via long-distance communication throughout the conception and writing of the entire manuscript. She also gave me the name of the then-director of PUP, Charles Watkinson. Charles was a tough but helpful publisher who encouraged me to submit a book proposal to the editorial board of PUP, but forbade me from mentioning in the proposal my two tours of duty at Purdue. Thanks, Marifran.

Omar Swartz is currently an associate professor of humanities and social science, director of the master of social science degree program, and coordinator of the law studies minor at the University of Colorado Denver. He became a valued colleague when my wife Elaine and I retired from the University of Colorado Boulder and moved to downtown Denver, just across Cherry Creek from CU Denver. I was intrigued with a man with a PhD in communication and a law degree from Duke University. Omar would not let me retire, inviting me to walk over the bridge to visit with him and his colleagues on campus. He invited me to give the keynote address to the Rocky Mountain Communication Association Convention in 2004. He got me appointed to the graduate faculty of CU Denver so that I could serve on an MA thesis committee; the student's topic was homelessness, a topic he had heard me discuss in a public lecture—yes, one that Omar had arranged. Omar also put me to work reading some of his work, plus writing an introduction for one of his books and a chapter for another. He helps me find documents electronically that at least one of us thinks I need to study. Reading his work and talking to him about it became an informal tutorial, a much-needed and *deeper* look at Richard Rorty and neo-pragmatism than I had made before.

Gregory Desilet and I met at a National Communication Association Convention in 1993. We played a lot of golf, and I now thank him for the strokes he generously gave me—and still took my money. (I gave him the nickname "Ace" after he made a hole in one and some money on the same swing.) Off the course he kept me reading philosophy, helping me learn most of what I know about Jacques Derrida and postmodernism. Over the years we have also been reading each other's work in the hope of improving it. His books have a central place in my bookcase. I want to thank Greg for reading the first draft of the Introduction and chapter 1 of this book, making some suggestions, and encouraging me to complete the other chapters.

I first met Carey Candrian when I served on her doctoral dissertation committee at the University of Colorado Boulder after my retirement. We scaled the distance between Boulder and Denver to develop our scholarly relationship. That distance was shortened when she did her dissertation research in Denver. I was fascinated by her work in an emergency room of a Denver hospital and in a Denver hospice where I had helped a friend and neighbor move into her final lodging. Carey and I became colleagues as she tutored me in health communication and I invited her to coauthor a book chapter on concertive control and communication in organizations quoted in this book. Chapter 4 also draws from a "working paper" we have seen move through several drafts. Carey is now an assistant professor of health communication at the University of Colorado School of Medicine.

I must acknowledge two medical doctors, Alan Lidsky and Richard Kem, for reading an earlier draft of chapter 4 and commenting on it. Thanks, Docs! I hope you approve of what I added after you read it.

Timothy Kuhn, who came to CU Boulder as I was retiring, served on Carey Candrian's committee. As I began to write this book, Tim was generous with ideas about recent developments in organizational communication. Chapter 5 recommends that the history of the U.S. Forest Service be studied using Kuhn's theory inspired by the Montreal School of organizational communication—an emphasis on texts and conversations. Thanks, Tim.

I was blessed to direct the doctoral work of Connie A. Bullis and her important research in the U.S. Forest Service, the scale of which was much greater and more ambitious than most dissertations I have read. I was proud to be the second author on an article published in *Communication Monographs* based on her dissertation that is summarized in the beginning of chapter 5 of this book. I also admire the courage with which she won a battle with a serious illness. Thanks, Connie. Gregory S. Larson, professor in the Department of Communication Studies at the University of Montana, was also a graduate student I advised who did important research discussed in some detail in this book. I was proud to be second author of an article written with him based on his dissertation research. In fact, Greg works so effectively in several different areas of teaching and research that he and that work are discussed in more than one chapter of this book.

George Cheney let me draw upon his vast resources for this book, sharing his knowledge of relevant articles and books, many of them written by him. I mention him also because of my fond memories of an earlier life when we worked together on research and theory projects discussed in this book. Jim Barker is another student from that era who conducted one of the important studies considered in detail in this book. He also helped with answers to questions I put to him while writing this book on complexity and risk. Jennifer Ziegler was in the fire seminar and she has continued to work on the fire line. She was helpful in bringing me up to date on her activities and publications.

I must say thanks to my son, Terry Tompkins, who gave me an inspirational book for Father's Day over 20 years ago, *Young Men and Fire*. That brilliant book inspired me to launch the fire seminar at CU Boulder mentioned in chapter 5. Terry has fought many a wildfire from California to Quebec, Canada, and in our state of Colorado. He is now an administrator for the U.S. Forest Service in the Mystic District of the Black Hills National Forest. He also granted me a couple of interviews quoted in chapter 5 of this book. Thanks also to Kristofer "Tofer" Lewis and his wife, Emily Tompkins Lewis, for helping me set up the new computer needed for a new and complex book, with producing figures for the book, for other technicalities and kindnesses, and for just being Tofer and Emily.

I am thankful for the systematic questions and suggestions supplied by Kelley Kimm, the PUP production editor assigned to this project. Her work made it a better book.

Michael Lampert was a bright undergraduate student of mine back in the early 1970s who has kept in touch during law school at Harvard and a career practicing and learning law in New York and London. Today he is a wise counselor. He came up with a copy of the learned paper we presented at the annual meeting of the Speech Communication Association (now National Communication Association) in 1980 that is cited in this book. Thanks also to Tom Luehrs for putting up with me as a volunteer for 17 years. He also read the first draft of chapter 8 about the risks and riskiness of our homeless guests. Thanks also to the staff and volunteers at St. Francis Center—and to the guests themselves. May we come to find the will to end their status as homeless humans. And thanks to Leonard Cox who, as a former student of mine, inspired me to seek greater heights—including that of a volunteer in a homeless shelter.

Jessica R. Snitko is a graduate student in the Brian Lamb School of Communication at Purdue University. She helped me as an author's research assistant, performing useful library tasks. Thanks, Jessica.

Now I give thanks and pay respects to two mentors of mine who have slipped the surly bonds of this world. One is W. Charles Redding, my doctoral adviser and guru who gave my name to Walter Wiesman, who in turn played a many-faceted role in the Apollo Project. Walt offered me a job at NASA on the basis of Charles's recommendation that changed my life in nothing but the best ways.

Finally, there is the one person without whom I could not have written this book. She helped with ideas, their expression, footnotes, references, and proofreading—thus helping manage the risk and complexity involved in seeing an idea become a book. Thanks, Elaine. This book is dedicated to you, Elaine, and to our "kids": Todd, Kari, Terry, and Emily.

Bibliography

Akerlof, George A. "The Market for 'Lemons': Quality Uncertainties and the Market Mechanism." *Quarterly Journal of Economics* 84, no. 3 (1970): 488–500. doi:10.2307/1879431.

Audi, Robert, ed. *The Cambridge Dictionary of Philosophy*, 2nd ed. Cambridge, UK: Cambridge University Press, 1995.

Barker, James R. *The Discipline of Teamwork: Participation and Concertive Control.* Thousand Oaks, CA: Sage, 1999.

———. "Tightening the Iron Cage: Concertive Control in Self-Managing Work Teams." *Administrative Science Quarterly* 38, no. 3 (1993): 408–37. doi:10.2307/2393374.

Barker, James R., and Phillip K. Tompkins. "Identification in the Self-Managing Organization: Characteristics of Target and Tenure." *Human Communication Research* 21, no. 2 (1994): 223–40. doi:10.1111/j.1468-2958.1994.tb00346.x.

Beck, Ulrich. *Risk Society: Towards a New Modernity.* London: Sage Publications, 1992.

Beckmann, Petr. *A History of Pi*, 3rd ed. New York: The Golem Press, 1976.

Berwick, Donald M. *Escape Fire: Designs for the Future of Health Care.* San Francisco: Jossey-Bass, 2004.

Berwick, Donald M., A. Blanton Godfrey, and Jane Roessner. *Curing Health Care: New Strategies for Quality Improvement.* San Francisco: Jossey-Bass, 1990.

Blakeman, Chuck. *Why Employees are Always a Bad Idea (and Other Business Diseases of the Industrial Age).* Highlands Ranch, CO: Crankset, 2014.

Block, Peter. Foreword to *The Age of Participation: New Governance for the Workplace and the World*, by Patricia McLagan and Christo Nel, ix–xiv. San Francisco: Berrett-Koehler, 1995.

Browning, Larry Davis. "Lists and Stories as Organizational Communication." *Communication Theory* 2, no. 4 (1992): 281–302. doi:10.1111/j.1468-2885.1992 .tb00045.x.

Bullis, Connie A., and Phillip K. Tompkins. "The Forest Ranger Revisited: A

Study of Control Practices and Identification." *Communication Monographs* 56, no. 4 (1989): 287–305. doi:10.1080/03637758909390266.

Burke, Kenneth. *Attitudes toward History*, 3rd ed. Berkeley: University of California Press, 1984.

———. *A Grammar of Motives*. New York: Prentice-Hall, 1945.

———. *Language as Symbolic Action*. Berkeley: University of California Press, 1968.

———. *Permanence and Change*, 2nd ed. Indianapolis: Bobbs-Merrill, 1965.

———. *A Rhetoric of Motives*. New York: Prentice-Hall, 1950.

Cass, Stein. "Risk Management in the Aerospace Industry: Past and Present." Paper presented at the quarterly meeting of the Colorado Chapter of the International Council of Systems Engineering, December 2004.

Cheney, George, and Dana L. Cloud. "Doing Democracy, Engaging the Material: Employee Participation and Labor Activity in an Age of Market Globalization." *Management Communication Quarterly* 19, no. 4 (2006): 501–40. doi:10.1177/0893318905285485.

Cheney, George, Lars Thoger Christensen, Theodore E. Zorn Jr., and Shiv Ganesh. *Organizational Communication in an Age of Globalization: Issues, Reflections, Practices*. Prospect Heights, IL: Waveland Press, 2004.

Cherry, Colin. *On Human Communication*, 2nd ed. Cambridge, MA: MIT Press, 1966.

Connell, Linda J. "Cross-Industry Applications of a Confidential Reporting Model." *ASRS Research Papers* 62 (2004): 1–13.

Cushman, Donald P., and Phillip K. Tompkins. "A Theory of Rhetoric for Contemporary Society." *Philosophy and Rhetoric* 13, no. 1 (1980): 43–67.

Deetz, Stanley, and Dennis Mumby. "Power, Discourse, and the Workplace: Reclaiming the Critical Tradition." In *Communication Yearbook 13*, edited by James A. Anderson, 18–47. Newbury Park, CA: Sage Publications, 1990.

Edwards, Richard. *Contested Terrain: The Transformation of the Workplace in the Twentieth Century*. New York: Basic Books, 1979.

Gasiorek, Jessica, and Howard Giles. "Communication, Volunteering, and Aging: A Research Agenda." *International Journal of Communication* 7 (2013): 2659–77.

Gawande, Atul. *Being Mortal: Medicine and What Matters in the End*. New York: Metropolitan Books, 2014.

———. *The Checklist Manifesto: How to Get Things Right.* New York: Picador, 2009.

———. *Complications: A Surgeon's Notes on an Imperfect Science.* New York: Picador, 2002.

———. "The Cost Conundrum: Expensive Health Care Can Be Harmful." *The New Yorker,* June 1, 2009, 36–44.

Gladwell, Malcolm. "Million Dollar Murray: Why Problems Like Homelessness May Be Easier to Solve than Manage." *The New Yorker,* February 13 and 20, 2006, 96–98, 161–67.

Halbfinger, David M., and Richard A. Oppel Jr. "Loss of the Shuttle: On the Ground; First the Air Shook with Sound, and Then Debris Rained Down." *New York Times,* February 2, 2003, 27.

Hall, Douglas T., Schneider, Benjamin, and Nygren, Harold T. "Personal Factors in Organizational Identification," *Administrative Science Quarterly* 15 (1970): 176–90.

Jacobsen, Annie. *Operation Paperclip: The Secret Intelligence Program that Brought Nazi Scientists to America.* New York: Little, Brown, 2014.

Jensen, Claus. *No Downlink: A Dramatic Narrative about the Challenger Accident and Our Time.* Translated by Barbara Haveland. New York: Farrar Straus and Giroux, 1996.

Kaufman, Herbert. *The Forest Ranger: A Study in Administrative Behavior.* Baltimore: The Johns Hopkins Press, 1967.

Kuhn, Timothy. "A Communicative Theory of the Firm: Developing an Alternative Perspective on Intra-Organizational Power and Stakeholder Relationships." *Organization Studies* 29, no. 8–9 (2008): 1227–54. doi:10.1177 /0170840608094778.

Kuhn, Timothy, and Stanley Deetz. "Critical Theory and Corporate Social Responsibility: Can/Should We Get Beyond Cynical Reasoning?" In *The Oxford Handbook of Corporate Social Responsibility,* edited by Andrew Crane, Abagail McWilliams, Dirk Matten, Jeremy Moon, and Donald S. Siegel, 173–96. Oxford: Oxford University Press, 2008.

Kusmer, Kenneth L. *Down and Out, On the Road: The Homeless in American History.* New York: Oxford University Press, 2002.

Larson, Gregory S., and Phillip K. Tompkins. "Ambivalence and Resistance: A Study of Management in a Concertive Control System." *Communication*

Monographs 72, no. 1 (2005): 1–21. doi:10.1080/0363775052000342508.

Lash, Scott, and Brian Wynn. Introduction to *Risk Society: Towards a New Modernity* by Ulrich Beck. London: Sage Publications, 1992.

Lepore, Jill. "Richer and Poorer: Accounting for Inequality." *The New Yorker,* March 16, 2015, 26–32.

Lupton, Deborah. *Risk,* 2nd ed. London: Routledge, 2013.

Lurie, Stephen. "The Astonishing Decline of Homelessness in America." *The Atlantic,* August 26, 2013. http://theatlantic.com/business/archive/2013/08 /the-astonishing-decline-of homelessness.

Maclean, Norman. *Young Men and Fire.* Chicago: University of Chicago Press, 1992.

McConnell, Malcolm. *Challenger: A Major Malfunction: A True Story of Politics, Greed, and the Wrong Stuff.* Garden City, NY: Doubleday and Co., 1987.

McCurdy, Howard E. *Inside NASA: High Technology and Organizational Change in the U.S. Space Program.* Baltimore: The Johns Hopkins University Press, 1993.

McKeon, Richard, ed. *Introduction to Aristotle,* 2nd ed. Chicago: The University of Chicago Press, 1973.

McLagan, Patricia, and Christo Nel. *The Age of Participation: New Governance for the Workplace and the World.* San Francisco: Berrett-Koehler, 1995.

Melville, Craig, and Phillip K. Tompkins. "Fighting the Mundane Fire, Smartly! Training for Smart Risk." Paper presented at the Wurth Forum: Center of the American West, University of Colorado Boulder, February 17, 2001.

Mlodinow, Leonard. *Euclid's Window: The Story of Geometry from Parallel Lines to Hyperspace.* New York: Simon and Schuster, 2001.

Mockenhaupt, Brian. "Confessions of a Whistleblower: Dr. Sam Foote Reveals How He Went to War with the VA." *AARP Bulletin* 4 (Sept. 2014): 26–27, 40.

NASA. *Columbia Accident Investigation Board Report,* Volume 1. Washington, DC: Government Printing Office, 2003.

———. *Managing the Moon Program: Lessons Learned from Project Apollo,* Monographs in Aerospace History, No. 14. Washington, DC: NASA History Division, 1999.

Nieburg, Harold L. *In the Name of Science.* Chicago: Quadrangle, 1966.

Papa, Michael J., Mohammad A. Auwal, and Arvind Singhal. "Dialectic of Control and Emancipation in Organizing for Social Change: A Multitheoretic Study of the Grameen Bank in Bangladesh." *Communication Theory* 5, no. 3 (1995): 189–223. doi:10.1111/j.1468-2885.1995.tb00106.x.

Papa, Michael J., Mohammed A. Auwal, and Arvind Singhal, "Organizing for Social Change within Concertive Control Systems: Member Identification, Empowerment, and the Masking of Discipline," *Communication Monographs* 64 (1997): 189–223.

Papa, Michael J., Arvind Singhal, and Wendy H. Papa. *Organizing for Social Change: A Dialectic Journey of Theory and Praxis.* Thousand Oaks, CA: Sage, 2006.

Pathways to Housing. "Results in 'Mental Health.'" Accessed March 19, 2015. https://pathwaystohousing.org/tags/mental-health.

Perinbanayagam, Robert S. *Discursive Acts.* Hawthorne, NY: Aldine de Gruyter, 1991.

Perrow, Charles. *Normal Accidents: Living with High Risk Technologies.* New York: Basic Books, 1984.

Pronovost, Peter, Dale Needham, Sean Berenholtz, David Sinopoli, Haitao Chu, Sara Cosgrove, Bryan Sexton, et al. "An Intervention to Decrease Catheter-Related Bloodstream Infections in the ICU." *New England Journal of Medicine* 355 (2006): 2725–32. doi:10.1056/NEJMoa061115.

Ramcharitar, Nadina. "Keeping Law and Order in the Norwegian Oil and Gas Industry: The Challenges of Safety Regulations." In *Culture, Development, and Petroleum: An Ethnography of the High North,* edited by Jan-Oddvar Sornes, Larry Browning, and Jan Terje Henriksen. London: Routledge, in press 2015.

Reason, James T. *Managing the Risks of Organizational Accidents.* Brookfield, VT: Ashgate, 1997.

Redding, W. Charles. *Communication within the Organization.* New York: Industrial Communication Council, 1972.

Reid, T. R. *The Healing of America: A Global Quest for Better, Cheaper, and Fairer Health Care.* New York: Penguin, 2010.

Rorty, Richard. "Anticlericalism and Atheism." In *The Future of Religion,* edited by Santiago Zabala, 29–40. New York: Columbia University Press, 2005.

Rowan, Katherine E. "Why Some Health Risks Upset Us and Others Do Not: Risk Perception and Risk Communiction." *Spectra* (March 2015): 13–17.

Semler, Ricardo. *Maverick: The Success Story Behind the World's Most Unusual Workplace.* New York: Hachette Book Group, 1993.

Silva, Jennifer M. *Coming Up Short: Working-Class Adulthood in an Age of Uncertainty.* New York: Oxford University Press, 2013.

Simon, Herbert A. "On the Concept of Organizational Goal." *Administrative Science Quarterly* 9, no. 1 (1964): 1–22. doi:10.2307/2391519.

Stewart, Matthew. *The Management Myth: Why the Experts Keep Getting It Wrong.* New York: W. W. Norton, 2009.

Stohl, Cynthia. "Globalization Theory." In *Engaging Organizational Communication Theory and Research: Multiple Perspectives,* edited by Steve May and Dennis K. Mumby, 223–61. Thousand Oaks, CA: Sage, 2005.

———. *Organizational Communication: Connectedness in Action.* Thousand Oaks, CA: Sage, 1995.

Stohl, Cynthia, and George Cheney. "Participatory Practices/Paradoxical Practices: Communication and the Dilemmas of Organizational Democracy." *Management Communication Quarterly* 14, no. 3 (2001): 349–407. doi:10.1177 /0893318901143001.

Swartz, Omar, Katia Campbell, and Christina Pestana. *Neo-Pragmatism, Communication, and the Culture of Creative Democracy.* New York: Peter Lang, 2009.

Thackaberry, Jennifer Anne [Ziegler]. "Blaming the Dead: The Ethics of Accident Investigations in Wildland Firefighting." In *Case Studies in Organizational Communication: Ethical Perspectives and Practice,* edited by Steve May, 265–86. Thousand Oaks, CA: Sage, 2006.

———. "'Discursive Opening' and Closing in Organizational Self-Study: Culture as Trap and Tool in Wildland Firefighting Safety," *Management Communication Quarterly* 17 (2005): 319–59. doi:10.1177/0893318903259402.

———. "Wisdom in the Lessons Learned Library: Work Ethics and Firefighter Identities in the Fire Orders." In *Proceedings of the 8th International Wildland Fire Safety Summit, April 26–28, 2005 Missoula, Montana,* edited by Bret W. Butler and Marty E. Alexander. Hot Springs, SD: International Assembly of Wildland Fires, 2005.

Tillich, Paul. *The Courage to Be.* New Haven: Yale University Press, 1952/1980.

Tompkins, Elaine V., Phillip K. Tompkins, and George Cheney. "Organizations as Arguments: Discovering, Expressing, and Analyzing Premises for Decisions." *Journal of Management Systems* 1, no. 2 (1989): 35–48.

Tompkins, Phillip K. *Apollo, Challenger, Columbia: The Decline of the Space Program.* Los Angeles: Roxbury, 2005.

———. *Communication as Action.* Belmont, CA: Wadsworth, 1982.

———. "The Functions of Human Communication in Organization." In *Handbook of Rhetorical and Communication Theory,* edited by Carroll C. Arnold and John Waite Bowers, 659–719. Boston: Allyn and Bacon, 1984.

———. "Management Qua Communication in Rocket Research and Development." *Communication Monographs* 44, no. 1 (1977): 1–26. doi:10.1080 /03637757709390111.

———. "On Risk Communication as Interorganizational Control: The Case of the Aviation Safety Reporting System." In *Nothing to Fear: Risks and Hazards in American Society,* edited by Andrew Kirby, 203–39. Tucson: University of Arizona Press, 1990.

———. "Organizational Metamorphosis in Space Research and Development." *Communication Monographs* 45, no. 2 (1978): 110–18. doi:10.1080/036377 57809375958.

———. "Organizational Communication and Technological Risks." In *Risky Business: Communicating Issues of Science, Risk, and Public Policy,* edited by Lee Wilkins and Philip Paterson, 113–29. New York: Greenwood Press, 1991.

———. *Organizational Communication Imperatives: Lessons of the Space Program.* Los Angeles: Roxbury, 1993.

———. *Who Is My Neighbor? Communicating and Organizing to End Homelessness.* Boulder, CO: Paradigm, 2009.

Tompkins, Phillip K., James Barker, and Karen Lee Ashcraft. "Communication, Unobtrusive and Concertive Control in Contemporary Organizations: A Theoretical and Empirical Update." Unpublished paper, 2002.

Tompkins, Phillip K., and Carey Candrian. "Organizing Health: Communication Cures." Unpublished manuscript in progress.

Tompkins, Phillip K., and George Cheney. "Communication and Unobtrusive Control in Contemporary Organizations." In *Organizational Communication: Traditional Themes and New Directions,* edited by Robert D. McPhee and Phillip K. Tompkins, 179–210. Beverly Hills, CA: Sage, 1985.

Tompkins, Phillip K., and Tamla Clarke. "Managing Communicative Manifestations of Psychiatric Disorders at a Homeless Shelter." In *Stretching Boundaries: Cases in Organizational and Managerial Communication,* edited by Jeremy P. Fyke, Jeralyn Faris, and Patrice M. Buzzanell. New York: Routledge, in press.

Tompkins, Phillip K., Jeanne Y. Fisher, Dominic A. Infante, and Elaine L. Tompkins. "Kenneth Burke and the Inherent Characteristics of Formal Organizations: A Field Study." *Speech Monographs* 42, no. 2 (1975): 135–42. doi:10.1080/03637757509375887.

Tompkins, Phillip K., Kurt Heppard, and Craig Melville. "Deviance from Normality or Normalization of Deviance? Making Sense of the *Challenger* Launch Decision." *Organization* 5, no. 4 (1998): 620–29. doi:10.1177/1350508 49854010.

Tompkins, Phillip K., and Michael A. Lampert. "Conspiracies, Corporations, Communication." Paper presented at the annual meeting of the Speech Communication Association, New York, November 14, 1980.

Tompkins, Phillip K., Yvonne J. Montoya, and Carey Candrian. "Watch Your Neighbor Watching You: Applying Concertive Control in Changing Organizational Environments." In *An Integrated Approach to Communication Theory and Research,* 2nd ed., edited by Don W. Stacks and Michael B. Salwen, 370–86. New York: Routledge, 2009.

Tompkins, Phillip K., and Elaine Vanden Bout Anderson. *Communication Crisis at Kent State: A Case Study.* New York: Gordon and Breach Science, 1971.

Tompkins, Terry, and Phillip K. Tompkins. "The Next Catastrophic Fire in the American West Will Be of Our Own Making." Paper presented at the Wurth Forum: Center of the American West, University of Colorado at Boulder, February 17, 2001.

Vaughan, Diane. *The Challenger Launch Decision: Risky Technology, Culture, and Deviance at NASA.* Chicago: The University of Chicago Press, 1996.

Webb, Tom, and George Cheney. "Worker-Owned-and-Governed Cooperatives and the Wider Cooperative Movement: Challenges." In *The Routledge Companion to Alternative Organization,* edited by Martin Parker, George Cheney, Valérie Fournier, and Chris Land, 64–88. London: Routledge, 2014.

Weber, Max. *Economy and Society: An Outline of Interpretive Sociology,* edited by Guenther Roth and Claus Wittich. Berkeley: University of California Press, 1978.

Weick, Karl E., "The Collapse of Sensemaking in Organizations: The Mann Gulch Disaster." *Administrative Science Quarterly* 38 (1993): 628–52.

Weick, Karl E., and Susan J. Ashford. "Learning in Organizations." In *The New Handbook of Organizational Communication: Advances in Theory, Research, and Methods*, edited by Frederic M. Jablin and Linda L. Putnam, 704–31. Thousand Oaks, CA: Sage, 2001.

Weick, Karl E., and Kathleen M. Sutcliffe. *Managing the Unexpected: Assuring High Performance in an Age of Complexity*. San Francisco: Jossey-Bass, 2001.

White, Orion F., Jr. "The Dialectical Organization: An Alternative to Bureaucracy." *Public Administration Review* 29, no. 1 (1969): 32–42. doi:10.2307/973983.

Wildavsky, Aaron B. *Searching for Safety*. New Brunswick, NJ: Transaction, 1991.

Wuchty, Stefan, Benjamin F. Jones, and Brian Uzzi. "The Increasing Dominance of Teams in Production of Knowledge. *Science* 316, no. 5827 (2007): 1036–39. doi:10.1126/science.1136099.

Ziegler, Jennifer Anne. "The Story Behind an Organizational List: A Genealogy of Wildland Firefighters' 10 Standard Fire Orders." *Communication Monographs* 74, no. 4 (2007): 415–42. doi:10.1080/03637750701716594.

Glossary of Acronyms and Technical Terms

Arsenal concept: The practice of the U.S. Army in which the R&D stages of developing weapons systems were done in-house.

Apollo: The U.S. space flight program that put astronauts on the Moon and safely returned them to Earth.

ASRS: The Aviation Safety Reporting System, discussed at length in chapter 9.

Automatic responsibility: A communication practice at NASA's Marshall Space Flight Center during the Apollo Program, articulated by Dr. Wernher von Braun, in which every employee who perceived a technical problem within his or her area of expertise automatically assumed responsibility for the problem; if the person lacked the expertise to solve the problem, she or he assumed responsibility to communicate the problem up the line so that it could receive the proper technical attention.

CAIB: The Columbia Accident Investigation Board, which issued a report in August of 2003.

Carte Vitale: The vital card or card of life in France. A green card carried by every French citizen that contains a digital record of every medical interaction experienced by its holder, including X-rays, diagnoses, and treatments. It is said to make French medical care very efficient.

Challenger: The orbiter or space shuttle that exploded during its launch in 1986, killing seven astronauts.

Columbia: The orbiter or space shuttle that disintegrated during reentry in 2003, killing seven astronauts.

Communication transgressions: Violations of the basic principles of open communication. They include lying, encouraging others to lie, failure to listen to employees and workers, plausible deniability, *ignorantia affectata* (pretended ignorance of illicit acts), the fear of speaking truth to power, suppression of voice, the absence of feedback loops to prevent illicit actions, and the absence of symmetrical information.

Complexity: A complex of variables or units related to each other whose relationships are difficult to comprehend in their totality. Problems attacked by today's organizations are thought to be increasing in complexity because the numbers of related units are increasing, partly because of subdivision into specializations, and because new technologies produce new variables.

Concertive control: A theory developed by Phillip K. Tompkins and George Cheney, it originally referred to an organization that practiced participatory decision making at all levels: control practiced unobtrusively by people working in *concert*. It has come to mean the process by which teams or work groups democratically reach decisions by applying accepted decision premises during intense oral discourse.

Dialectic: Originally, *dialegein* in Greek meant "to argue." Today it has a meaning of two forces in direct opposition.

Discursive closure: The closing of openness and candor in organizational communication by those with formal power. It is sometimes limited to particular problems threatening to management.

Enthymeme: Discovered by Aristotle, the rhetorical syllogism or deductive argument in which one or more of its parts is missing because the speaker or writer assumes it is in the mind of receivers, who will supply it to complete the argument. Enthymeme^2 is the process by which organizations inculcate key decision premises in the mind of their employees so that they will make the preferred decisions.

Faster, Better, Cheaper: The slogan introduced by NASA administrator Daniel Goldin in the 1990s. The concept was not supposed to be applied to manned space flight. The effect is thought to have significantly compromised quality or reliability.

Formal vs. informal organization and communication: The formal organization is depicted by the lines and boxes of the organizational chart. The lines represent the formal channels of communication (i.e., command and reporting relationships). The informal organization, by contrast, develops naturally and outside the formal lines of authoritative communication.

Hierarchy: The graded, vertical series of status levels in an organization. It is usually thought of as formal or official; that is, it is specified and acknowledged by signs of status. There can be an informal hierarchy at odds with the formal one and often based more on trust, credibility, and open communication.

Ideal managerial climate: Defined by W. Charles Redding, based on his encyclopedic knowledge of theory and empirical research of his day. The defining characteristics are supportiveness, participative decision making, trust, confidence, credibility, openness and candor, and an emphasis on high performance goals.

Idiographic: A form of knowledge, that of individual and unique aspects of reality, as opposed to the nomothetic form of knowledge characterized by the search for generalizations or laws. The distinction was made by a German philosopher, Wilhelm Windelband (1848–1915).

Marshall Space Flight Center (MSFC): The NASA field center in Huntsville, Alabama, where the *Saturn V,* the Moon rocket, was created.

Matrix management: The method of managing an organization of relatively permanent substantive or technical departments such as labs with project offices that come and go. The lines of communication in this kind of organization are vertical, horizontal, and diagonal, thus resembling a matrix.

Monday Notes: A communication practice created by Dr. Wernher von Braun at NASA's Marshall Space Flight Center (MSFC) in which informality, openness, and candor were achieved in upward-directed reporting and feedback from the boss. The practice is explained at length in chapter 1.

Mission management team: The group of managers responsible for each orbiter or space shuttle mission.

NASA: The U.S. National Aeronautics and Space Administration.

Normalization of deviance: A sociological concept specifying a gradual acclimatization to, or acceptance of, unexpected and undesired results. This idea was applied by Diane Vaughan in her book, *The Challenger Launch Decision: Risky Technology, Culture, and Deviance at NASA,* discussed in chapter 6.

Normalization of risk: This concept leads to an atmosphere or culture in which risk, troubles, and failure can be discussed openly; *open communication* is a term used by Howard E. McCurdy in writing about this concept in his book *Inside NASA: High Technology and Organizational Change in the U.S. Space Program*, and discussed in chapter 6.

Nomothetic: Knowledge in the form of generalizations or laws. See idiographic.

Organizational communication: The study of organizations as communication systems and messages. Communication *constitutes* organization in the sense that organizations must have goals, rewards, and penalties that are expressed to and understood by their members. It is usually assumed that there is an inverse correlation between effective communication and organizational failure. The study of such phenomena can be done empirically, interpretatively, and critically.

Organizational culture: The rough draft of individual behavior within an organization. Individuals are suspended in webs of significance or meaning of their collective making. The stronger the culture, the more the actions of employees will be similar. The weaker the culture, the more they will be different and less predictable. Language, symbolism, and meaning are the heart of culture.

Organizational identification: A person identifies with an organization when she or he seeks to select the alternative that best fits the perceived interests of the organization. The higher the degree of identification, the more the individual's identity is shaped by membership in the group, and the more the person develops a "we-self." Identification was stressed by Kenneth Burke as the modern rhetoric, involving a considerable degree of self-persuasion. Organizational commitment is the behavioral expression of identification.

OTC: The original technical culture of NASA during its glory days of the 1960s. Categories of OTC were in-house technical capacity, research and testing, capable people, open communication, normalization of risk, and high degrees of organizational identification.

Penetration: A communication practice in which the organization buying a product or components of a product from another organization, a contractor, gains access to (penetrates) the selling organization to ensure that the product or components will meet requirements. Contractors can practice penetration in two directions: with their subcontractors and with their customer. There is an internal practice as well in which managers try to penetrate two levels up and down within their organization so that they may anticipate problems, risks, and new directions.

R&D: Research and development, the process of conceiving, designing, fabricating, and testing hardware. It precedes the actual serial production of the product.

Redundancy: More information than is ideally or logically necessary (e.g., repetition or restatement). An organization can also create redundant channels of communication to ensure that crucial information gets up and down the levels of the hierarchy. The word is also used in a technomorphic sense, as when engineers decide to design backup components in technology.

Risk: The likelihood and impact of potential problems or undesirable events which might occur and prevent the achievement of an objective or project. The impact could range from not succeeding in making a product or harming or killing workers, users, or bystanders. In risk management it is expressed as $RF = L \times I$ (Risk Factor equals Likelihood times Impact).

Risk aversive: Refers to decision makers who are fearful of deciding to act because they might fail.

Saturn V: The Moon rocket, the R&D for which was done at NASA's MSFC.

Semantic-information distance: Refers to the degrees of difference in the meanings of key terms or jargon and degrees of knowledge among people at different hierarchical levels of an organization, either vertical or horizontal.

Smart risk: The willing and courageous acceptance of the probability of a threat because it is balanced by the ability and resources to resist non-being.

Topoi: A Greek term for places to look for arguments. The three *topoi* for rocket R&D are reliability or safety, time or schedule, and cost. Difficult decisions often involve compromise and tradeoffs. The singular form is *topos*.

V-2: A military missile, the first, developed during World War II by the German rocket team under the direction of Dr. Wernher von Braun at the rocket center Peenemünde on the Baltic Sea.

Voice: A metaphor for the degree to which employees participate and have influence in organizational decision making—the degree to which their views are listened to by those at the top of the hierarchy.

Index